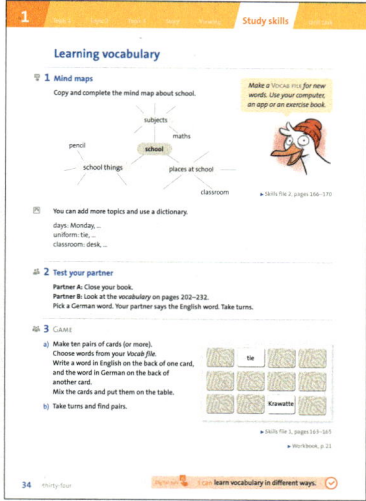
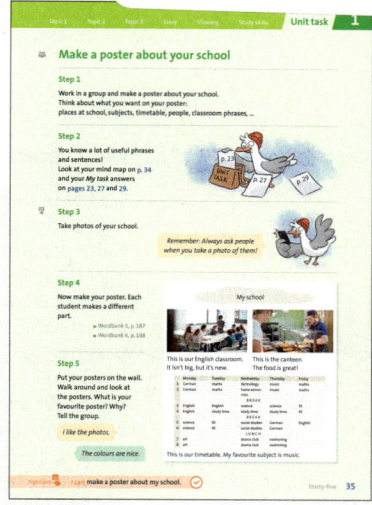

Lern- und Arbeitstechniken

Auf der *Study skills*-Seite übst du wichtige Lern- und Arbeitstechniken, z. B. wie du neue Wörter am besten lernst.

Eine Aufgabe am Unit-Ende

In der *Unit task* erstellst du ein größeres Produkt, z. B. eine Präsentation. Dabei wendest du das Gelernte aus der Unit an.

Im *Checkpoint* wiederholst du

Hier überprüfst du, wie gut du die Lernziele der Unit schon erreicht hast.

Nach Units 2 und 4 findest du ein *Text file* mit interessanten Texten zum Thema der Unit.

Diese Verweise führen dich in die *Diff bank* am Ende der Unit

▶ More help	▶ Parallel exercise	▶ More practice
Hilfen zu den Aufgaben	einfachere Variante einer Übung	weitere Übungen

Diese Lernangebote findest du im hinteren Teil des Buches

▶ Skills file	▶ Language file	▶ Wordbank
eine Übersicht über die Lern- und Arbeitstechniken	die wichtigsten Sprachregeln	zusätzliche Wörter zu bestimmten Themen

Let's talk	**Vocabulary**	**Dictionary**
Redewendungen nach wichtigen Themen und Situationen geordnet	eine Liste der neuen Vokabeln einer Unit mit hilfreichen Tipps	alphabetische Wörterlisten zum Nachschlagen (Englisch–Deutsch, Deutsch–Englisch)

lighthouse 1 BASIC

Im Auftrag des Verlages herausgegeben von
Ulrike Rath, Aachen
sowie
Martin Bastkowski, Schellerten;
Sonja Mahne, Basel;
Berit Schaarschmidt, Aschaffenburg

Erarbeitet von
Olivia Wintgens, Aachen; Rebecca Robb Benne, Kopenhagen; Zoe Thorne, Royston
sowie
Jennifer O'Hagan, Bristol (*Checkpoints*);
Ulrike Rath, Aachen (*Skills file*)

In Zusammenarbeit mit der Englischredaktion
Klaus Unger (Projektleitung),
Silvia Wiedemann (koordinierende Redakteurin),
Kathrin Spiegelberg
Ursula Fleischhauer, Hannover (*Vocabulary*)
Ingrid Raspe, Düsseldorf (*Vocabulary, Dictionary E–D*)

Beratende Mitwirkung
Sabine Bay, Cloppenburg; Armin Düpmeier, Warendorf; Lina Hein-Gehrmann, Wuppertal; Daniel Henn, Frankfurt/Main; Tobias Pfeifer, Dossenheim
sowie
Vertr.-Prof. Dr. Christian Ludwig, Berlin; Prof. Dr. Bernd Rüschoff, Essen; Prof. Dr. Michaela Sambanis, Berlin

Medienmanagement
Silke Kirchhoff

Illustrationen
Harald Ardeias, Schelklingen; Irina Zinner, Hamburg

Fotos
Anja Poehlmann, Brighton
Für die freundliche Unterstützung danken wir der *Varndean School, Brighton*

Umschlaggestaltung
Rosendahl, Berlin

Layoutkonzept
Klein & Halm, Berlin

Designberatung
Ungermeyer, Berlin

Layout und technische Umsetzung
Straive

Druck
Mohn Media Mohndruck, Gütersloh

PEFC zertifiziert
Dieses Produkt stammt aus nachhaltig bewirtschafteten Wäldern und kontrollierten Quellen.
www.pefc.de
PEFC/04-31-1033

www.cornelsen.de

Soweit in diesem Lehrwerk Personen fotografisch abgebildet sind und ihnen von der Redaktion fiktive Namen, Berufe, Dialoge und Ähnliches zugeordnet oder diese Personen in bestimmte Kontexte gesetzt werden, dienen diese Zuordnungen und Darstellungen ausschließlich der Veranschaulichung und dem besseren Verständnis des Buchinhaltes.

Dieses Werk berücksichtigt die Regeln der reformierten Rechtschreibung und Zeichensetzung.

Die Webseiten Dritter, deren Internetadressen in diesem Lehrwerk angegeben sind, wurden vor Drucklegung sorgfältig geprüft. Der Verlag übernimmt keine Gewähr für die Aktualität und den Inhalt dieser Seiten oder solcher, die mit ihnen verlinkt sind.

Die Cornelsen App ist eine fakultative Ergänzung *zu Lighthouse*, die die inhaltliche Arbeit begleitet und unterstützt. Als solche unterliegt sie nicht der Genehmigungspflicht.

© 2023 Cornelsen Verlag GmbH, Berlin

Das Werk und seine Teile sind urheberrechtlich geschützt. Jede Nutzung in anderen als den gesetzlich zugelassenen Fällen bedarf der vorherigen schriftlichen Einwilligung des Verlages.

Hinweis zu §§ 60a, 60b UrhG: Weder das Werk noch seine Teile dürfen ohne eine solche Einwilligung an Schulen oder in Unterrichts- und Lehrmedien (§ 60b Abs. 3 UrhG) vervielfältigt, insbesondere kopiert oder eingescannt, verbreitet oder in ein Netzwerk eingestellt oder sonst öffentlich zugänglich gemacht oder wiedergegeben werden.
Dies gilt auch für Intranets von Schulen.

Alle Drucke dieser Auflage sind inhaltlich unverändert und können im Unterricht nebeneinander verwendet werden.

ISBN 9783060362639 broschiert
1. Auflage, 1. Druck 2023

ISBN 9783060357680 gebunden
1. Auflage, 1. Druck 2023

ISBN 9783060345816 E-Book

lighthouse

BASIC 1

Cornelsen

Inhalt

	I can ...	Kompetenzen	Sprachliche Mittel	Seite
Hello! Nice to meet you	... say hello. ... talk about a picture. ... talk about what I like. ... understand classroom English.	**L/S** Sich begrüßen, Informationen austauschen und sich verabschieden **S** Sagen, welche Tiere, Farben, Hobbys und Dinge man mag, was man auf einem Bild sieht, wie es einem geht **L** Songs verstehen und mitsingen **L/R** Classroom English verstehen	**Voc** Hello, I'm ... · What's your name? · I'm from ... What about you? · How are you? – I'm fine. · My favourite ... is ... · I like/don't like ... · I remember/ I can see ... · Open your books. · Put your hand up.	10

Unit 1
My new school

Lead-in	... understand students at a British school.	**S** Über sich Auskunft geben **L** Vier britische Schulkinder kennenlernen	**Voc** Hello, I'm ... · I'm ... years old. · My favourite sport/hobby is ...	18
Topic 1 Time for school	... understand and use classroom English.	**L/S/R** Dialoge in der Schule verstehen und führen **S** Sich zur Schuluniform äußern **IC** Schule, Schuluniform **My task** Fragen und Antworten für Gespräche im Klassenraum sammeln	**Voc** school things · The uniform is nice/great/ ... · What page is it? · Let's ask Mr Lee. · Can you help me with ...? **G** a/an, plural of nouns	20
Topic 2 My timetable	... write my timetable in English.	**L** Dialogen und Songs Informationen zum Stundenplan entnehmen **S** Sich über Lieblingsfächer austauschen **My task** Meinen Stundenplan schreiben	**Voc** days of the week · school subjects · My favourite subject/ day of the week is ... **G** to be (positive) · personal pronouns	24
Topic 3 It's a big school!	... describe my school.	**R** Dialog über Schulräume verstehen **My task** Über meine Schule schreiben	**Voc** places at school **G** to be (negative)	28
Story After school	... understand a story about friends.	**R/S** Eine Geschichte verstehen und nachspielen · Charaktere beschreiben **S/W/LS** Eine(n) Freund(in) beschreiben	**Voc** He/She is brave/nice/... · I (don't) like ... because ... · ... is my friend because ...	30
Viewing The Brighton dares: School		**V/IC** Filmszenen verstehen **S** Sich zu den Szenen äußern	**Voc** I think the dare / Mr ... is bad/clever/...	33
Study skills Learning vocabulary	... learn vocabulary in different ways.	**MK** Mindmap zum Wortfeld Schule erstellen · ein VOCAB FILE anlegen · Vokabelspiel ausarbeiten und spielen	**Voc** school words	34
Unit task Make a poster about your school	... make a poster about my school.	**MK** Fotos machen **W** Meine Schule beschreiben **S** Feedback geben	**Voc** school words · feedback phrases	35
Checkpoint	Kompetenzen und sprachliche Mittel (Unit 1) üben, Lernfortschritte erkennen			36
Diff bank	Partner B, Parallel exercises, More help, More practice			40

4 four

	I can ...	Kompetenzen	Sprachliche Mittel	Seite

L Listening · **R** Reading · **S** Speaking · **W** Writing · **M** Mediation · **V** Viewing · **IC** Intercultural competence · **MK** Medienkompetenz · **LS** Life skills · **Voc** Vocabulary · **G** Grammar

Unit 2
My family and home

	I can ...	Kompetenzen	Sprachliche Mittel	Seite
Lead-in	... talk about my family.	**L** Dialogen Informationen über Familienverhältnisse entnehmen **S** Sich über Familie, Freunde und Nachbarn austauschen	**Voc** family words · ... is my brother/mum/...	44
Topic 1 My pets	... talk about pets.	**R/L** Dialoge über Haustiere verstehen **S** Sich über Haustiere austauschen **R** Tierbeschreibungen verstehen **My task** Ein Interview über Haustiere führen	**Voc** pets · My favourite pet is ... because ... **G** to be (questions and short answers)	46
Topic 2 Different homes	... describe my home or dream home.	**L** Ein Gespräch über Wohnsituationen verstehen **V** Einer Tour durch Sunitas Haus Informationen entnehmen **My task** Über das eigene (Traum-) Zuhause schreiben	**Voc** rooms and things in a house **G** There's / There are	50
Topic 3 In my room	... describe my room.	**S** Sunitas Zimmer beschreiben · sagen/ fragen, wo sich etwas befindet **My task** Sich über das eigene Zimmer austauschen und es anhand der Beschreibung zeichnen	**Voc** things in a room · prepositions · question words	52
Story At home with Sunita	... understand a problem and talk about it.	**L** Einen Song über eine Wohnung verstehen **R** Eine Geschichte über einen Konflikt zu Hause verstehen **S/LS** Über Probleme und mögliche Lösungen sprechen (role-play)	**Voc** I have a problem when you ... – I'm sorry. I can ... – That's a good idea. Thanks! – You're welcome.	56
Viewing The Brighton dares: Family		**V/IC** Filmszenen verstehen **S** Ergebnisse vergleichen	**Voc** I think it's true. – Me too. / No, I think it's false.	59
Study skills Spelling	... spell words correctly.	**L/S** Das Alphabet kennenlernen **L/S/W** Buchstabieren · Rückfragen zur Schreibung stellen und beantworten	**Voc** the numbers 0–9 · the alphabet · name, address, phone number	60
Unit task Present your dream room	... present my dream room.	Wortschatz in einer Mindmap sammeln · die korrekte Schreibung überprüfen **MK** Bilder aus dem Internet verwenden **W/S** Mein Traumzimmer beschreiben	**Voc** things in a room · colours · pets · adjectives · prepositions	61
Checkpoint	Kompetenzen und sprachliche Mittel (Unit 2) üben, Lernfortschritte erkennen			62
Text file	Varndean Teen Zine: Pets, homes and families			66
Festivals	Teen Zine special: Festivals (Christmas, Chinese New Year)			68
Diff bank	Partner B, Parallel exercises, More help, More practice			70

Inhalt

	I can ...	Kompetenzen	Sprachliche Mittel	Seite
Unit 3 **My day**				
Lead-in	... talk about my school journey.	**L** Sprachnachrichten Informationen über den Schulweg entnehmen **S** Sich über den Schulweg austauschen · Umfrageergebnisse versprachlichen	**Voc** I go to school by bus/ bike/... It's a ... journey. – I walk to school. · Some students in our class ...	76
Topic 1 A weekday	... describe my daily routine.	**L/IC** Zeitangaben verstehen **L/S** Song zum Tageslauf verstehen, mitsingen **S** Sagen, wieviel Uhr es ist und wann etwas regelmäßig stattfindet **R** Artikel über Zanes Tag verstehen **My task** Post zum Tageslauf verfassen	**Voc** the numbers 10–60 · the time **G** the simple present	78
Topic 2 School clubs	... talk about my free time.	**L/IC** Hörtexten Informationen über AGs und Hobbys entnehmen **S** Sagen, welche Aktivitäten man regelmäßig, oft, nie macht **M** Wesentliche Inhalte eines AG-Aushangs ins Deutsche vermitteln **My task** Eine Nachricht über meine Freizeitgestaltung schreiben	**Voc** sports and hobbies · I like singing, but I don't like ... · adverbs of frequency: I sometimes/often/never go/ play/...	82
Topic 3 Meeting friends	... make plans to meet friends.	**R** Chat-Nachrichten Details über eine Verabredung entnehmen **L** Eine Verabredung am Telefon verstehen **My task** Verabredungen treffen	**Voc** planning to meet: Are you free on/at ...? Let's ... – I'd love to. / Sorry, I can't / I'm busy.	86
Story The competition	... understand feelings in a story.	**R** Eine Geschichte verstehen und ihr die Gefühle der Protagonisten entnehmen **S** Über Zanes Pläne spekulieren **L/IC** Zanes Rede entnehmen, wie er sein Preisgeld einsetzen möchte **S/LS** Überlegen, wem man einen Preis verleihen würde	**Voc** He/She is/feels angry/ happy/sorry/sad/surprised/ tired/...	88
Viewing The Brighton dares: Sports and hobbies		**V/IC** Filmszenen verstehen	**Voc** sports and hobbies	91
Study skills Look up and remember words	... look up and learn new words.	Neuen Wortschatz alphabetisch ordnen, im *Dictionary* nachschlagen und im VOCAB FILE systematisieren	**Voc** free-time activities	92
Unit task Share your highlights of the week	... share the highlights of my week.	**S/W/MK** Zum Thema Höhepunkte der Woche einen Comic zeichnen oder ein Video aufnehmen und vorstellen **S** Feedback geben	**Voc** free-time activities · days of the week · feedback phrases	93
Checkpoint	Kompetenzen und sprachliche Mittel (Unit 3) üben, Lernfortschritte erkennen			94
Diff bank	Partner B, Parallel exercises, More help, More practice			98

6 six

	I can …	Kompetenzen	Sprachliche Mittel	Seite
 **Unit 4 Where I live**			**L** Listening · **R** Reading · **S** Speaking · **W** Writing · **M** Mediation · **V** Viewing · **IC** Intercultural competence · **MK** Medienkompetenz · **LS** Life skills · **Voc** Vocabulary · **G** Grammar	
Lead-in	… understand information about Brighton.	**V/IC** Filmszenen Informationen über Brighton entnehmen **S** Fotos von Brighton beschreiben · sagen, welche Orte in Brighton man mag	**Voc** sights in Brighton	104
Topic 1 My neighbourhood	… describe my neighbourhood.	**S** Sagen, was man sieht und hört · darüber sprechen, was man an seiner Wohngegend (nicht) mag **R** Einem Text über Lilys Gegend Informationen und Adjektive entnehmen, Posts verstehen **My task** Einen Online-Post über meine Wohngegend schreiben	**Voc** I can see/hear/smell … · adjectives and their opposites · places · I don't like … · She doesn't like … · I live in a … · My neighbourhood has … **G** simple present: negative sentences	106
Topic 2 My town or village	… talk about my town or village.	**IC** Informationen über Städte im UK **L** Song über eine Kleinstadt verstehen · Fragen über Brighton verstehen und beantworten **S** Sich über den eigenen Wohnort und Tourismus austauschen **M** Website-Informationen über Brighton ins Deutsche sprachmitteln **My task** Orte durch Fragen erraten	**Voc** places in a town or village · Does your town have …? – Yes, it does. / No, it doesn't. · Do you like …? – Yes, I do. / No, I don't. **G** simple present: questions and short answers	110
Topic 3 Brighton in all weathers	… talk about sights in Brighton and the weather.	**L** Einer Stadtführung Informationen über Brighton und das Wetter entnehmen **R** Einer Online-Bewertung Informationen entnehmen **My task** Fragen über Aktivitäten bei jedem Wetter stellen und beantworten	**Voc** weather words · sights **G** simple present: wh-questions	114
Story Lily's idea	… understand a story about green activities.	**R** Eine Geschichte verstehen **W/LS** Eine Tauschaktion planen und dafür ein Plakat erstellen	**Voc** my neighbourhood	116
Viewing Brighton dares: In town		**V/IC** Filmszenen verstehen	**Voc** Brighton sights	119
Study skills Give a short talk	… plan and practise a short talk.	**S** Eine Kurzvortrag strukturieren, formulieren, üben und vortragen · Feedback geben **MK/W** Folien für eine Präsentation erstellen **MK** Sich filmen	**Voc** places in Brighton · phrases for short talks	120
Unit task Present your top three places for kids	… give a short talk to a group.	**S** Themen für eine Präsentation diskutieren · eine Präsentation halten · Feedback geben **MK** Karten und Fotos aus dem Internet nutzen **MK/W** Folien für eine Präsentation erstellen	**Voc** discussion phrases · places for kids · phrases for presentations · feedback phrases	121
Checkpoint	Kompetenzen und sprachliche Mittel (Unit 4) üben, Lernfortschritte erkennen			122
Text file	Varndean Teen Zine: Brighton			126
Diff bank	Partner B, Parallel exercises, More help, More practice			128

Inhalt

	I can ...	Kompetenzen	Sprachliche Mittel	Seite
Unit 5 Enjoy!		L Listening · R Reading · S Speaking · W Writing · M Mediation · V Viewing · IC Intercultural competence · MK Medienkompetenz · LS Life skills · Voc Vocabulary · G Grammar		
Lead-in	... talk about food.	R/IC Rezeptbuch-Einträge verstehen S Sich über Lebensmittel und Gerichte austauschen	Voc food and drinks	134
Topic 1 Time for a party	... talk about birthdays and parties.	R Einer Einladung Informationen entnehmen S Von Geburtstagstraditionen erzählen · sich darüber austauschen, wann man Geburtstag hat · sagen, was man gerade macht · beschreiben, was in einem Bild gerade geschieht W Eine Einladung schreiben My task Partyfotos beschreiben	Voc months and dates · ordinal numbers · calling a friend · What are you doing? – I'm ... G the present progressive	136
Topic 2 Party shopping	... talk about party food and activities.	L Dialogen Informationen entnehmen · einen Song verstehen S Sich auf ein Geburtstagsgeschenk einigen: Vorschläge machen und darauf reagieren · ein Geschenk annehmen · eine Einkaufsliste besprechen L ein Rezept verstehen M Spielregeln auf Deutsch wiedergeben My task Ein Klassenfest planen	Voc party shopping · Why don't we buy ...? / Let's get a ... / What about ...? – That's a great idea! / I'm not sure. / It's too ... · food and drinks G much, many, a lot of	140
Topic 3 Let's cook!	... describe my favourite dish.	V Ein authentisches Koch-Video verstehen R/IC Einen Blog-Eintrag verstehen My task Einen Blog-Eintrag über das eigene Leibgericht schreiben	Voc cooking and baking (recipes) · food	144
Story A different kind of party	... understand and talk about differences.	R Eine Geschichte verstehen und ihr neuen Wortschatz entnehmen S/LS Über kulturelle und persönliche Unterschiede sprechen	Voc party words · feelings · I like/eat/ ... – I like/eat/ ... too. So that's the same. / I don't like/eat/... So that's different.	146
Viewing The Brighton dares: A birthday		V/IC Filmszenen verstehen S Über die Brighton dares diskutieren	Voc birthday words · discussion phrases	149
Study skills Explaining words	... explain words.	Oberbegriffe, Adjektive und weitere Informationen zum Erklären von Wörtern nutzen	Voc food and drinks · umbrella words · adjectives	150
Unit task Make a class recipe book	... write a recipe for a sandwich.	W Ein Rezept schreiben · Feedback geben	Voc food, cooking things and activities · feedback phrases	151
Checkpoint		Kompetenzen und sprachliche Mittel (Unit 5) üben, Lernfortschritte erkennen		152
Diff bank		Partner B, Parallel exercises, More help, More practice		156

Anhang

Skills file — 162

SF 1 Wörter lernen leichtgemacht	163	SF 4 Arbeit mit dem Wörterbuch — 169
SF 2 Sammeln und ordnen – Mindmaps	166	SF 5 Einen Kurzvortrag halten — 171
SF 3 Buchstabieren	168	SF 6 Wörter umschreiben — 173

Language file — 174

LF 1 Der s-Genitiv und die of-Fügung	174	LF 10 Die einfache Form der Gegenwart:
LF 2 Der Artikel	175	a) Bejahte Aussagesätze — 179
LF 3 Der Plural der Nomen	175	LF 11 b) Die Wortstellung — 179
LF 4 Die Personalpronomen	176	LF 12 c) Verneinte Aussagesätze — 180
LF 5 Die Possessivbegleiter	176	LF 13 d) Fragen mit do/does — 180
LF 6 Das Verb be:		LF 14 e) Kurzantworten — 181
a) Bejahte Aussagesätze	177	LF 15 f) Fragen mit Fragewörtern — 181
LF 7 b) Verneinte Aussagesätze	177	LF 16 Die Verlaufsform der Gegenwart — 182
LF 8 c) Fragen und Kurzantworten	178	LF 17 Much – many – a lot of — 183
LF 9 There is … / There are …	178	Grammatical terms — 183

Wordbanks — 184

WB 1 Numbers	184	WB 8 Pets — 190
WB 2 Colours	184	WB 9 Things in my room — 190
WB 3 Animals	185	WB 10 The times of the day — 191
WB 4 Free time	186	WB 11 Places — 192
WB 5 School subjects	187	WB 12 Food — 193
WB 6 Places at school	188	WB 13 Cooking — 194
WB 7 Family	189	

Let's talk (Redewendungen für wichtige Situationen, z. B. Diskussionen, Feedback geben etc.) — 195

Vocabulary (Lernwortschatz Unit für Unit) — 201

English-German Dictionary (alphabetische Wörterliste Englisch—Deutsch) — 236

German-English Dictionary (alphabetische Wörterliste Deutsch—Englisch) — 247

The English alphabet, English sounds — 257

English numbers — 258

Quellenverzeichnis — 259

Typical tasks (häufige Arbeitsanweisungen) — 263

Classroom English — 264

Die Angebote des Schulbuchs sind nicht obligatorisch abzuarbeiten. Die Auswahl der Übungen und Übungsteile richtet sich nach den Schwerpunkten des schulinternen Curriculums.

Hello!
Nice to meet you

1 Hello Scout

Look at pictures 1–3. Right or wrong?

1 Scout is a seagull.
2 Scout is white and green.
3 Scout is hungry.
4 Scout is nice.

Right!

Wrong!

🔊 2 What about you?

Look at picture 4. Listen. Then listen again and repeat.

▶ Numbers, p. 258   ▶ Wordbank 1, p. 184

3 Hello class

WALK AROUND Say hello to four other students. Ask and answer the questions. Look at picture 4 for help.

Hello! I'm ...
What's your name?

Hi! I'm ...

I like ...
What about you?

I like ...

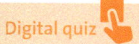 **I can** introduce myself. ✓

Hello!

Goodbye, holidays!

1 In the picture

a) Find, point and say.

Scout the seagull   Leo's mum   Ben
two numbers   two colours   two drinks
two animals   two things to eat

I can see …   *Here's …*

I can see the colour …

▶ Wordbank 2, p. 184

b) Look at the picture and listen. Match sounds 1–6 to A–F in the picture.

c) Look at the picture for 30 seconds again. Close your books. What can you remember?

I remember Scout.

I remember Scout and a dog.

I remember Scout and a dog and a …

12   twelve

Hello!

🔊 **2** Song **Scout's song**

Listen and act out the song. Then listen again, act and sing.

Hi, hello
Nice to meet you today.

How are you?
I'm fine, I'm OK.

I live in Brighton
Right by the sea.

"Look out! It's Scout!"

I'm a seagull, I'm Scout the seagull.

I can fly in the sky
SO HIGH

Over the sea!

I can **talk about a picture.** ✓

▶ Workbook, p. 8

Hello!

About me

1 My favourite animal

a) What animals can you see? Match the words to the pictures.

In picture 1, I can see ...

a cat • a dog •
an elephant • a horse •
a lion • a monkey •
a parrot • a snake

b) Listen. Write five animals from a).

c) Mime, draw or make an animal noise. Your partner says the animal.   *It's a dog!*

d) GAME Look at the animals on the page and choose one. Stand in a circle. One student stands in the middle and says their favourite animal. Students with the same favourite animal change places.

My favourite animal is a fish.

▶ Wordbank 3, p. 185
▶ Workbook, p. 9

Hello!

2 My hobbies and sports

a) Look at the box. Say Scout's hobbies and sports.

> dancing • drawing • football • listening to music • swimming • taking photos

Number 1 is football.

b) **What's your favourite hobby and your favourite sport?** *My favourite hobby is …*

c) DOUBLE CIRCLE Talk to a partner. One circle moves to find a new partner.

*My favourite hobby is …
What about you?*   *I like …*   *I love …*

*My favourite sport is …
What about you?*   *I don't like …*

▶ Wordbank 4, p. 186

3 My favourite things

a) Listen and point.

a cap   a football   a rucksack   a phone   a bike

b) Look and read. Match sentences 1–5 to the pictures.

1. My favourite thing is cool and green.
2. I love it – it's big and blue.
3. This thing is black and white.
4. I can take photos with it.
5. It's red and I put things in it.

▶ Workbook, pages 9–10

fifteen **15**

Hello!

4 SONG My favourites

Listen and sing.

> What's your favourite animal?
> My favourite animal is a kangaroo.
> What's your favourite colour?
> My favourite colour is blue. What about you?
>
> What's your favourite hobby?
> Dancing is my favourite thing to do.
> What's your favourite sport?
> I like swimming too. What about you?

5 Scout's top five

Write the correct words.

orange • singing • swimming • a fish • my hat

> My favourite animal is …
> My favourite colour is …
> My favourite sport is …
> My favourite thing is …
> My favourite hobby is …

6 My top five

a) Write your top five. Look at Scout's top five for help.

1 My favourite animal is …
2 …

b) WALK AROUND Ask and answer questions.

> What's your favourite …?

> My favourite … is …
> What about you?

> My favourite … is …

Im DOSSIER kannst du deine wichtigen und schönen Arbeiten sammeln.

c) Put your top five in your DOSSIER.

▶ Workbook, p. 10

Digital quiz   I can **talk about what I like.**

16   sixteen

Hello!

Ready for school

1 Listen, please!

a) Listen. Point to the correct pictures.

b) Match the pictures to the speech bubbles.

1 Open your books.

2 Listen.

3 Sit down.

4 Put your hand up.

5 Look at the board.

6 Stand up.

c) Listen. Do the actions in the pictures.

2 Song The school song

a) Listen and act out the song.

b) Listen again, act and sing.

*First sit down and then stand up.
Don't forget, put your hand up.*

*Open your book at page four.
Look at me, look at the board.*

*Quick, put all your things away.
Now it's break, it's time to play.*

3 My new English book

Find Scout with these hats. Which part of the book is she in? Match the letters A–G to the numbers 1–7.

1 So lernst du mit Lighthouse
2 Skills file
3 Language file
4 Let's talk
5 Vocabulary
6 Dictionary
7 Classroom English

I can understand classroom English.

▶ Workbook, p. 11

seventeen **17**

Unit 1
My new school

Name	Sunita Chandra
How old?	11
Hobby	coding
Sport	yoga

Name	Noah Williams
How old?	11
Hobby	taking photos
Sport	walking

1 LISTENING Four students at Varndean School

a) BEFORE YOU LISTEN Tell a partner about you.

> Hello, I'm … I'm … years old.
> My favourite hobby is …
> My favourite sport is …
> What about you?

b) Look at the pictures of four students from Brighton and read about them. Then listen and put pictures A–D in the correct order.

▶ More practice 1, p. 40

18 eighteen

Nach dieser Unit kann ich ...
- mich im Klassenzimmer auf Englisch verständigen
- meinen Stundenplan schreiben
- meine Schule beschreiben
- Vokabeln auf verschiedene Arten üben

Unit task
- ein Poster über meine Schule anfertigen

C

Name	Zane Adebayo
How old?	11
Hobby	cooking
Sport	swimming

D

Name	Lily Hall
How old?	11
Hobby	drawing
Sport	parkour

c) Choose Sunita, Noah, Zane or Lily. What's the same for you? What's different to you? Talk to a partner.

Sunita is ... years old. I'm ...

Sunita's favourite hobby is ... My favourite hobby is ...

Sunita's favourite sport is ... My favourite sport is ...

▶ Language file 1, p. 174
▶ Workbook, p. 12

Digital quiz   **I can** understand students at a British school.

nineteen **19**

1 Topic 1   Topic 2   Topic 3   Story   Viewing   Study skills   Unit task

Time for school

1 LISTENING At school

a) BEFORE YOU LISTEN **Look at the photo.
Point and say the names of the students.**

> Lily • Zane • Sunita • Noah

b) **Listen. Write the correct name or names in your exercise book.**

1 … is busy and tired.
2 … is happy about the school tie.
3 … and … like the uniform.
4 … and … are in class 7C.

Good to know
British schools have a school uniform.
▶ Digital help

2 SPEAKING School uniform

Is the Varndean school uniform great or horrible? Tell a partner.   nice • cool • horrible • not cool

> The uniform is great.
> I like the colour.

> The uniform is OK.
> I don't like ties.

▶ Workbook, p. 13

3 WORDS Sunita's desk

a) Look at the picture. Listen and point.

b) Listen and repeat.

4 LOOKING AT LANGUAGE a/an

Write *a* or *an*.

▶ Language file 2, p. 175

... pencil case
... exercise book
... apple
... desk
... pen
... orange

5 I can remember

Close your books. What things from Sunita's desk can you remember?

I can remember a pink pen.

I can remember an orange.

▶ Workbook, pages 13–14

1 Topic 1

6 SPEAKING Your desk

Put your school things on your desk.
Close your eyes.
Tell your partner about your school things.
Take turns.

a pencil   two pencils

> I have a ruler.
> I have two pencils.

▶ More practice 2, p. 40
▶ More practice 3, p. 41
▶ Language file 3, p. 175

7 READING Hello class 7C!

a) Read and find Mr Lee, Emma and Ravi in the photo.

Mr Lee Hello class 7C! I'm Mr Lee, your class teacher and English teacher.
Emma Sorry I'm late, Mr Lee.
Mr Lee OK, please sit down.
Ravi Can I open the window, please?
Mr Lee Yes, you can.
Now, please take your English books. Let's start.

Good to know

In England the first year of secondary school is year 7.

b) Act out the dialogue in a).

8 SONG The class 7C song

Listen and sing.

We're in class 7C
It's a great place to be.

It's a big, new school
But we think it's really cool.

Our teacher's Mr Lee
He is nice and so are we.

We're in class 7C
It's a great place to be.

▶ More practice 4, p. 41
▶ Workbook, p. 14

22   twenty-two

9 SPEAKING **In class**

a) Listen. Match what Noah and Sunita say.

1 What page is it?
2 Can you help me with exercise 2?
3 What's the answer to question 3?
4 Can I use your book?
5 Thanks.

a Yes, here you are.
b Page 9.
c Yes, I can.
d I don't know. Let's ask Mr Lee.
e You're welcome.

b) Listen to the questions in a). Say the answers.

c) WALK AROUND Practise the questions and answers in a) with different partners.

My task

10 My classroom questions and answers

a) Use the questions and answers in 9a) and change the blue parts.
Can you help me with ~~exercise 2~~? => the new words
Let's ask ~~Mr Lee~~. => Frau Keller

b) Practise with your partner.

c) Make two groups in class. Ask and answer questions.

▶ Workbook, p. 15

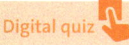 I can understand and use classroom English.

twenty-three 23

My timetable

1 The English lessons

a) Read the conversation.

Mr Lee 7C, please look at your timetable. Can you see the English lessons? They're in room 2.
Lily Mr Lee, look at Tim. I think he's tired.
Mr Lee You're right, Lily. And Emma — she's tired too. Emma and Tim, I know you're tired. We're all tired! But break is in five minutes.
Tim I'm sorry, Mr Lee.

b) Match the sentences A–D to 1–4.

1 The English lessons are in room 2.
2 Tim is tired.
3 Break is in five minutes.
4 Emma is tired too.

A She's tired too.
B They're in room 2.
C He's tired.
D It's in five minutes.

c) Complete the sentences with the words in the box.

> He • She • It • They

1 …'s our teacher. 2 …'s yellow. 3 …'re in class 7C. 4 …'s 11.

▶ More practice 5, p. 41   ▶ Language file 4, p. 176

Erklär-film

2 LOOKING AT LANGUAGE 'm / 're / 's

Look at **1** again.
Copy and complete the table.

I'm
you're
he's / she's / it'…
we'…
you'…
they'…

▶ Language file 6, p. 177
▶ Workbook, pages 15–16

3 Varndean students and teachers

a) Match the correct name(s) to the sentences.

> Emma and Tim • Lily • Mr Lee •
> Sunita and Noah • Zane

1 I'm an English teacher.
2 He's a good swimmer.
3 We're tired.
4 She's in a parkour class.
5 They're a girl and a boy in 7C.

b) Say sentences about people in your class. The class guesses the person.

She's in a football / ... team.
He can sing / make music / ...
She likes sandwiches / the colour blue / ...

He can draw.
They're good friends.
He's ... years old.

4 Messages

Complete the messages from Noah and his mum with the words in the box.

▶ Parallel exercise, p. 42

> They're • You're • it's • He's • It's • I'm

Hi, Mum! I like the classroom. (1) ... big.
I like Mr Lee, my teacher, too. (2) ... cool.
And I like my new friends. (3) ... nice. 😊

👍 Great! (4) ... lucky, Noah! Varndean School is big, but (5) ... a good school. Sorry, (6) ... busy now. See you! 😊

▶ More practice 6, p. 42

5 SONG Days of the week

a) WORDS Listen and put the days in the correct order. *1 Monday, 2 ...*

Thursday   Tuesday   Sunday   Friday
Monday   Wednesday   Saturday

b) Now sing the song.

c) Complete the sentence: *My favourite day of the week is ...*

▶ Workbook, p. 17

6 Words School subjects

a) Look at the timetable for 7C. German and other languages can help you. Which words can you understand?

Lesson	Monday	Tuesday	Wednesday	Thursday	Friday
	REGISTRATION AND ASSEMBLY				
1	English	art	French	computing	
2	English	maths	French	computing	
	BREAK				
3	history	English	science	geography	
4	geography	music	science	history	
	LUNCH				
5	maths	science	design and technology	PE	
6	maths	science	computing	PE	

▶ Digital help

b) Match the pictures to the subjects in the timetable. Then listen and check. *1 art, 2 …*

7 Listening 7C's timetable

Listen to Lily and Zane. Complete 7C's timetable for Friday in your exercise book.

Lesson 1: …
Lesson 2: …
…

▶ Workbook, pages 17–18

8 Song The timetable song

a) Listen. Stand up when you hear a school subject.

b) Listen again. Write the correct subject (a–e) for 1–5.

On Monday morning I have (1) ...
The next lesson is (2) ...
After lunch we have biology
And then at three, go home to play.

On Tuesdays I study (3) ... at ten.
After break, (4) ... with Mr Wren.
Finally, it's time for (5) ... and then
We do it all again another day.

a French
b geography
c history
d maths
e PE

9 Speaking My subjects

a) Talk about your subjects. Say three sentences.

b) Speed dating Make two lines. Tell your partner.

*I like maths.
My favourite subject is PE.
I don't like history.*

My task

10 My timetable

Write your timetable in English for an English friend. Put your timetable in your Dossier.

▶ Wordbank 5, p. 187

▶ Workbook, p. 19

I can write my timetable in English.

twenty-seven 27

Topic 3

It's a big school!

1 Words Places at school

a) Match the pictures A–E to the rooms 1–5.

1 the art room
2 the canteen
3 the computer room
4 the English classroom
5 the sports hall

b) Read the conversation.

Zane Hi, Lily!
Lily Hi, Zane. This is Sunita and this is Noah.
Sunita Nice to meet you, Zane.
Noah I'm hungry. My sandwich isn't in my bag. Where's the canteen?
Sunita Is it here? … No, this room isn't the canteen, it's the art room.
Zane This room is the computer room. And the toilets are here.
Lily Look at this map! We're in building 1. The canteen and the sports hall are in building 2. It's a big school!
Noah They aren't in this building. We aren't near the canteen!
Zane I have two sandwiches and I'm not hungry. Here, you can have one.
Noah You aren't hungry, Zane … I'm always hungry! Thanks!
Zane You're welcome.

c) Listen and repeat the places.

▶ More practice 7, p. 42

2 What's right?

Choose the correct words.

1 I'm / I'm not hungry.
2 My sandwich is / isn't in my bag.
3 This room is / isn't the computer room.
4 They're / They aren't in this building.
5 We're / We aren't near the canteen.
6 You're / You aren't hungry, Zane.

▶ Workbook, p. 19

Erklär-film

3 LOOKING AT LANGUAGE *to be* (negative)

Look at exercise 2. Copy and complete the box with *isn't* (2x) and *aren't* (3x).

I'm	→	I'm not
you're	→	you …
he's	→	he …
she	→	she isn't
it's	→	it …
we're	→	we …
you're	→	you aren't
they're	→	they …

Your sandwich isn't in your bag. It's in here.

Language file 7, p. 177

4 The new school

Choose the correct picture (A or B) for each of the sentences 1–6.

1 The school isn't big.

2 We aren't scared!

3 The teacher is nice.

4 The food isn't bad.

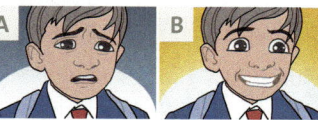

5 I'm happy at my school.

6 My new school is cool!

▶ More practice 8+9, p. 43

My task

5 My school

a) Read Lily's email to her grandma about her school.

b) Write to Scout about your school. You can use Lily's email and change the blue words. Put your text in your DOSSIER.

Hi, Grandma!
The name of my school is Varndean School. I'm in class 7C. My class teacher is Mr Lee. My favourite place at school is the art room. My favourite day is Tuesday because lesson 2 is art.
My school is great.
See you, Lily

▶ Digital help ▶ More help, p. 43 ▶ Wordbanks 5+6, pages 187–188

▶ Workbook, p. 20

Digital quiz   I can describe my school.

twenty-nine 29

After school

1 Before you read A good friend

Describe a good friend.

A good friend is ...   A good friend isn't ...

> friendly • helpful • horrible • mean • nice

2 Reading Who is ...?

Read the story. Answer the questions.

1 Who is busy?
2 Who is mean?
3 Who is sad?
4 Who is helpful?
5 Who is scared, then helpful?
6 Who is friendly?

Lily Hey, Zane! Let's go to the beach!
Zane Sorry, I'm busy! Bye!
Lily Zane is always busy.
Sunita You're right.

Kyle You're too slow, Noah!
Jade Noah is so weird.
Noah I'm not weird!
Lily Who are they?
Sunita They aren't from Varndean. They're bullies.

Lily That's Noah from our class. He's in trouble!
Sunita Can we help him?
Lily I don't know. I'm scared of bullies!

Noah Hello, seagull. You're nice.
But the bullies aren't nice.
They're mean!
I'm sad. They think I'm weird.
But I'm not weird.
I'm Noah and I'm clever!

1

Lily Oh no! Noah is sad ...
Sunita Let's help him!

Jade Look! The weird boy's still here!
Sunita Stop! He's our friend.
Lily Go away!

Noah That's my friend, the seagull! And her friends too – they're very helpful!
Kyle Ugh! Let's go!
Jade The seagulls are horrible!

Noah Thanks. You're good friends.
Sunita That seagull is very clever! You're good with animals, Noah.

Noah Hi, Dad. These are my friends.
Dad Hello! Nice to meet you. This is Noah's dog, Buddy. He's very friendly.
Lily He's cool.

3 READING What's wrong?

Correct the sentences.
Change the words in blue.

1 Zane **is** free after school.
2 Kyle and Jade **are** nice to Noah.
3 Sunita and Lily **aren't** scared of the bullies at first.
4 Lily and Sunita **aren't** Noah's friends.
5 The seagulls **are** nice to Kyle and Jade.
6 Noah's dog **is** mean.

thirty-one 31

4 WORDS Opposites

Match the phrases 1–5 to their opposites A–E.

1 I'm OK.
2 I'm busy.
3 You're right.
4 They're nice.
5 He's happy.

A I'm free.
B He's sad.
C I'm in trouble.
D They're mean.
E You're wrong.

5 SHOWTIME Action!

a) Make groups of seven students:
Noah, Lily, Sunita, Zane, Kyle, Jade and Noah's dad.
Read the scenes.

b) Act out the scenes for the class or another group.
Use actions and feelings.

6 SPEAKING People in the story

Talk about Noah, Lily, Sunita, Scout and Buddy.

> I like Noah.
> He's good with animals.
> What about you?

> I like Lily.
> She's helpful.

a good friend • clever • cool • friendly • good with people / animals • helpful • nice

7 LIFE SKILLS Your best friend

Read Noah's text.
Write three sentences or more about your best friend.

*My best friend is my dog, Buddy.
He's always nice to me.
He's helpful when I'm sad.*

▶ Workbook, p. 21

 I can understand a story about friends.

The Brighton dares[1]: School

1 Before you watch The people in the video

Say who you can see in the picture.

a girl / a boy • British / German • friends • students • teachers

I can see … I think they are / aren't …

2 Viewing What are the dares?

Watch the video. Match the pictures (A–C) to the dares.

1 Wear a beard[2]
2 Speak backwards[3]
3 Walk backwards

3 Who says what?

Match the people to the sentences.

1 "She has a maths test in lesson one. She needs her ruler."
2 "Old – years – eleven – am – I."
3 "Come see me after assembly."
4 "It's a really good book."

4 My opinion

Tell a partner your opinion.

I think …

bad • clever • cool • friendly • good • great • horrible • mean • nice • OK • weird

1 the beard dare is …
2 the backwards dare is …
3 Mr Campbell is …
4 Mrs Collins is …
5 the film is …
6 it's OK to say no to a dare.

---

[1] **dare** *die Mutprobe*   [2] (to) **wear a beard** *einen Bart tragen*   [3] **backwards** *rückwärts*

Learning vocabulary

1 Mind maps

Copy and complete the mind map about school.

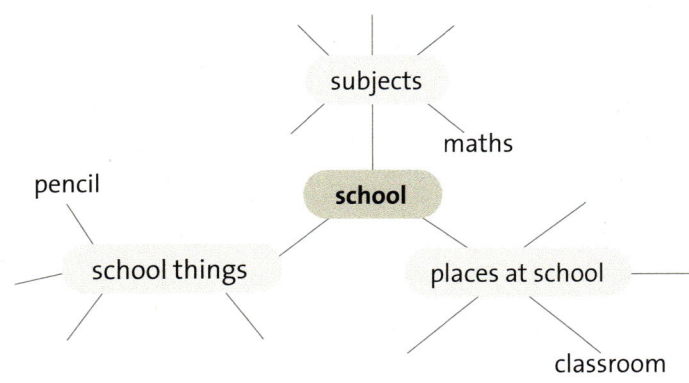

Make a VOCAB FILE for new words. Use your computer, an app or an exercise book.

▶ Skills file 2, pages 166–167

You can add more topics and use a dictionary.

days: Monday, ...
uniform: tie, ...
classroom: desk, ...

2 Test your partner

Partner A: Close your book.
Partner B: Look at the *Vocabulary* on pages 202–213.
Pick a German word. Your partner says the English word. Take turns.

3 GAME New words

a) Make ten pairs of cards (or more).
   Choose words from your VOCAB FILE.
   Write a word in English on the back of one card, and the word in German on the back of another card.
   Mix the cards and put them on the table.

b) Take turns and find pairs.

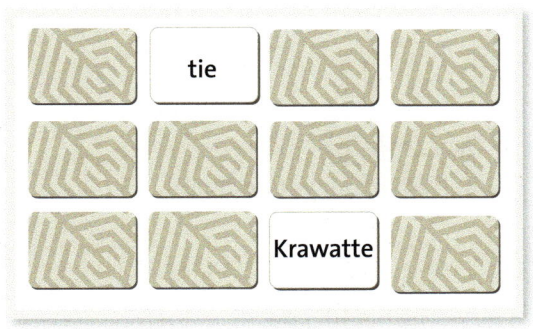

▶ Skills file 1, pages 163–165

▶ Workbook, pages 22–23

I can learn vocabulary in different ways.

| Topic 1 | Topic 2 | Topic 3 | Story | Viewing | Study skills | **Unit task** | **1** |

Make a poster about your school

Step 1

Work in a group and make a poster about your school.
Think about what you want on your poster:
places at school, subjects, timetable, people, classroom phrases, …

Step 2

You know a lot of useful phrases and sentences!
Look at your mind map on p. 34 and your *My task* answers on pages 23, 27 and 29.

Step 3

Take photos of your school.

Remember: Always ask people when you take a photo of them!

Step 4

Now make your poster. Each student makes a different part.
▶ Digital help
▶ Wordbank 5, p. 187
▶ Wordbank 6, p. 188

My school

This is our English classroom. It isn't big, but it's new.

This is the canteen. The food is great!

	Monday	Tuesday	Wednesday	Thursday	Friday
1	German	maths	technology	music	maths
2	German	maths	home economics	music	maths
			BREAK		
3	English	English	science	science	PE
4	English	study time	study time	study time	PE
			BREAK		
5	science	RE	social studies	German	English
6	science	RE	social studies	German	
			LUNCH		
7	art		drama club	swimming	
8	art		drama club	swimming	

This is our timetable. My favourite subject is music.

Step 5

WALK AROUND Put your posters on the wall.
Look at the posters. What's your favourite poster? Why?
Tell the group.

I like the photos.

The colours are nice.

Digital quiz   **I can** make a poster about my school.

thirty-five 35

1 Checkpoint   Digital checkpoint

1 LISTENING At break
I can understand students at a British school.

a) Listen to the conversation. What places can you hear? Put the pictures in the correct order.

 A
 B
 C
 D

b) Listen to the next part of the conversation.
Copy and complete the table with the words in the box.

computing • geography • PE • cool • fun • nice

	Favourite lesson today	Why?
Zane	…	The teacher is …
Sunita	…	It's …
Lily	…	It's …

2 SPEAKING Mr Lee's desk
I can understand and use classroom English.

Say what you can see in the picture.

In the picture, I can see a white computer, …

3 WORDS In the classroom

The students talk to the teacher. Choose the correct word.

1 Can you help / say me, please?
2 Can I answer / open the window, please?
3 Sorry / Please I'm late, Ms Miller.
4 What's the answer to this question / ruler, please?

Check

Die Übungen kannst du auch digital machen

1

4 LANGUAGE Sunita's email

I can write my timetable in English *(to be)*.

Sunita and her friend Jasmine are at different schools.
Complete Sunita's message with *'m / is / are*.

Hi, Jasmine!
How (1) … you? I (2) … now in class 7C at Varndean School. My timetable (3) … great! English lessons (4) … on Mondays, Tuesdays and Fridays. Science lessons (my favourite lessons) (5) … on Tuesdays and Wednesdays. And PE (6) … on Thursdays. Is your timetable OK? See you, Sunita.

5 LANGUAGE Jasmine's school

I can describe my school *(to be – negative)*.

Jasmine talks about her school. Look at the picture and complete Jasmine's sentences with *'m not / isn't / aren't*.

This is my school in Hove. The students (1) … in the building because it's break. The uniform is nice – the tie (2) … red, it's blue.
I like the canteen! The food is great. But the classrooms are in building 1 – they (3) … near the canteen. That's horrible, (4) I … happy about that! The sports hall (5) … in building 1 – it's near the canteen.

6 WRITING Seb's school

Complete Seb's email to Lily with the words in the box.

are • big • class • is • It's • place

Hi, Lily!
My school … Schiller School. … in Bochum.
It's a … school.
The students … friendly.
Our … teacher is Ms Lang.
My favourite … is the sports hall.
See you,
Seb

Check

thirty-seven 37

1 Checkpoint   Digital checkpoint

7 Reading Zane's homework

I can understand a story about friends.

a) Read the story.

Mr King So, class 7B. This is your homework. Make a poster about your favourite band, with facts and photos.

Zane Erm … Sir … Can I ask a …
Mr King Sorry Zane, I'm busy. Let's talk at break.

Sunita Why are you sad, Zane? You like music! And you're in a band!
Zane I want to make a great poster. But my computer is old and slow.
Sunita Where's your computer? I can help with that.

Zane Wow. You're good with computers. Thanks, Sunita!
Sunita You're welcome.

b) Complete the sentences with the words in the box.

1 Mr King is …
2 Sunita is … and …
3 Zane is … then …

busy • clever • happy • helpful • sad

c) Choose the correct answer.

1 Mr King is the music teacher / maths teacher.
2 Mr King can talk now / at break.
3 Zane likes computers / music.
4 Zane's computer isn't new / old.
5 Sunita is good with computers / music.

Check

8 STUDY SKILLS All about Lily   I can learn vocabulary in different ways.

Copy the mind map about Lily.
Complete it with the words in the box.

drawing • friendly • nice •
parkour • pencil • phone

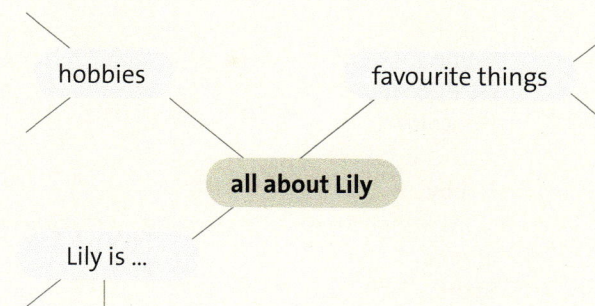

9 READING AND WORDS Noah's poster   I can make a poster about my school.

a) Look at Noah's poster. Match the pictures A–D to the texts 1–4.

1 This is my
   timetable.
   My favourite …
   is maths.

2 This is
   the art room.
   It's my favourite …

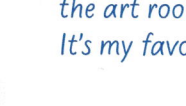

Welcome to Varndean

3 This is
   my uniform.
   The … is red.

4 This is Mr Lee.
   He's my class …
   He's nice!

Lesson	Monday	Tuesday	Wednesday	Thursday	Friday
			REGISTRATION AND ASSEMBLY		
1	English	art	French	computing	music
2	English	maths	French	computing	maths
			BREAK		
3	history	English	science	geography	English
4	geography	music	science	history	French
			LUNCH		
5	maths	science	design and technology	PE	art
6	maths	science	computing	PE	design and technology

b) Complete the sentences in Noah's poster with the words in the box.

place • teacher • lesson • tie

Check

thirty-nine 39

1 Diff bank

▶ Page 18

More practice 1 Four students at Varndean school

Watch the videos again. Write *a*, *b* or *c* for the answers.

Name Sunita Chandra How old? a 10 b 11 c 12 Hobby a coding b drawing c reading Sport a badminton b dancing c yoga	Name Noah Williams How old? a 10 b 11 c 12 Hobby a listening to music b reading c taking photos Sport a basketball b football c walking
Name Zane Adebayo How old? a 10 b 11 c 12 Hobby a coding b cooking c listening to music Sport a basketball b football c swimming	Name Lily Hall How old? a 10 b 11 c 12 Hobby a drawing b listening to music c reading Sport a dancing b parkour c yoga

▶ Page 22

More practice 2 WORDS Lily's things

Write what's in Lily's rucksack.

In Lily's rucksack I can see one ...
I can see two ... and three ...
I can see two keys with an ...

40 forty

More practice 3 SPEAKING **Different desks**

Partner A: Go to page 21 and look at Sunita's desk.
Partner B: Look at Noah's desk. Talk to partner A and find four different things.
Partner B: *In my picture, I can see two brown pencils.*
Partner A: *In my picture, I can see one brown pencil.*

More practice 4 **Rules for class 7C**

Complete the rules.
Use the words in the box.

Be • Listen • Put • Remember • Stand

1 … your school things.
2 … up when the teacher comes into the classroom.
3 … to the teacher.
4 … your hand up to speak.
5 … nice to other students.

▶ Page 24

 More practice 5 **Help Scout**

Complete the sentences with the words in the box.

I • you • ~~he~~ • she • it • we • you • they

1 Zane is a busy boy. **He**'s always tired.
2 Noah and Sunita are good students. …'re clever.
3 Lily is nice. …'s always happy.
4 The kids and I are from Brighton. …'re friends.
5 …'re new here, *Blue Bird*. Welcome to Brighton!
6 Brighton is a nice place. …'s on the sea.
7 …'m hungry.
8 *Blue Bird* and *Black Bird*, I think …'re hungry too. Let's find lunch!

forty-one **41**

1 Diff bank

▶ Page 25

Parallel exercise **4 Messages**

Complete the messages from Noah and his mum.

Hi, Mum! I like the classroom. (1) *It's / They're* big. I like Mr Lee, my teacher, too. (2) *She's / He's* cool. And I like my new friends. (3) *They're / We're* nice. ☺

👍 Great! (4) *It's / You're* lucky, Noah! Varndean School is big, but (5) *she's / it's* a good school. Sorry, (6) *you're / I'm* busy now. See you! ☺

More practice 6 **Scout's day**

Complete the sentences.

1. I... tired!
2. This is my friend *Black Bird*. He... tired too.
3. And my new friend *Blue Bird*? She... tired too.
4. We... all tired!
5. Today is a nice day. But it... busy. What about you?

▶ Page 28

More practice 7 WORDS **Places at school**

a) **Write the correct place.**

1. You can use computers in this room.
2. You can draw pictures here.
3. You can go to different rooms from here.
4. You can do sport in this place.
5. You can eat lunch and snacks here.
6. You have lessons in this room.

b) **Complete the sentence.**

My favourite place at school is ...

Yum! School lunch is good!

▶ Page 29

More practice 8 It's all wrong!

Complete the sentences with *isn't* and *aren't*.

1 Varndean School ... in London. It's in Brighton.
2 The canteen and the sports hall ... in building 1. They're in building 2.
3 The school uniform ... green. It's blue.
4 Mr Lee ... a maths teacher. He's an English teacher.
5 English and geography ... on Tuesday. They're on Monday.
6 The English lessons ... in room 5. They're in room 2.

More practice 9 Describe the pictures

Complete the sentences with *is, isn't, are* or *aren't*.

1 The dog *is* big.
It ... small.

2 Lily and Noah ... nice.
They ... horrible.

3 The book ... new.
It ... old.

4 The sandwiches ... good.
They ... bad.

5 The seagull ... grey.
It ... black.

6 Zane ... tired.
He ... hungry.

More help 5 MY TASK My school

b) Write to Scout about your school.

The name of my school is ... I'm in class ... My class teacher is ...
My favourite place at school is *the art room / the canteen / the sports hall / ...*
My favourite lesson is *maths / English / PE / ...*
My school is *great / nice / cool / OK / ...*

Unit 2
My family and home

That's my family.

🔊 **1** WORDS **Sunita's family**

a) Listen to Sunita and Lily. Point at the people in Sunita's family.

b) Listen again and complete the sentences with the words in the box. ▶ Parallel exercise, p. 70

A Meera is Sunita's …
B Nish is Sunita's …
C Ben is Meera's …
D Ben is Willow's …
E Priya is Sunita's …
F Rahi is Sunita's …
G and H Jay and Anika are Sunita's …
I Grandma Chandra is Meera's …
J Grandpa Chandra is Meera's …

aunt • brother • cousins •
mum (2x) • dad (2x)
partner • uncle

Nach dieser Unit kann ich ...

○ über meine Familie und unsere Haustiere sprechen
○ mein Zuhause und mein Zimmer beschreiben
○ Wörter buchstabieren

Unit task

○ mein Traumzimmer präsentieren

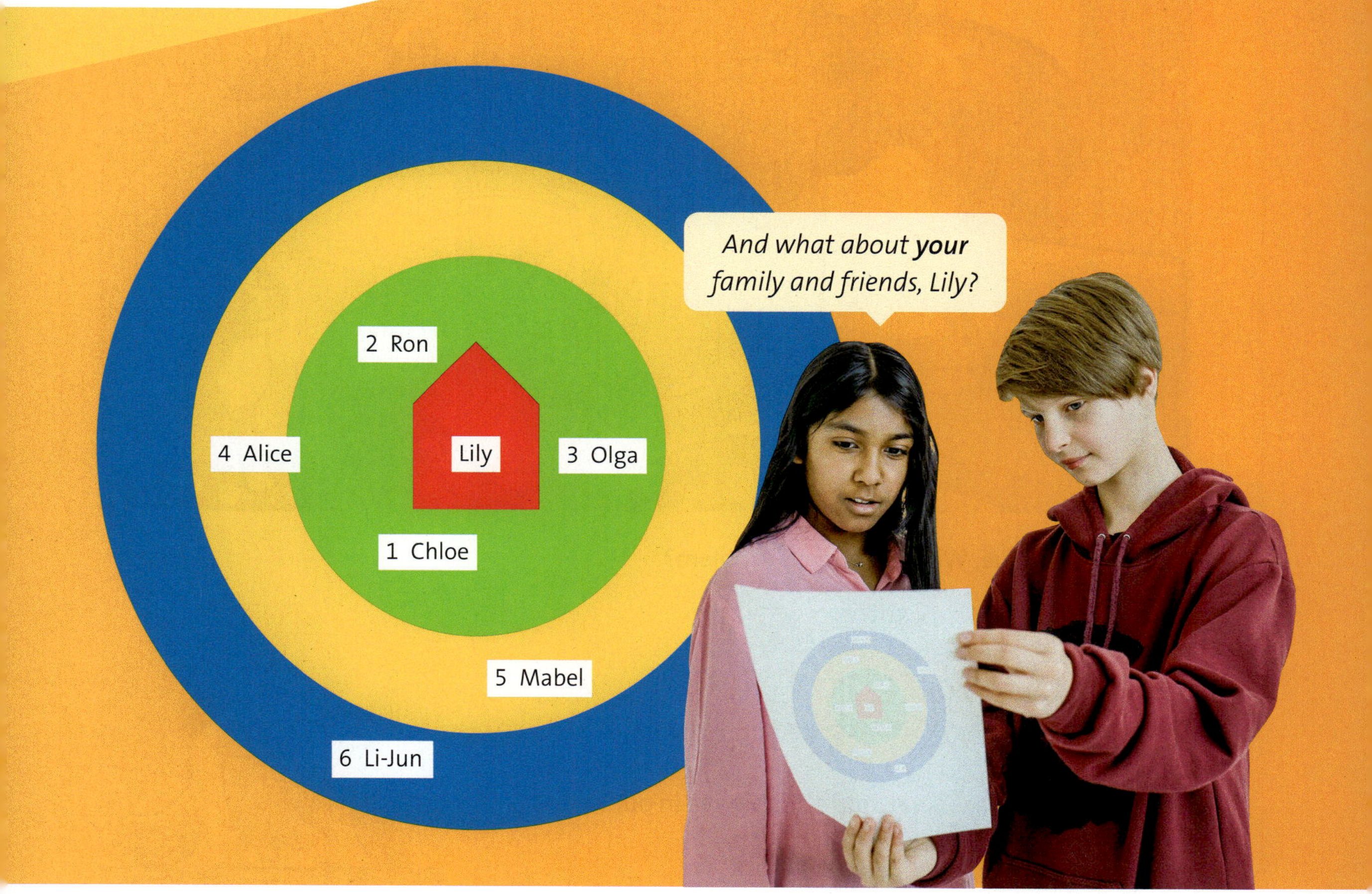

> And what about **your** family and friends, Lily?

2 Ron
4 Alice   Lily   3 Olga
1 Chloe
5 Mabel
6 Li-Jun

2 LISTENING A circle of family, friends and neighbours

a) **Look at Lily's circle. Listen and make six sentences.**

1 Chloe is Lily's sister.
2 Ron is Lily's ...

b) SPEAKING **Draw your circle of important people and tell a partner about them.**

Gabriela is my ...

▶ More practice 1, p. 70   ▶ Wordbank 7, p. 189

▶ Workbook, p. 26

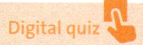   I can **talk about my family.**

2 Topic 1

My pets

1 READING A lot of animals!

a) BEFORE YOU READ One animal in the box isn't in the picture. Find the animal.

> a cat • a fish • a horse • a parrot • a rabbit • a snake • two hamsters

b) Read the dialogue. What's George's problem?

Scout	Hello, I'm Scout.
George	Hi, I'm George.
Scout	Are you OK?
George	No, I'm not. It's not quiet at home!
Scout	Why?
George	Meera is a vet, and animals live in our house at weekends.
Scout	Oh, are they loud?
George	Yes, they are! And the house is so messy!
Scout	Is Meera Sunita's mum?
George	Yes, she is.
Scout	I know Sunita! Are you Sunita's pet?
George	Yes, I am. Are you and Sunita friends?
Scout	Yes, we are!

2 WORDS A cat, a fish, …

Listen and repeat the words from the box in 1a).

▶ Workbook, p. 27

3 LOOKING AT LANGUAGE Questions and short answers

a) Read the dialogue on p. 46 again. Match the questions and answers.

1 Are they loud?
2 Is Meera Sunita's mum?
3 Are you Sunita's pet?
4 Are you and Sunita friends?

A Yes, we are.
B Yes, they are.
C Yes, she is.
D Yes, I am.

b) Match the questions and answers.

1 Is Scout Meera's pet?
2 Are you OK?
3 Is it quiet in Sunita's house?
4 Are George and Scout rabbits?

A No, they aren't.
B No, she isn't.
C No, I'm not.
D No, it isn't.

It's not polite to answer only *yes* or *no*. Use short answers:
Are you OK? Yes, I am.
　　　　　　No, I'm not.

▶ Language file 8, p. 178

4 Scout's questions

a) Scout has some questions for you about animals. Complete the questions with *is* or *are*.

1 … you good with animals?
2 … your favourite animal friendly?
3 … it loud in your house?
4 … you scared of snakes?
5 … you and your family cat fans?

b) Ask your partner the questions in a). Answer your partner's questions with short answers.

Are you good with animals?

Yes, I am.

No, I'm not. What about you?

▶ More practice 2+3, p. 70

▶ Workbook, p. 28

2 Topic 1

5 LISTENING Is that your pet?

a) BEFORE YOU LISTEN What animals can you see?

> I can see …

A

B

C

D

b) Listen to the dialogue about pets. Which picture (A–D) is correct for:

1 Noah?   2 Zane?   3 Lily?

c) Listen again and write the answers.

▶ Parallel exercise, p. 71

1 Are you OK, Sunita? — No, I'm not.
2 Is it hard to do your homework? — Yes, …
3 Is your dog Buddy loud? — No, …
4 Are you too busy for pets? — Yes, …
5 Are they your pets? — No, …

6 READING FindAPet

a) BEFORE YOU READ Look at the pictures. Which pet is your favourite?

b) Now read about the pets. Read about Lily's dream pet too.

> My dream pet is interesting. It's not too big or too loud!

Rex is a big and happy dog.
He's very friendly, but he's very loud!

Axel is a special pet – he's a small, green lizard.
He's quiet and very fast.

c) Which pet is right for her? Say why.

> I think … is right for Lily because …

Maude is an old and slow cat.
She's cute, but she isn't very friendly!

7 WORDS Animals

Complete the sentences with the words in the box.

> big • cute • clever • fast • friendly • loud • quiet • small

The rabbit is …

The snake is …

The dog is …

The cat is …

The horse is …

The monkey is …

The parrot is …

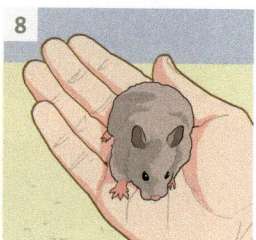
The mouse is …

My task

8 My pet or dream pet

a) Write about your pet or dream pet.

I have a … *My dream pet is a …*
Her name is … *His name is …*
She's … *He's …*
She isn't … *He isn't …*

▶ Digital help   ▶ More help, p. 71   ▶ Wordbank 8, p. 190

b) Think of questions to ask your partner. You can use the words in exercise 7.

Is your pet cute? Is your pet …?

c) Interview your partner about their pet or dream pet.

I have a cat. Her name is Molly.

Is Molly cute?

Yes, she is.

Is she …?

▶ Workbook, p. 29

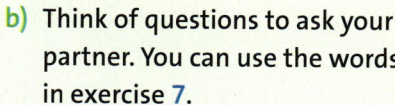
I can talk about pets.

2 Topic 2

Different homes

1 LISTENING Four homes

a) BEFORE YOU LISTEN Look at the photos. Is it a flat or a house? Guess.

A — tree, garden

B — ground floor

C — top floor

D

b) Listen to Zane, Sunita, Noah and Lily. Write the correct photo for each person.

Zane: B, Sunita: ...

2 About the homes

Listen again. Choose the correct words.

Zane	There's / There are two flats.
Sunita	There's / There are a big garden and there's / there are a lot of trees.
Noah	There's / There are a small garden.
Lily	There's / There are friendly neighbours.

▶ More practice 4, p. 71   ▶ Language file 9, p. 178

3 VIEWING A tour of Sunita's home

a) BEFORE YOU WATCH What can you remember from exercise 1 about Sunita's home?

It's a ... house.   *Yes, and there's a ...*

b) Watch the tour of Sunita's house. Can you see Sunita's room?

4 Words Rooms

a) Match photos A–F to rooms 1–6.

1E, 2…

1 bathroom
2 mum's bedroom
3 hall
4 dining area
5 living room
6 kitchen

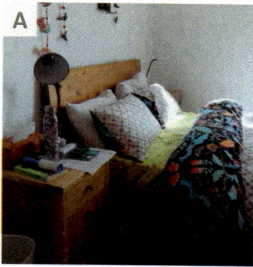

b) Watch the video again. In what order can you see the rooms?

c) Right or wrong?
1 The living room is on the ground floor.
2 Nish's room is on the ground floor.
3 Mum's bedroom is on the top floor.
4 There are three bathrooms.
5 Mum's office is in the living room.
6 Sunita's room is on the top floor.

My task

5 My home

a) Read Lily's message to her new friend about her home. Complete her chat with the words in the box.

> small and nice • mum and dad •
> your • Brighton • flat •
> a living room and two bedrooms

I live with my (1) …
We live in a (2) … in (3) …
It's (4) …
There's a kitchen,
a bathroom, (5) …
Tell me about (6) … home!

b) Write a chat message to a new friend about your home or dream home. Use Lily's chat.

▶ Digital help   ▶ More help, p. 72

▶ Workbook, pages 30–31

I can describe my home or dream home.

In my room

1 Speaking Sunita's room

a) Look at the picture. What can you see?

I can see …   *There's a …*   *There are two/three …*

b) Right or wrong? Correct the wrong sentences.

1 There are three red cushions on the bed.
2 There's a robot on the sofa.
3 There's a small table with a blue lamp.
4 There's a green chair.
5 There are two cushions on the sofa.
6 There's a computer on the desk.
7 There's a white wardrobe.

▶ Parallel exercise, p. 72

2 Words Things in a room

Match the blue and red word parts and write the things.

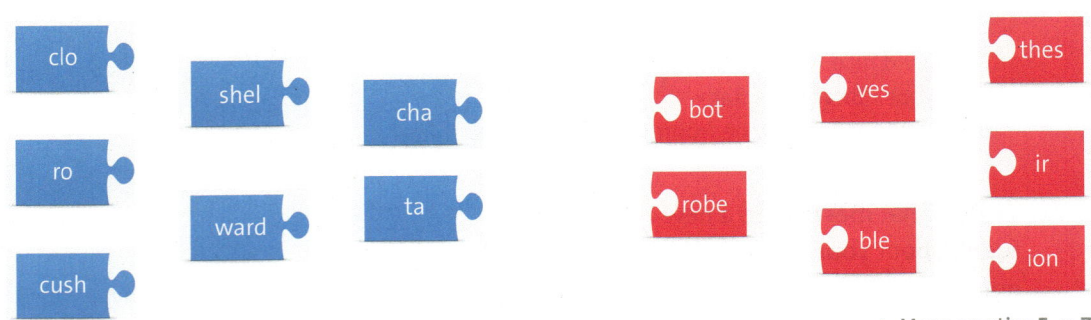

▶ More practice 5, p. 72

▶ Workbook, p. 32

3 Where is it?

a) BEFORE YOU READ Look at the picture of Sunita's room.
What's different to the room in ex. 1 on p. 52? *The room in this picture is …*

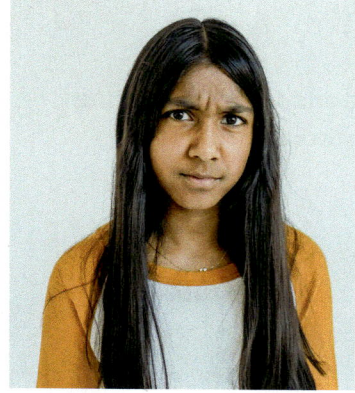

*Oh no! Look at my room! It's so messy!
The cushions are on the floor.
And the lamp is on the floor too, next to the bed.
And one book is on the desk, in front of the computer.
Who is in here? Who is that behind the door? Is it George?
And who is that under the bed? Is it Scout?
Where's Robbie the robot?
And where's my chocolate? It isn't on my desk.
Chocolate is Nish's favourite thing!
Hey Nish, where's my chocolate?*

b) Read what Sunita says. Look at her room and answer the questions with the words in the box.

1. Who is behind the door? … is behind the door.
2. Who is under the bed? … is under the bed.
3. Where are the cushions? The cushions are …
4. Who is Robbie? Robbie is Sunita's …
5. Where's Robbie? He's …

> on the chair • Scout • robot • George • on the floor

c) OPINION LINE Is your room messy or tidy? Stand in a line. Then count the students.

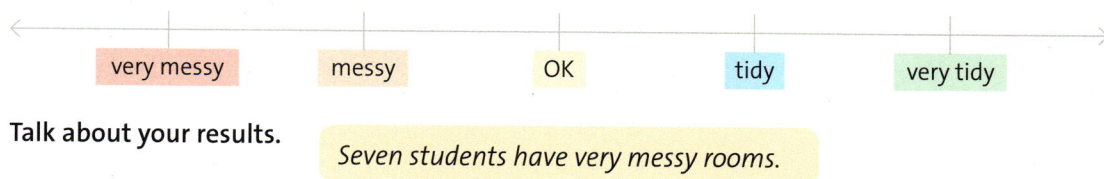

Talk about your results.

Seven students have very messy rooms.

4 Where's Scout?

a) **Partner A:** Choose a picture. Tell your partner where Scout is. Use the words in the box. *Scout is under the bed.*
Partner B: Say which picture it is. *That's picture …*

> behind • in • in front of • on • next to • under

b) WALK AROUND Draw another picture with Scout. Walk around and show your picture to different students. Look at the new pictures and say where Scout is.

▶ More practice 6+7, p. 73

5 Question words

a) Look at the picture and answer the questions.

WHO is George?
WHERE is George?
WHAT is George's favourite food?

b) What are the three question words in German?

6 Questions for you

a) Your teacher has a questionnaire for you. Choose the correct question word.

1 Who / Where is your home?
2 What / Who is your favourite person in your family?
3 Who / What is your favourite room in your home?
4 Where / Who is your room in your home?
5 Who / What is your favourite thing in your room?
6 Where / Who are your neighbours?

b) Ask and answer the questions with a partner.

▶ Workbook, p. 33

7 Where are my things?

a) Sunita can't find her things. Complete Sunita's questions with *who*, *where* or *what*.

1 … are my sandwiches? – Nish: They're in your bag.
2 … has my tie? – Mum: Not me! I think it's in the hall.
3 … has my sweets? – Nish: Not me! I like chocolate.
4 … is my black shoe? – Nish: Is it under your bed?
5 … animals are in the house today? – Mum: A dog, a cat and a snake.
6 … is the snake? – Mum: It's in its terrarium.

b) Look at the pictures. Which answer in a) (1–6) isn't right?

▶ More practice 8, p. 74

My task

8 My room

a) SPEAKING Ask your partner questions about their room. Make notes. You can ask more questions.

Questions	Answers
Is your room big or small?	It's big / small.
Is it your own room?	Yes, it's my own room. No, it's not my own room. It's my sister's room too.
What's in your room?	There are / There aren't a lot of things in my room. There's a bed and a wardrobe, a desk and …
Are there pets in your room?	Yes, there are. I have a … No, there aren't.

▶ Digital help   ▶ Wordbank 9, p. 190

b) Use your notes.
Draw your partner's room.

c) Swap pictures with your partner.
Are all your things in the picture?

▶ Workbook, p. 34

I can describe my room.

2 Story

At home with Sunita

1 Song Ben's song

a) Listen to Ben's song. What is it about?

  A Ben's pet   B Ben's partner, Meera   C Ben and Willow's flat

b) Talk about the song: *I like it. / I don't like it. / It's a nice song. / …*

▶ More practice 9, p. 74

2 Reading Feelings

a) Before you read Talk about how the people in pictures 1–3 feel.

Sunita is …   Nish is …
Lily is …   Ben is …

angry • happy • sad • tired

b) Read Sunita and Lily's messages. Check your answers to a).

> Hi, Lily. Are you at home?

>> Hi, Sunita. Yes, I am. I'm alone and it's very quiet 😌. My parents are at work, of course.

> It isn't quiet here! My mum is at work, but my brother is in his room. Willow is at her mum's house, but Ben is here.

>> Ben is nice, right?

> Yes, he is. He's funny and he's a great cook! But he's always in the living room with his guitar. And his music is horrible! 😠

>> Tell him!

> But he's so nice. And mum is a big fan of his music.

>> Sorry, Sunita. It's time for parkour. Speak later! Remember: Talk to Ben!

c) Now it's time for dinner. Look at the pictures and listen. What's Sunita's problem?

A Dinner is bad.   B Nish is mean.   C Ben's music is too loud.

d) Read the end of the story. Is it a happy ending?

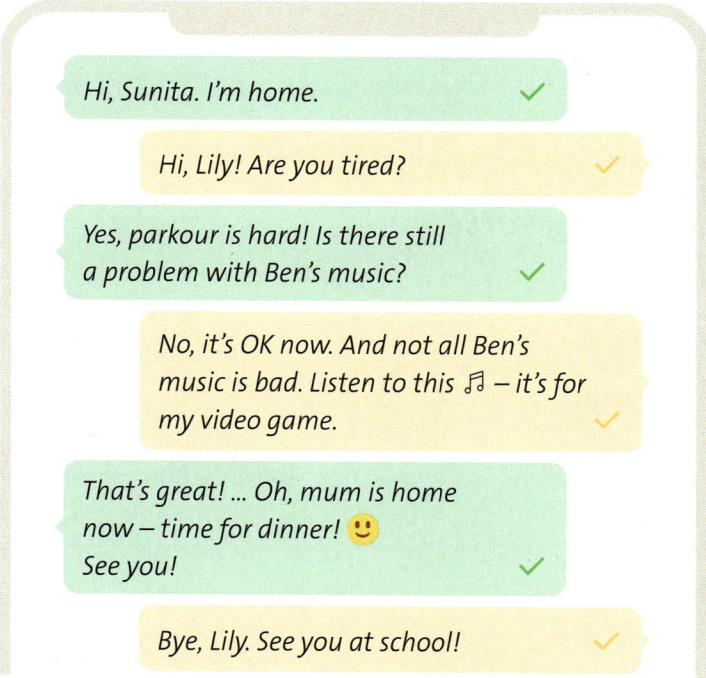

2 Story

3 Reading The story

Put sentences A–D in the correct order.

A Ben plays his new song, but Nish and Sunita aren't happy.
B Sunita is on her phone with Lily: She isn't happy about the noise at home.
C Sunita and Lily listen to Ben's music for the video game. It's great!
D Ben has an idea: He can use headphones. Then he helps Sunita with her video game.

4 Who is it?

Choose the correct names.

1 Sunita / Lily is alone at home.
2 Nish / Ben is in his room.
3 Meera / Ben is nice and a great cook.
4 Nish / Sunita can't code because it's loud.
5 Sunita / Lily is tired because parkour is hard.

5 Words Word snake

Find the words and match them to the pictures. You don't need three words.

guitarroomcookparkourheadphonessofamessagesdinnerphone

A  B 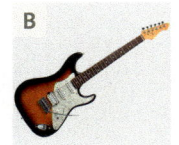 C  D 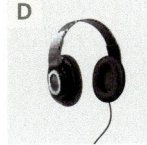 E  F

6 Life skills Talk about problems

SPEAKING Do the role-plays.
Use the ideas in the table.
Take turns to be A and B.

A I have a problem when you …
B I'm sorry. I can …
A That's a good idea. Thanks.
B You're welcome.

Partner A	Partner B
play loud music	be quiet
are in the bathroom a long time	be fast
make the kitchen messy	be tidy
take my computer	ask you first

▶ Workbook, p. 35

I can understand a problem and talk about it.

The Brighton dares: Family

1 BEFORE YOU WATCH Can you guess the dares?

Look at the pictures and read the sentences.
Daisy and Emir do two new dares this week.
Can you guess them? Say the numbers.

1 Make a 3D family tree
2 Hug a tree
3 Hug a postbox
4 Write a love letter to a student in your class.

(to) hug
umarmen

postbox
Briefkasten

letter
Brief

family tree
*Familien-
stammbaum*

2 VIEWING The story

a) Watch the video and check your guesses in **1**. Which dares are in the video?

b) Put the pictures in the correct order.

c) Choose the correct answer.

1 The postbox is in front of Luke's / Emir's house.
2 Mrs Collins wants to find her father / cousin.
3 Emir makes his family tree at the park / on the beach.
4 Gloria stops / helps Emir.
5 Mrs Collins and Mr Campbell / Robert Collins speak on the phone.
6 Emir's tree is / isn't very good.

Spelling

1 Song The alphabet

a) Look at the alphabet song in the box and listen. Then listen again and sing.

b) Sing or say the alphabet in pairs.
Partner A: black lines.
Partner B: blue lines.

A B C D E
F G H I J
K L M N O
P Q R S T
U V W
X Y Z
That's the alphabet!

2 Name, address and phone number

Sunita is on the phone about a coding course. There are three mistakes. Listen and find them.

First name: Sunita
Family name: Chondra
Address: 22 Palmeira Road, Brighton, BN3 2JN
Phone number: 07700-900576

! You say phone numbers in English like this: 07700 900638
oh–seven–seven–oh–oh
nine–oh–oh–six–three–eight

▶ More practice 10, p. 74

3 Spell, write and say

a) Write three long words from this unit in your exercise book. Don't show your partner!

bathroom, ...

b) **Partner A:** Spell a word for partner B.
Partner B: Write the word. Then say it and check the spelling. Take turns.

B-A-T-H-R-O-O-M

B-A-T-H-R-O-O-M

Can you say that again, please?

It's "bathroom".
Your spelling is correct.

▶ Skills file 3, p. 168

I can spell words correctly.

| Topic 1 | Topic 2 | Topic 3 | Story | Viewing | Study skills | Unit task | 2 |

Present your dream room

Step 1

a) Collect words and phrases for your dream room. Use a mind map.

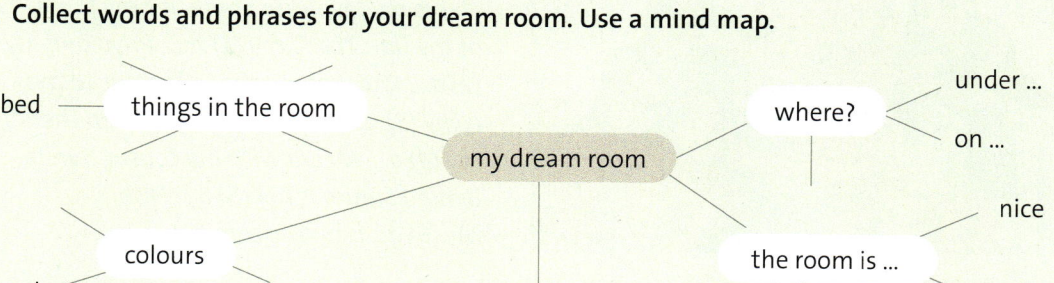

b) Check the spelling in the *E–G Dictionary* (pages 236–246). ▶ Digital help

Step 2

Think about your dream room. Draw it, find photos or make it on the computer.

Step 3

a) Write about your dream room (at least five sentences).

There's a big red sofa. There's a dog on the bed. There are a lot of posters. It's quiet. …

▶ Digital help   ▶ More help, p. 75   ▶ Wordbank 9, p. 190

b) Read your partner's sentences and check the spelling.

c) Practise with your partner: Read your sentences and show your picture.

Look at my picture. This is my dream room. …

Step 4

a) Present your dream room to your group. Read your description and show your picture.

b) Give other students feedback on their dream room.

Your dream room is cool.   *I like the posters.*

▶ Skills file 5, p. 171   ▶ Let's talk: Feedback geben, p. 200

I can present my dream room.

2 Checkpoint   Digital checkpoint

1 Words Jay's favourite picture

I can talk about my family.

Jay is Sunita's cousin. Look at his picture and complete his sentences.

This is my favourite photo. It's my family at my flat. That's my (1) m..., Priya and my (2) d..., Rahi behind the sofa. Next to me is my (3) s..., Anika. She's nice! Then there's my (4) a..., Meera with my cousin, Sunita. Behind Sunita is her (5) b..., Nish. My (6) g... is on the sofa too.

2 Words Priya's pictures

Priya is Sunita's aunt. Look at her pictures. Choose A or B for each sentence.

1. That's me and Rahi. We're Jay and Anika's parents.
2. These are Jay's cousins, Sunita and Nish.
3. That's their parrot George.
4. That's Jay. He's 11.
5. That's my sister – she's Jay's aunt.
6. And that's Anika, she's Jay's sister.

3 On the phone to *FindAPet*

I can talk about pets (questions and short answers).

a) LANGUAGE Lily is on the phone with Ms Taylor from *FindAPet*. Complete Ms Taylor's questions with *Is* or *Are*. Then complete Lily's answers with *am / 'm not / are / aren't / is / isn't*.

1. ... you good with animals? – Yes, I ...
2. ... your flat big? – No, it ...
3. ... your home quiet? – Yes, it ...
4. ... you and your family cat fans? – No, we ...
5. ... your neighbours dog fans? – No, they ...
6. ... you scared of lizards? – No, I ...

b) SPEAKING Ask your partner four questions from a). He/She answers. Take turns.

Check

Die Übungen kannst du auch digital machen **2**

4 WRITING Amira's email to Ben

I can describe my home or dream home.

Look at Amira's mind map about her home. Write her message to her new British friend.

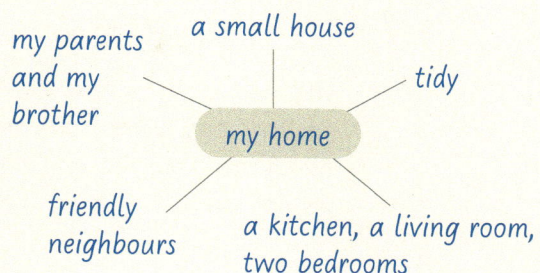

Start your sentences like this:

I live with …
We live in …
It's …
There's / There are …
Our neighbours are …

5 LISTENING Noah's room

I can describe my room.

a) Listen to Noah. What's in his room? Write three letters.

b) Listen again. Choose the correct answer. Write A or B.

1 Is Noah's room tidy?   A No, it isn't tidy.   B Yes, it's very tidy.
2 Where is Noah's desk?   A It's in front of the shelves.   B It's behind the shelves.
3 Where is Buddy?   A He's under the bed.   B He's behind the bed.
4 Is Noah's room quiet?   A No, it isn't quiet.   B Yes, it's always quiet.

Check

sixty-three **63**

2 Checkpoint Digital checkpoint

6 Reading Lily wants a new pet

I can understand a problem and talk about it.

a) Read the messages.

Friday, 16.00

NOAH
Hi, Lily. Buddy says "hello"! That's his favourite ball.

LILY
Hi, Noah, hi, Buddy! You're so lucky. My pets don't play with me.

Saturday, 11.00

NOAH
We're near your flat. Are you at home?

LILY
That's great! Yes, I'm at home. You and Buddy can meet my two fish. And we can play with Buddy.

Saturday, 13.00

LILY
I'm very sorry, Mum. Noah and Buddy are in our flat, and now it's very messy.

MUM
Why is Buddy in the flat?

LILY
Mum, I REALLY like animals! I'm often alone in the flat. I'm sorry. Are you angry?

MUM
No, I'm not angry. Let's talk to Noah's parents. You can go to their house sometimes.

Sunday, 10.30

LILY
Hi, Mum. This is me and Buddy in Noah's garden. See you!

---

b) Put the pictures in the correct order.

A B C D E

c) What's Lily's problem? Choose the right sentence. Write A **or** B.

A Lily's mum is angry because Buddy is in the flat.
B Lily is often alone and wants to play with a pet.

Check

64 sixty-four

Die Übungen kannst du auch digital machen

2

7 STUDY SKILLS Sunita's messages

I can spell words correctly.

One word is wrong in each message. Write the correct word.

1. Ben's music is too DOUL – again!
2. Hi, Lily, the art EWORKHOM is hard – can you help me?
3. Coding is hard to NEARL, but it's fun!
4. Nish, thank you for the OLATECHOC!
5. I'm at home today. It's very quiet because I'm OALEN.
6. Mum, what's for NERDIN? I'm really hungry.
7. Hi, Zane. Do you know Noah's DRESSAD please?
8. Hi, Noah, it's time for homework. KASPE later.

8 LISTENING At the vet

There are two new animals at the vet. Copy the forms. Listen and complete them.

1
Pet's name: *Queenie*
Animal: …
Family name: *Fruin*
Phone number: …

2
Pet's name: *Hermes*
Animal: …
Family name: …
Phone number: *07700* …

9 SPEAKING Zane's dream room

I can present my dream room.

Look at Zane's picture of his dream room. Talk about it. Say at least five sentences. You can use the words in the boxes.

| bag • bed • cat • computer • cushions • desk • football posters • guitar • sofa |

| big • cool • great • green • messy • nice • quiet |

This is Zane's dream room.
It's … and …
The … is / are …
There's / There are …
The … is on the …

Check

sixty-five **65**

VARNDEAN Teen Zine

This month's topics: pets, homes and families

Our school magazine: by students for students

Lucy's Poems[1]

I love writing poems! Here are two poems about pets.

I have a dog
She has a blog
She's always fine
When she's online!

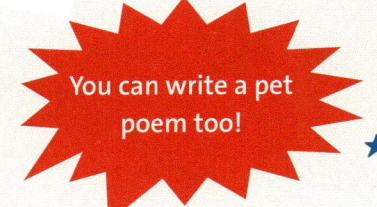

You can write a pet poem too!

I have a snake
His name is Jake
He's white and green
And very mean!

My pet by Max

I have a bearded dragon[2] or a 'beardie'. Here's a photo of him. Isn't he cute? His name is Drago and he's grey and yellow.

Beardies can swim and move fast. They can live for 10–12 years. Drago is four. He's active in the day and he's very funny.

Drago has a big terrarium with a lamp. It's nice and warm under the lamp.

I think Drago is great!

Hello!

We like Drago too! What about you?
Is your pet great? Write to us and send a photo!

---

[1] **poem** *das Gedicht*   [2] **bearded dragon** *Bartagame (Echsenart)*

Puzzle time

What am I? Can you say the animal?

> I have four legs[1], but I'm not a dog
> I can run fast, but I'm not a lion
> I like carrots, but I'm not a rabbit
> You can ride me, but I'm not a camel
> What am I?

Where do they live?

Emma, Zendaya, Leon and Danny all live in the same street[2]. What are their house numbers?

1. Emma's house number isn't 2 or 6.
2. Zendaya's house is between[3] Emma and Leon's houses.
3. Leon's house is next to Danny's house.

Make a paper family

You need:

- a piece of paper (DIN A4)
- a pencil
- scissors[4]
- coloured pens

1

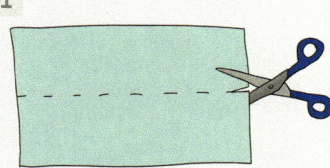

Fold[5] an A4 piece of paper in half. Cut[6] it in two.

2

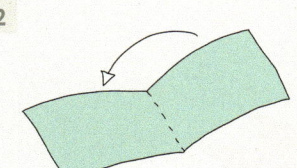

Take one piece. Fold it in half.

3

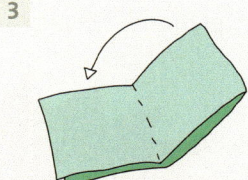

Fold it in half again.

4

Draw a person on one side of the folded paper.

5

Cut out the person.

6

Open the paper. You can draw on the paper.

---

[1] **leg** *das Bein* [2] **street** *die Straße* [3] **between** *zwischen* [4] **scissors** *die Schere* [5] **(to) fold** *falten*
[6] **(to) cut** *schneiden*

Teen Zine Special: Festivals

Christmas

I'm Lyle and this is my sister Astra. I want to tell you all about Christmas in my family:

Before Christmas

★ We write Christmas cards to family and friends.
★ We decorate[1] a Christmas tree.
★ My friends and I go to the neighbours' houses and sing Christmas songs.

Christmas Eve[4] (24th December)

★ We hang up[5] our stockings[6].
★ We make Christmas cookies[7].
★ We put cookies and milk under the tree for Father Christmas, and a carrot for reindeer[8] Rudolph.

Christmas Day (25th December)

★ We open our presents[9] in the morning.
★ My parents make the turkey[10] for dinner.
★ My grandparents and my aunt and uncle and cousins eat with us.
★ After dinner we play a game.

We wish[2] you a merry Christmas[3]
We wish you a merry Christmas
We wish you a merry Christmas
and a happy new year.

Is Christmas important for you? Tell us about your holidays!

---

[1] (to) **decorate** schmücken [2] (to) **wish** wünschen [3] **Merry Christmas** frohe Weihnachten
[4] **Christmas Eve** der Heiligabend [5] (to) **hang** sth. up etwas aufhängen [6] **stocking** der Strumpf
[7] **cookie** der Keks, das Plätzchen [8] **reindeer** das Rentier [9] **present** das Geschenk [10] **turkey** der Truthahn

Chinese New Year

I'm Vivian and my family is Chinese. There are about 400,000 Chinese people in Britain and Chinese New Year is a very important festival for us.
It can be in January or February. Brighton has a big party for Chinese New Year!

There are 15 days of the Chinese New Year. Here are my favourite days:

New Year's Eve: The day before Chinese New Year we see our families and eat a special dinner.

Day 1 It's New Year's Day! We have new clothes for this important day and go to our grandma and grandpa's house. They give[1] us money in red packets[2]. Red is a lucky colour.

Day 15 It's the Lantern[3] Festival! I like taking photos of the different lanterns. We always go to the parade. There are a lot of animals and people in it – dancing! The lion and the dragon[4] are my favourite animals. Happy New Year!

Kung Hey Fat Choi! Happy New Year!

Tell us about you and your family's New Year's traditions: the food you eat, the things you do …

---

[1] (to) **give** *geben, schenken*   [2] **packet** *das Päckchen*   [3] **lantern** *die Laterne*   [4] **dragon** *der Drache*

2 Diff bank

▶ Page 44

 Parallel exercise **1 WORDS Sunita's family**

Listen to Sunita and Lily. Choose the correct answer.

A Meera is Sunita's sister / mum.
B Nish is Sunita's brother / partner.
C Ben is Meera's partner / grandpa.
D Ben is Willow's partner / dad.
E Priya is Sunita's aunt / mum.
F Rahi is Sunita's brother / uncle.
G and H Jay and Anika are Sunita's uncles / cousins.
I Grandma Chandra is Meera's mum / aunt.
J Grandpa Chandra is Meera's uncle / dad.

▶ Page 45

More practice 1 **WORDS Family words**

**Copy and complete the table.
Use the words from the box.**

| aunt • brother • cousin • dad • grandpa • grandma • mum • partner • sister • uncle |

brother
...

...

...

▶ Page 47

More practice 2 **Scout's family and friends**

Read the sentences. Make questions.

1 Sally is Scout's cousin.
   → Is Sally Scout's cousin?
2 Scout's mum and dad are from Brighton.
3 Scout's brothers are loud.
4 She is very friendly.
5 We are all Scout's friends.

More practice 3 **HOT SEAT Act out!**

a) **Find a partner. First write the questions together.**

1 you / a vet / are / ?
2 Sunita / is / your sister / ?
3 your house / this / is / ?
4 are / happy / you and Ben / ?
5 cats / your favourite animals / are / ?

b) **Now write short answers together and act out the dialogue.**

70 seventy

▶ Page 48

Parallel exercise **5** LISTENING **Is that your pet?**

c) Listen again and match the answers to the questions.

1 Are you OK, Sunita?
2 Is it hard to do your homework?
3 Is your dog Buddy loud?
4 Are you too busy for pets?
5 Are they your pets?

a No, they aren't.
b Yes, I am.
c No, I'm not.
d No, he isn't.
e Yes, it is.

▶ Page 49

More help **8** MY TASK **My pet or dream pet**

Read about Nish's dream pet and look at the box for more ideas. Change the words in blue.

My dream pet is a horse.
He's brown and very big.
He's friendly.
He's not slow or loud.

big • black • brown • cute •
fast • friendly • green • grey •
happy • loud • old • quiet •
slow • small • white

▶ Page 50

More practice 4 **A special house**

a) Zane's friend has a special house. Choose the correct words for Zane's sentences.

1 There's / There are eleven floors. The ground floor is white. The other floors are red, white, red, …
2 There's / There are one room on each floor.
3 There's / There are eleven rooms. The top two floors are red.
4 There's / There are a red lamp at the top of the building.
5 There's / There are no garden.

b) Draw the house with a partner. Then compare with the photo on p. 75.

2 Diff bank

▶ Page 51

More help **5** MY TASK **My home**

b) Write a chat message to a new friend about your home or dream home.
You can add other things.

I live with my	dad / mum / grandma / grandpa / brother / sister.
We live in a	house / flat in …
It's	old / new / big / small / nice / quiet / loud.
There's a kitchen, a bathroom and	a living room / an office / a toilet / three bedrooms / a garden.
Tell me about your home!	

▶ Page 52

Parallel exercise **1** SPEAKING **Sunita's room**

b) Choose the correct answer.

1 There are three red / blue cushions on the bed.
2 There's a robot on the sofa / desk.
3 There's a small table with a blue / yellow lamp.
4 There's a green / brown chair.
5 There are two / three cushions on the sofa.
6 There's a computer on the desk / bed.
7 There's a white / brown wardrobe.

More practice 5 **Nish's room**

Help Nish. Complete his homework about his room. Write the words. Example: *1 bed, 2 …*

In my room there's a big (1)  . There's a nice blue (2) with my (3)

and (4)  . And there is a big (5) and a (6) .

There are brown (7)  with (8)  and a (9) .

There are a lot of music (10)  . There are two (11)  .

> ▶ Page 54

More practice 6 **Where is it?**

Say where the things or animals are. Your partner says the thing or animal. Take turns.

> *I see a brown thing or animal under the desk.*

> *It's a rabbit.*

More practice 7 **Different homes**

a) **Partner A:** Choose a picture – don't tell your partner! Talk about the home.
In this picture there's … / there are …
Partner B: Guess the picture. *I think it's picture 2.*

small brown house • one big window • a red door • a big garden with trees

big grey house • very old • two old trees next to it

a new, big pink building • big windows • three trees in front

an old, pink house • small windows • a big garden • no trees

a brown house • a black door • two big windows • a lot of trees behind the house

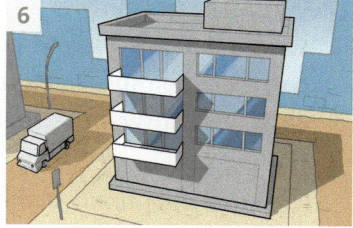

a new, grey building • no garden

b) **Swap roles.**

2 Diff bank

▶ Page 55

More practice 8 — **Questions**

Complete the questions with *who, where* or *what*. Then write the name of the student.

1. ... is the name of your school?   The name of my school is Varndean.
2. ... is your home?   It's in Hove.
3. ... is your sister?   My sister is Sunita.
4. ... is your favourite thing?   It's chocolate.
5. ... is your name?   My name is ...

▶ Page 56

More practice 9 — **Ben's song**

a) Listen to the song about Ben and Willow's flat. Put lines a–i in the correct order: *1f, 2c, 3...*

b) Listen again and check.

c) Describe the flat in one sentence. It's ...

My little flat

a And the living room is always very messy
b There are two small bedrooms, there aren't three
c And it isn't new or modern at all
d There aren't expensive pictures on the wall
e But my little flat is perfect for me
f People ask, 'Is your flat big?' No, it's small
g There's my family, that's enough
h My little flat is perfect for me
i Because there's music, there's love

▶ Page 60

More practice 10 — **Name, address and phone number**

First name:
Family name:
Address:
Phone number:

Find a partner and copy the form.

Partner A: Ask partner B the questions in the yellow speech bubbles and complete the form.
Use the green speech bubbles to check.
Partner B: Answer the questions.

> What's your family name?

> What's your address?

> What's your phone number?

> Can you spell that, please?

> Can you say that again, please?

> Is that right?

Now change roles: Partner B asks the questions, and partner A answers.

▶ Numbers, p. 258

▶ Page 61

More help | UNIT TASK **Present your dream room**

a) **Step 3** Write about your room. Write at least five sentences.

There's	a big red sofa.
	a dog on the bed / a parrot / ...
	a very big wardrobe for my clothes.
	a guitar.
There are	a lot of posters / photos / lamps / cushions / ...
	two cats / hamsters / ...
It's	big / small.
	quiet.
	tidy / messy.

▶ Page 71

More practice 4 **A special house**

Compare your drawing with the photo.

Unit 3
My day

Five of our students tell us about their school journeys. ❤️
😊 #greenschooljourneys

1 LISTENING School journeys

a) BEFORE YOU LISTEN **Guess: Who says what? Match sentences 1–5 to photos A–E.**

1 I go to school by bike.
2 I go to school by car.
3 I go to school by bus.
4 I go to school by train.
5 I walk to school.

b) **Listen to the students and check your answers from a). Then read sentences 1–5. True or false?**

1 Zane's flat is near the school.
2 Sunita's school journey is short.
3 Noah goes to school by car with his mum.
4 Lily has a long journey to school.
5 Alice is alone on her school journey.

▶ Language file 5, p. 176

Nach dieser Unit kann Ich ... ✓

- über meinen Schulweg sprechen
- meinen Alltag beschreiben
- mich verabreden
- neue Wörter nachschlagen und lernen

Unit task ✓

- die Höhepunkte meiner Woche vorstellen

2 SPEAKING My school journey

a) WALK AROUND Talk about your school journey. Find three students with the same transport.

I go to school by bus. What about you?   *Me too.*

I	go to school by	bike.
		bus.
		car.
		train.
walk to school.		

b) **Tell the class:** *Anna, Erdem, Sami and I go to school by bus.*

▶ More practice 1, p. 99

▶ Workbook, p. 40

Digital quiz 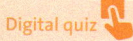 **I can** talk about my school journey.

seventy-seven **77**

3 Topic 1

A weekday

1 Words Big numbers

a) Listen and repeat the numbers. Stand up for the blue numbers. Sit down for the black numbers.

10 15 20 25 30 35 40 45 50 55 60

b) Listen to the numbers. If the number is under 20, make yourself small. If it's over 20, make yourself big.

▶ Numbers, p. 258   ▶ More practice 2, p. 99

2 Speaking What's the time?

Partner B: Go to p. 98. Partner A:

a) Ask the time: *What's the time?* Listen to your partner and write the five times.

b) Look at the clocks. Tell your partner the time: *It's ... o'clock.*

A	B	C	D	E
9.00	11.00	3.00	4.00	8.00

Good to know
Britain uses the 12-hour clock with a.m. and p.m.

▶ More practice 3, p. 99

3 Listening It's time for ...

a) Before you listen Match the times. *1D, 2...*

1 It's twelve forty-five.
2 It's one fifteen.
3 It's three oh five.
4 It's ten twenty.
5 It's one thirty.
6 It's twelve oh five.

A	B	C
12.05	1.30	3.05

D	E	F
12.45	1.15	10.20

b) Listen to a school tour with a new student. Write the times.

1 The start of school is at ...
2 Assembly is at ...
3 Lesson 1 is at ...
4 Break is at ...
5 Lunch is at ...
6 The end of school is at ...

▶ More practice 4+5, p. 100   ▶ Wordbank 10, p. 191
▶ Workbook, p. 41

4 Reading Before and after school

a) BEFORE YOU READ What's true about Zane? Talk to a partner.
Then check on the pages in Unit 1.

1. His hobby is parkour. (U1, p. 19)
2. He's a swimmer. (U1, p. 19)
3. He's always busy. (U1, p. 30)

> His hobby is parkour.

> I think that's right / wrong. Let's check.

b) Zane's family is in the newspaper.
Look at the picture, the title and the first paragraph. Choose the correct answer.

Who is Louise Adebayo? – She's Zane's teacher / mum.
Who can win the competition? – The best kid / pet.

My son is the best!

This text for our 'Best Kids Competition' is from Louise Adebayo. It's about her son Zane (11).

I use a wheelchair. My husband Eno
5 has a cafe and he works long days.
On weekdays, my son Zane helps me.

Zane gets up at 7 o'clock and has
a shower. Eno makes breakfast for us
and we all eat breakfast. Zane walks with
10 his sister Holly to her school at 8.15
and then he goes to his school. Then
I work on the computer. I write books.

Zane meets Holly at her school at 3.20
and they walk home. Then he does his
15 homework. It takes an hour. Sometimes
Zane helps me with dinner.

Or he talks to his friends or watches TV.
On Friday he goes swimming.

20 Zane, you're a really good kid. You're not
in trouble at school and you always help
me. You're the best!

c) Zane's weekday
Read about Zane's day. Put his activities in the correct order: *1E, 2...*

- A Zane does his homework.
- B He eats breakfast with his family.
- C He walks with Holly to her school at 8.15.
- D Zane talks to his friends or watches TV.
- E He gets up at 7 o'clock and has a shower.
- F Zane meets Holly at her school at 3.20.

5 LOOKING AT LANGUAGE Simple present

a) Read these sentences from the text and find the rule.

I *use* a wheelchair.
We all *eat* breakfast.

> Die Zeitform der Verben *use* und *eat* heißt *simple present*.
> Was ist richtig? Wähle A oder B.
> Mit dem *simple present* sagst du,
> A was jeden Tag oder oft passiert.
> B was schon passiert ist.

Now complete these sentences with the verbs in the box.

help • walk • work • write

1. I … on the computer.
2. I … books.
3. They … home.
4. You … me a lot.

b) Read these sentences from the text and find the rule.

Eno *has* a cafe.
He *works* a lot.

> Wann verwendest du das Verb mit s? Wähle A oder B.
> A mit *he, she, it*
> B mit *I, you, we, they*

Now complete these sentences with the verbs in the box.

does • goes • takes • talks

1. He … to school.
2. He … his homework.
3. It … an hour.
4. He … with his friends.

▶ Language file 10, p. 179   ▶ More practice 6, p. 100

6 On Saturday

Zane's mum tells a friend about the family's weekend. Choose the correct verb.

On Saturday Zane and Holly often (1) **get up / gets up** late. Eno (2) **get up / gets up** first and he (3) **do / does** the shopping. Then he (4) **make / makes** breakfast for us and we all (5) **eat / eats**. In the afternoon I (6) **work / works**. Eno and the kids (7) **go / goes** to the park or they (8) **play / plays** a game at home.

▶ More practice 7, p. 100   ▶ More practice 8+9, p. 101

▶ Workbook, pages 41–43

7 Song The morning song

a) BEFORE YOU LISTEN Match the activities 1–6 to the photos A–F.

A 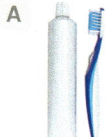 B 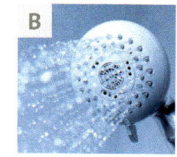 C  D  E  F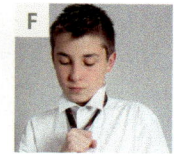

1 eat your breakfast
2 go to school
3 have a shower
4 get dressed
5 brush your teeth
6 get up

b) Listen to the song. What happens first? What happens next? Put the pictures in the correct order. You don't need one picture.

c) Listen to verse 6. Say how the song ends. The girl says: *Today is …*   ▶ More help, p. 101

My task

8 My school day

a) Read Zane's post and pick A or B:
He wants to know about your
 A class project   B school day.

b) Complete Leni's post with the words in the box.

| ends • get up • live • play • starts • takes |

 Hi, everybody!
My class has a project about the school day in other countries. Please tell us about your school day. Thanks.

Hi, Zane!
My name is Leni and I (1) … in Bochum. This is my day.
I (2) … at 6.30. I have a shower and eat breakfast.
I go to school by bus at 7.30. The journey (3) … 20 minutes.
School (4) … at 8 o'clock. I have lunch at school.
School (5) … at 3.15. In the afternoon I often (6) … football.
I go to bed at 8.45.
What about you?
Bye, Leni

c) Write to Zane about your day. You can use the text in b) for help. Change the words in blue if necessary. Put your text in your DOSSIER.

▶ Digital help   ▶ Wordbank 10, p. 191

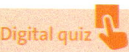 I can describe my daily routine.

School clubs

1 LISTENING Sports and hobbies

a) BEFORE YOU LISTEN Talk about the sports and hobbies with a partner.

Table tennis is great/fun/OK/…
I don't know cricket.

table tennis

cricket

dancing

singing

running

windsurfing

trampolining

playing computer games

b) Listen to some Varndean students.
Read the sentences 1–4 and choose the correct answer.

1 Annie / Brahim plays cricket.
2 Rin / Annie is in the school band.
3 Brahim / Annie doesn't like running.
4 Liam / Rin does a sport in the sea.
5 Liam / Brahim likes trampolining.

Good to know

Most schools in Britain have school clubs. Students learn new hobbies and sports there.

2 What about you?

a) Collect all the sports and hobbies that you know.

b) Use your mind map and tell your partner which sports and hobbies you like and don't like.

I like basketball, but I don't like table tennis. What about you?

I like windsurfing and running.

▶ Wordbank 4, p. 186
▶ Workbook, p. 44

3 How often?

a) Listen again to the Varndean students. Choose the correct words. ▶ Parallel exercise, p. 102
1 Annie sometimes / often / never plays cricket.
2 Brahim often / sometimes / never goes running.
3 Rin always / sometimes / never does dancing.
4 Liam always / never / sometimes does art.

b) Match the blue words from 3a) with the correct symbol.

1 never   2 ...   3 ...   4 ...

▶ Language file 11, p. 179

4 SPEAKING Scout's surfing sentences

a) Look at the picture. Make sentences. Your partner checks your verbs.

He sometimes ~~play~~ football. — No, that's wrong. He sometimes plays football.

Swap roles with your partner.

b) Use the words in the picture and say sentences about you.

I often go cycling.

▶ More practice 10, p. 102

▶ Workbook, p. 45

5 MEDIATION A very special school club

a) Look at the poster from Varndean School and read the text.

> Du brauchst nicht jedes Wort zu übersetzen. Gib nur das Wichtigste wieder.

b) **Partner A:** Ask partner B these questions in German:

1 Was baut man in dieser AG?
2 Wer nimmt am Rennen teil?
3 Wann findet die AG statt?

Partner B: Answer partner A's questions in German.

c) Swap roles.
Partner B: Ask partner A these questions:

1 Welche Eigenschaften sollte man für die AG haben?
2 Wie lange dauert die AG?
3 Arbeiten die Schüler/innen allein oder haben sie Hilfe?

Partner A: Answer partner B's questions.

FORMULA 24 CLUB

Are you active and good in a team?
Are maths, design and technology or art fun for you?
If you want an interesting hobby, then join the Formula 24 Club at Varndean!

We make electric cars from old materials.
Then we race with 700 other teams from Britain and other countries.

We meet every Friday afternoon at 3.30 for two hours. Mr Price and Ms Haffar sometimes help us, but we work hard too. It's always a lot of fun!

6 SPEAKING What's right?

a) Say three sentences about yourself. One sentence is right, two sentences are wrong. Use *always, often, sometimes* or *never*. Your partner guesses which sentence is right.

I never go swimming.

I sometimes eat chocolate.

I always play computer games.

Wrong!

Wrong!

Right!

b) Swap roles with your partner.

My task

7 My free time

Read about Annie and answer her post.
You can use the sentences in **ex. 6**. Put your text in your DOSSIER.

Hi, I'm Annie from Varndean School.
I want a new online friend!
Are you in a school club?
Tell me what activities you do.

Hi, Annie!
Nice to meet you.
My name is …
I'm in the … club at my school.
My hobbies are …
I like …, but I don't like …
What about you?
Bye,
…

▶ Digital help   ▶ Wordbank 4, p. 186

▶ Workbook, pages 46–47

I **can** talk about my free time.

3 Topic 3

Meeting friends

1 Reading Are you busy?

Read the messages. Is it Lily or Zane?

1 wants to meet at the weekend
2 says sorry
3 is free on Saturday and Sunday
4 likes swimming
5 is very busy

> Hi, Zane! Are you free on Saturday?
>
> Sorry, Lily. I'm busy on Saturday.
>
> Oh, OK. Let's meet on Sunday.
>
> Sorry, I can't. On Sunday I have a swimming competition.
>
> Oh, OK. You're very busy, Zane!

2 Listening Let's meet

a) **Before you listen** Copy and complete the table.

~~Let's ...~~ • ~~I'd love to.~~ • Sorry, I'm busy. • Good idea! • Are you free on ...? • Sorry, I can't. • Yes, please! • Can we meet ...?

Ask to meet	Say *yes*	Say *no*
Let's ...	I'd love to.	...

b) Now Lily asks to meet Noah. Listen and tick the phrases from your table in 2a). One phrase is not in the dialogue. Which phrase is it?

c) Say when Lily and Noah meet.

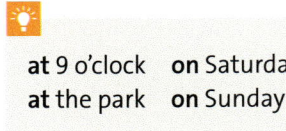

at 9 o'clock   on Saturday
at the park   on Sunday

▶ Workbook, p. 48

3 ROLE-PLAY **Can we meet this weekend?**
Go to p. 98 and act out Lily and Noah's conversation.

My task

4 Are you free?

a) Copy the calendar.

	Saturday	Sunday
9.00	activity: with:	activity: with:
1.00	activity: with:	activity: with:

b) DOUBLE CIRCLE **Stand in two circles.**
Choose an activity from the box or your own idea.
Talk to a partner and make plans.

> go to the beach • go to the skatepark •
> go swimming • go cycling •
> play football • meet at my house / flat

Let's go to the beach.

Good idea!

Are you free on Saturday at 9 o'clock?

Sorry, I'm busy on Saturday. Can we meet on Sunday at 1 o'clock?

Yes, please!

c) One circle moves to the right. Talk to a new partner. Complete your calendar from a).

d) Tell the class about your plans. Change the words in blue.

On *Sunday* at *1* o'clock I want to *go cycling* with *Lea*.

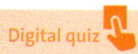 I can **make plans to meet friends.**

The competition

1 READING About the story

a) BEFORE YOU READ Look at the title and the pictures. Choose A, B or C.

A Zane isn't the winner of the competition.
B Zane is the winner. His friends are really happy for him.
C Zane wins the competition. His friends are angry at him.

b) Read the story and check your ideas from 1a).

"Look, Lily! It's Zane!" Lily's mum says.
Lily looks at the newspaper.
"What?" Lily is really surprised.
"Zane's mum is in a wheelchair?"
She takes a photo of the newspaper and tells Sunita and Noah.

After school, Lily, Sunita and Noah talk to Zane.
"Hi, Zane," Sunita says.
"We know about your mum. But why is it a secret?"
"I'm sad because it's hard for her," says Zane.
"So I often help at home. But I don't like to talk about it."

"Zane, you help your mum – that's cool," says Lily.
"But we're your friends. You can tell us."
"Don't be angry, Lily," says Zane.
"People see mum in her wheelchair and they are sorry for her. But please don't be sorry for her – she's great. And don't be sorry for me!"

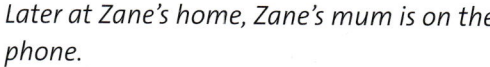

Later at Zane's home, Zane's mum is on the phone.
"Hello, Louise Adebayo.
... Really? Thank you! Bye."
"Zane! You're the *Best Kids Competition* winner!"
His mum is happy.
"Thanks, Mum," says Zane. "I love you!"

Zane tells his friends. Everybody is happy! But Zane's mum is tired and she is in bed for two days.
"The prize show isn't a good idea, Mum."
"Why not? I can do it."
"OK, Mum!" Zane says.

At the prize show ...
"Thank you! I'm so happy. Mum and Dad and Holly – you're the best! And thanks to my friends Lily, Sunita and Noah!
There's some prize money for the winner. I'd like to ..."

2 Which part?

Match sentences a–f to parts 1–6. *1c, 2...*

a Zane says *thank you* to his friends.
b Zane's friends tell him they know.
c Zane's friends read about his mum.
d Zane tells his friends he's the winner.
e Zane tells his friends about his feelings.
f Zane's mum is happy.

3 Who is it?

Complete the sentences. ▶ Parallel exercise, p. 102

1 ... sees Zane in the newspaper first.
2 ... takes a photo of the newspaper.
3 ... asks Zane about his secret.
4 ... tells his friends about his mum.
5 ... tells Zane that he is the winner of the competition.

3 Story

4 Feelings

Complete the sentences and say how people in the story feel.

1. In part 1, Lily is …
2. In part 2, Zane is …
3. In part 3, Lily is …
4. In part 4, Zane's mum is …
5. In part 5, everybody is … and Zane's mum is …
6. In part 6, Zane is …

5 Zane's prize money

a) Zane's prize money is £500. Decide what Zane does with the money.
You can use the ideas in the box or your ideas. Write two ideas in your exercise book.

I think he pays for a cleaner. And he pays for a big party with family and friends.

Ideas
- He gets a new games console / …
- He gets a new TV for his family.
- He gives some money to his mum and dad.

Good to know
The money in Britain is the pound (£). How much is £500 in euros?

b) Listen to Zane's ideas in his speech. Are they the same as your group's ideas?

Zane wants to … Our idea is the same / different.

6 Life skills Be kind

a) **Think** Zane is kind because he helps his mum. You can choose one person for a prize.
Who is kind in your group of friends, your family or where you live? Think about reasons why:

| My | trainer
brother
sister
friend
grandma
grandpa
… | is kind because | he
she | helps me with my homework / my computer / …
gives me sweets / books / …
sends me nice messages / funny pictures / …
shares his / her lunch with me.
shares his / her good ideas with me.
… |

Make sentences. Change the words in blue:

My *teacher* is really kind because *she often helps me with problems*.

b) **Pair** Tell a partner about the person. *My kind person is …*

c) **Share** Tell the class your ideas.

 I can understand feelings in a story.

| Topic 1 | Topic 2 | Topic 3 | Story | **Viewing** | Study skills | Unit task | **3** |

The Brighton dares: Sports and hobbies

1 BEFORE YOU WATCH Sports and hobbies

Can you find the German words for photos A–F?

head

football match

play air guitar

beanie

play street music

underpants

2 VIEWING What happens?

a) Watch the first scene. Look at the photos in 1. Complete the sentences about the dares.

Daisy: play …
Emir: play in a … with … on his …

b) Watch all the video. Look at the pictures and say where the kids are in the video.

1 They're at …

2 Daisy is at Gloria's …

3 They're at the …

4 Daisy is in her …

5 Emir is at his … match.

6 They're in Emir's …

▶ Workbook, p. 49

ninety-one **91**

Study skills

Look up and remember words

1 Look up free-time activities

A new English friend writes to you about free-time activities. You need to look up the words in blue.

a) First write the blue words in a list in alphabetical order. For words with the same first letter, look at the second letter: c**o**llecting
   c**r**afts

I do a lot of free-time activities! I like crafts. My favourite hobby is jewellery making. I like jigsaw puzzles too. I love collecting things with cats on them.

b) Look up the words in the *English-German Dictionary* on pages 236–246.

c) Listen and check your answers. Then listen and repeat the English words.

2 Find more free-time activities

Look at *Wordbank 4* on free time (p. 186). What are these activities in English?

1 Backen 2 Boxen 3 Klettern 4 Nageldesign

3 Write and remember

Choose five English words from 1 and 2. Write them in your VOCAB FILE.

English	Write a sentence or draw a picture	German + my other languages
collecting	I like collecting football cards.	Sammeln, toplamak
jigsaw puzzles	🧩	...

4 Odd word out

Find the three words in the same word group. Then say the odd word out.

1 running swimming cycling drawing
2 often cricket never sometimes
3 new angry sad happy
4 afternoon evening Sunday morning

It's helpful to learn words in groups.

▶ Skills file 4, pages 169–170

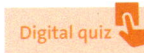 I can look up and learn new words.

| Topic 1 | Topic 2 | Topic 3 | Story | Viewing | Study skills | Unit task | 3 |

Share your highlights of the week

Step 1

Think about what you do every week. Write sentences about the best things. Choose 3–5 activities.

*On Saturday I always get up at 10 o'clock.
My dad and I play video games.*

▶ Wordbank 4, p. 186

YOU CHOOSE Step 2

Choose a task: A video recording or a comic (on p. 103).

A video recording

Practise your sentences from step 1 before you record.
Can you find things to show in your video?
Record your sentences from step 1 on your phone.

> Check that the light is good for your recording. Speak clearly.

Step 3

Play your video for a partner. Get feedback.

Step 4

Give other students feedback.

Your video is	funny. interesting. cool. …
You	speak clearly. have good scenes. have good ideas.
I like	the start. the scene with … the end.

▶ Feedback phrases, p. 200

Digital quiz   I can share the highlights of my week.

ninety-three 93

3 Checkpoint Digital checkpoint

1 Reading Zara's school journey

I can talk about my school journey.

a) Read the email from Zane's friend Zara.

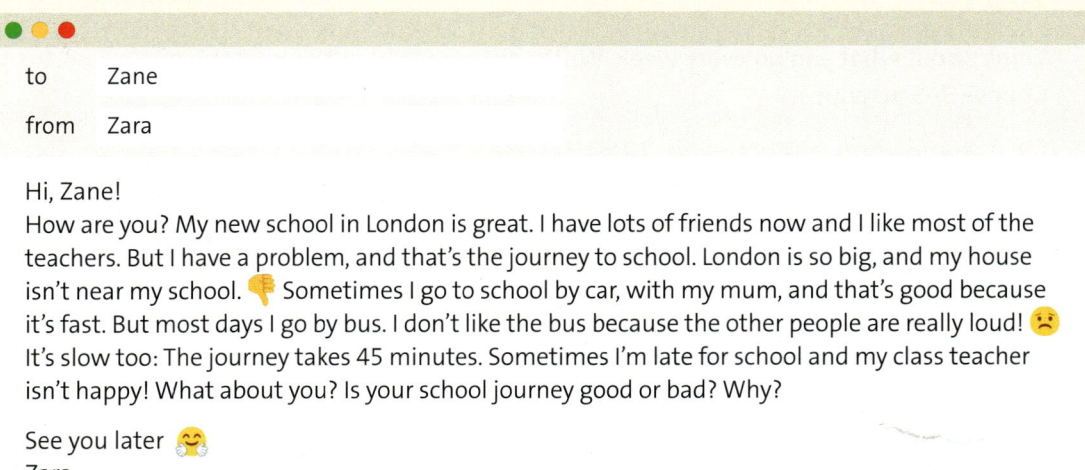

to Zane

from Zara

Hi, Zane!
How are you? My new school in London is great. I have lots of friends now and I like most of the teachers. But I have a problem, and that's the journey to school. London is so big, and my house isn't near my school. 👎 Sometimes I go to school by car, with my mum, and that's good because it's fast. But most days I go by bus. I don't like the bus because the other people are really loud! 😟 It's slow too: The journey takes 45 minutes. Sometimes I'm late for school and my class teacher isn't happy! What about you? Is your school journey good or bad? Why?

See you later 🥰
Zara

b) Read the sentences. True or false?

1 Zara isn't happy at her school.
2 Her school journey is long.
3 Zara goes to a different school in Brighton.
4 The bus is often quiet.
5 She's sometimes in trouble with her teacher.

c) Answer the questions.

1 Is Zara's car journey good or bad? – *Zara's car journey is … because it's …*
2 Is Zara's bus journey good or bad? – *Zara's bus journey is … because the bus is … and …*

d) Speaking Talk about your school journey with a partner.

*I go to school by 🚗 / 🚲 / 🚆 / 🚌.
I 🚶 to school.
My school journey is 👍 / 👎 because it's long / short / loud / quiet / fast / slow.
That's 👍 / 👎 because …*

Check

Die Übungen kannst du auch digital machen

2 WORDS Sunita's morning

I can describe my daily routine (*simple present*).

Sunita talks about her morning routine. Complete her sentences with the words in the box.

> brush my teeth • eat breakfast • get dressed • get up • go to school • have a shower

1 I … at six fifteen.   2 At six thirty, I …   3 And I …

4 After that I …   5 Then I …   6 I … at 8 o'clock.

3 LANGUAGE Sunita's evening

Complete Sunita's sentences with the verbs in the box.

> does • eat • go • makes • read • takes • tidies • watch • do

I come home from school at 4 o'clock.
Sometimes Nish (1) … a snack for us – we're always hungry after school! Then I (2) … my homework. That (3) … thirty minutes. We (4) … dinner at 7 o'clock, and then Ben (5) … the kitchen. After dinner, I (6) … TV and Nish (7) … his homework on the computer. Mum and Ben often (8) … the newspaper. On weekdays I (9) … to bed at 9 o'clock.

4 SPEAKING A conversation with Ryan

I can talk about my free time.

Lily and Ryan talk about their free time. Look at Lily's calendar and say her answers.

What's your hobby?   *My hobby is …*   *What clubs are you in?*   *I'm in the …*

Mon.	Tue.	Wed.	Thu.	Fri.	Sat.	Sun.
parkour	parkour	homework club	art club		parkour	

Check

3 Checkpoint   Digital checkpoint

5 WORDS Next weekend

I can make plans to meet friends.

Lily and Alice talk about the weekend. Choose the correct ending for each sentence. Copy the sentences into your exercise book.

Lily	Are you free on (1) …	a	OK.
Alice	Sorry Lily, I'm (2) …	b	11 o'clock.
Lily	Oh, (3) …	c	cycling.
Alice	What about Sunday? Are you (4) …	d	busy.
Lily	Yes, (5) …	e	idea!
Alice	Great. Let's go (6) …	f	I am.
Lily	Good (7) …	g	free?
Alice	Let's meet at the park at (8) …	h	Saturday?

6 LISTENING Saturday plans

I can understand feelings in a story.

a) Listen to Noah's conversations.
What are the students' plans for Saturday?
Copy and complete the table.
Use the words in the box.

do my homework • free (3x) • see grandpa • go shopping • go swimming • do yoga

	Saturday morning	Saturday afternoon
1 Zane		
2 Lily		
3 Noah		
4 Sunita		

b) Listen again. Say how they feel. Write the correct ending.

1 Zane is …
2 Lily is …
3 Noah is …
4 Sunita is …

angry

tired

sad

surprised

happy

sorry

Check

7 STUDY SKILLS **The Computer Club**

I can look up and learn new words. ✓

a) Read about the Computer Club on a British school's website.

b) Look at the text again. Write the blue words in alphabetical order.

c) Look up the words in the *English – German Dictionary* (pages 236–246).

d) Write the blue words from b) in the right group.

Hi, we're the Computer Club! We swap ideas about technology. We love memes. We help our classmates with computer problems. We give them useful information. It's great. We meet on Wednesdays at 3.30 p.m. in the computer room.

emails	...	good	give
headphones	friends	interesting	tell people
...	students	great	share
websites	teachers	...	...

8 WRITING **Fabian's week**

I can share the highlights of my week. ✓

Fabian shares the highlights of his week with his British friend Ali. Look at the pictures and write his sentences.

1 On Monday afternoon I go cycling with my friend. ...

Monday afternoon – cycling

Tuesday – guitar lesson

Wednesday – grandpa's house

Thursday afternoon – school drama club

Friday evening – computer games

Saturday and Sunday – big breakfast

Check

3 Partner page

Partner page

▶ Page 78

2 SPEAKING What's the time?

Partner B

a) Look at the clocks. Tell your partner the time.

It's … o'clock.

1	2	3	4	5
06.00	12.00	02.00	05.00	10.00

b) Ask the time.
Listen and write the five times.

What's the time?

▶ Numbers, p. 258

▶ Page 87

3 ROLE-PLAY Can we meet this weekend?

a) Read Lily's and Noah's conversation. Then act it out.

Lily	Hi, Noah! Can we meet this weekend?
Noah	I'd love to, Lily.
Lily	Great! Let's go to the skatepark.
Noah	Sorry, I can't go to the skatepark. It's too loud for me. What about the cafe?
Lily	Good idea! Are you free on Saturday?
Noah	Sorry, I'm busy on Saturday. But I'm free on Sunday.
Lily	OK, let's meet at the cafe at 10.30 a.m.
Noah	Let's ask Sunita too. See you on Sunday!

b) Swap roles and act out the conversation again.

c) Change the blue words and make a new conversation. Act it out for another pair.

Places	Days
the park a cafe the skatepark my house your house the beach	Monday Tuesday Wednesday Thursday Friday this week

98 ninety-eight

Diff bank

▶ Page 77

More practice 1 **I go to school by ...**

Say how these students go to school.
Complete their sentences.

1 Ahmed: I go to school by ...
2 Ruby: I go to school ...
3 Archie: I ...
    to school.
4 Zelal: I ...
5 Billy: I ...

▶ Page 78

More practice 2 **Your special numbers**

a) Write three special numbers for you. These ideas can help you:

> **Ideas**
> - how old you are
> - how old your pet is
> - your favourite number
> - your favourite football shirt number
> - your house number
> - your lucky number

b) Show your partner your numbers.
He/She guesses what the number is.

More practice 3 **The time**

Look at the box with times.
Listen and clap the rhythm.
Say the times from 8 o'clock to 9 o'clock.

8.00 =	eight o'clock
8.05 =	eight oh five
8.10 =	eight ten
8.15 =	eight fifteen

3 Diff bank

▶ Page 78

More practice 4 **Telling the time**

a) Write the numbers 1 to 5 in your exercise book. Listen to five conversations. Write the times in numbers.

b) Check with a partner.

> Number 1 is eight fifteen.

> Yes, that's right.

> No, that's wrong. It's …

More practice 5 GAME **Is it a match?**

- Each student: Make 3–4 pairs of cards like these.
- Put all your cards on the table. Mix them up.
- Take turns to turn over two cards.
- Is it a match? Say "Match!"

▶ Numbers, p. 258

▶ Page 80

More practice 6 **Who is it?**

Who is it: Zane, Holly, Louise or Eno?

1 She uses a wheelchair.
2 He has a cafe.
3 He gets up at 7 o'clock.
4 He makes breakfast.
5 She goes to school with her brother.
6 She writes books.
7 Her lessons end at 3.20.
8 He sometimes helps with dinner.

More practice 7 **Zane's swimming training**

a) Complete the sentences.
Find the correct form of the verb.

Zane (1 go) … to swimming training every week. He (2 walk) … to his swimming pool. Zane and the other swimmers (3 have) … training for an hour. They always (4 work) … really hard. Zane often (5 swim) … in competitions. All the swimmers (6 like) … to be the winner! But Zane is really good. He (7 love) … swimming.

b) Tell your partner about a sport you do and a sport somebody in your family does.

> I often play handball / go swimming / … My mum sometimes goes running.

100 one hundred

3

:busts_in_silhouette: **More practice 8** **Funny sentences**

Throw the dice and make funny sentences.
Make 5–8 different sentences.

Step 1	Step 2	Step 3
Throw the dice. Now you have a person.	Throw the dice again. Now you have an action.	Throw the dice again. Now you have a time or place.
1 Zane	1 go / to dancing lessons	1 at 5 a.m.
2 Holly	2 watch / horror films on TV	2 at school.
3 Mr and Mrs Adebayo	3 cook / spaghetti	3 in the car.
4 Sunita	4 draw / manga pictures	4 at lunchtime.
5 Lily and Noah	5 listen / to loud music	5 at 10 p.m.
6 Scout	6 do / yoga	6 on the bus.

💡 *He, she, it,* das **S** muss mit!

Sunita cook**s** spaghetti on the bus.

:busts_in_silhouette: **More practice 9** **GAME Weekdays**

Talk about your weekday like this:

Student 1	I get up at six thirty.
Student 2	She gets up at six thirty. I have a shower.
Student 3	He has a shower. I eat breakfast.
Student 4	…
Student 1	…

get dressed • go to school •
listen to the teacher •
meet friends at break •
eat lunch • go home •
do homework • watch TV • …

▶ Page 81

🔊 **More help 7 SONG The morning song**

What?
(Today is Saturday!)
Is it? Well, then
It's eight o'clock, go back to bed.
It's eight o'clock, go back to bed.
Who gets up at eight when you can sleep in till late?
It's eight o'clock, go back to bed!

one hundred and one 101

3

▶ Page 83

Parallel exercise **3 How often?**

Listen again. Choose the correct words.

1. Annie sometimes / often plays cricket.
2. Brahim never / often goes running.
3. Rin always / sometimes does dancing.
4. Liam always / never does art.

never
sometimes
often
always

More practice 10 **Scout's routine**

**Write about Scout's routine.
Use the verbs in the box in the correct form.**

eat • ~~get up~~ • walk • meet • swim • watch

Every day Scout *gets* up at 9 o'clock.

She often ... to the beach.

She sometimes ... in the sea with *Black Bird*.

Scout often ... people on the beach.

She sometimes ... a burger for lunch.

She often ... her friends.

▶ Page 89

Parallel exercise **3 Who is it?**

Sunita • Lily • Zane • Zane's mum • Lily's mum

Complete the sentences with the words in the box.

1. ... sees Zane in the newspaper.
2. ... takes a photo of the newspaper.
3. ... asks Zane about his secret.
4. ... tells his friends about his mum.
5. ... tells Zane that he is the winner of the competition.

| Topic 1 | Topic 2 | Topic 3 | Story | Viewing | Study skills | **Unit task** | **3** |

▶ Page 93

Share your highlights of the week

Step 1

Think about what you do every week. Write sentences about the best things. Choose 3–5 activities.

On Saturday I always get up at 10 o'clock. My dad and I play video games.

▶ Wordbank 4, p. 186

 You Choose **Step 2**

Choose a task: A video recording (on p. 93) or a comic.

A comic

Draw some pictures or cut them out of a magazine.
Write your sentences from step 1 under the pictures.

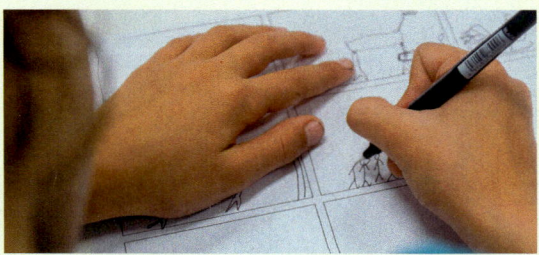

Draw simple pictures.

 ### Step 3

Show your comic to a partner. Get feedback.

Step 4

Give other students feedback.

Your comic is	funny.
	interesting.
	cool.
	great.
You have	good scenes.
	interesting highlights.
I like	your ideas.
	your pictures.

▶ Feedback phrases, p. 200

 I can **share the highlights of my week.**

one hundred and three **103**

Unit 4
Where I live

This is my city!

1 VIEWING **This is Brighton**

a) BEFORE YOU WATCH Choose a photo. Say what you can see. Your partner guesses the photo.

I can see   a building / a cinema / a lot of boats / a marina / a pier / shops / a skatepark / ...
This place is nice / busy / cool / interesting / old / quiet / ...

b) Watch the video. Match the letters of the places to the numbers of the photos. *1b, 2...*

a Brighton beach   b ~~Brighton Palace Pier~~   c Duke of York's cinema   d Hove Skatepark
e Brighton Marina   f Pavilion Gardens   g North Laine

Nach dieser Unit kann ich ...

○ Informationen über Brighton verstehen
○ meine Nachbarschaft beschreiben
○ über meine Stadt oder mein Dorf sprechen
○ über Sehenswürdigkeiten und
  das Wetter reden
○ Präsentationen halten

Unit task

○ die besten Orte in meiner Umgebung präsentieren

c) Read sentences a–g. Match them to photos 1–7. Watch the video again and check. *1e, 2...*

  a There are a lot of cool shops and cafes here.
  b This is a good place to have a picnic and listen to music.
  c This is a very old cinema and you can watch old films here.
  d People love skateboarding here.
  e You can eat fish and chips and play games here.
  f This is a good place for bowling and great food.
  g This place is very long. People like windsurfing here.

▶ More practice 1, p. 129

▶ Workbook, p. 56

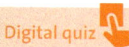 I can **understand information about Brighton.**

4 Topic 1

My neighbourhood

1 From Lily's window

🔊 a) Look at the photo and listen. You're Lily. What can you see and hear?

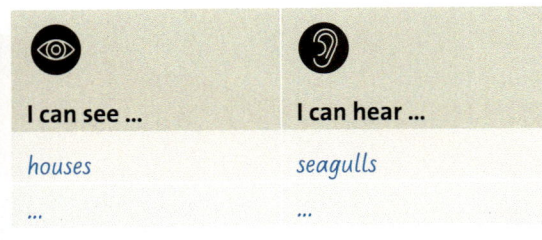

👁 I can see …	👂 I can hear …
houses	*seagulls*
…	…

▶ More help, p. 129

👥 b) Compare your answers. Take turns to say them. Add new ideas to your table.

2 READING Lily's homework

a) BEFORE YOU READ Make five pairs of opposites to describe a neighbourhood: *clean – dirty, …*

> ~~clean~~ • big • ~~dirty~~ • friendly • great • loud • small • unfriendly • horrible • quiet

b) Read Lily's text. Say which words from the box in a) Lily uses for:

▶ Parallel exercise, p. 129

1 her neighbours: *friendly*
2 the shop: …
3 activities at the youth centre: …
4 the park: …
5 some places on the estate: …
6 the cars: …

My neighbourhood

I live on the Whitehawk Estate with my mum and my dad. My sister doesn't live with us. She's 20 and has her own flat.

I like our neighbours, they're really friendly. There is one small shop in the neighbourhood, a youth centre and a sports centre. I like the youth centre because
5 it has great activities. I like the sports centre too. It doesn't have parkour, but I like playing table tennis there.

And I like the big park near our home. I walk there with my dad. But we don't go very often because he doesn't have a lot of free days.

Some places here are dirty because some people are messy. They don't put their
10 rubbish away. I don't like the rubbish – and I don't like all the cars, they're very loud.

But I really like my neighbourhood. I think it's nice!

▶ Workbook, p. 57

3 LOOKING AT LANGUAGE Simple present: negative sentences

Read these sentences from Lily's text. Pick A or B and find the rules.

1 We don't go very often.
2 They don't put their rubbish away.
3 I don't like the rubbish.
4 My sister doesn't live with us.
5 It doesn't have parkour.
6 He doesn't have a lot of free days.

I don't like rain.

Mit *don't* oder *doesn't* sagst du, was normalerweise
A geschieht.
B nicht geschieht.

Mit *I, you, we, they* verwendest du:
A *don't* + Verb (go, put, like, …).
B *doesn't* + Verb.

Mit *he, she, it* verwendest du:
A *don't* + Verb.
B *doesn't* + Verb.

▶ Language file 12, p. 180

4 SPEAKING Your neighbourhood

a) Think about what you like and don't like about your neighbourhood. Collect ideas on the board.

| I like … | the animals • the cars • the flats • my friends • the gardens • the houses • |
| I don't like … | the ice cream shop • my friendly / unfriendly neighbours • the park • my school • the sports centre • the swimming pool • the trees • … |

b) SPEED DATING Talk to different partners.

Hi, Masoud. I like the sports centre. What about you?

I like my friends. I don't like my neighbour's dog.

▶ More practice 2, p. 129   ▶ More practice 3, p. 130

▶ Workbook, pages 58–59

4 Topic 1

5 The youth centre

a) Lily tells Sunita, Noah and Zane about the youth centre. Put in *don't* or *doesn't*.

I go to the homework club on Wednesday. It (1) *doesn't* open on other days. There are a lot of activities: video games, table tennis, crafts and football. There's a girls' group on Tuesday, but I (2) ... go there, I (3) ... have time then. Sometimes I play football at the youth centre with my neighbour Niles. He (4) ... go to Varndean and his school (5) ... have a lot of clubs. We (6) ... pay for the activities – they're all free. A lot of people in our neighbourhood (7) ... have a lot of money.

b) Talk about the activities in **a)** with a partner.

I go / I don't go	to a youth centre • to a homework club • ...
I like / I don't like	video games • table tennis • crafts • football • ...
I play / I don't play	video games • table tennis • football • ...

▶ More practice 4, p. 130

6 WORDS Places (1)

In your VOCAB FILE you can explain words.

a) Match the explanations to the places.

1. shop
2. sports centre
3. pool
4. cinema
5. park

a. You swim here.
b. You watch films here.
c. You go walking here.
d. You do lots of sports here.
e. You buy things here.

b) Start a mind map for places in your VOCAB FILE.
Add the places in **a)** plus four more places from pages 104–108.

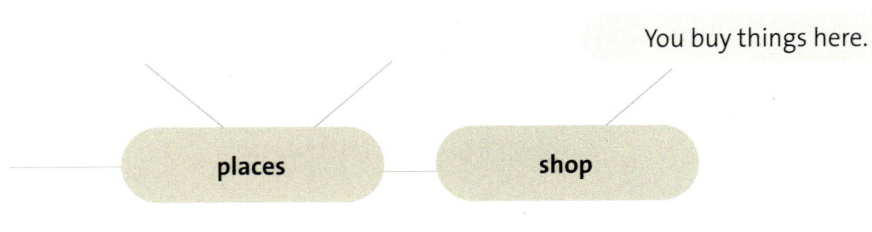

You buy things here.

places — shop

▶ More practice 5+6, p. 131   ▶ Wordbank 11, p. 192

▶ Workbook, p. 60

7 Reading My neighbourhood

Read the posts. Say what Jing and Alexis think about their neighbourhoods.

 www.my-neighbourhood.example.net

Hi, everybody! Tell me about your neighbourhood.
I live in a big city. It's very loud in my neighbourhood. There are a lot of cars and people. Everybody is very busy. I don't like my neighbourhood. I want to live in a small town.
Jing, China

 www.my-neighbourhood.example.net

I live in a village in the country. Our village doesn't have many fun places for kids. There's only one shop. It's not very interesting, but I like living here. Our neighbours are very friendly and there are a lot of other kids.
Alexis, France

Jing likes / doesn't like her neighbourhood because …
Alexis likes / doesn't like his neighbourhood because …

My task

8 A post about my neighbourhood

Write a post like in **ex. 7**. Use the mind map on **p. 108** and the ideas below. Write at least five sentences. Put your post in your Dossier.

I live in	a village / a town / a city / the country.
My neighbourhood is / isn't	great / clean / dirty / horrible / interesting / loud / nice / quiet.
My neighbourhood has / doesn't have	a cinema / a park / shops / a swimming pool / a youth centre.
The neighbours are	friendly / loud / nice / quiet / unfriendly.
I like / I don't like	my neighbourhood.

▶ Digital help

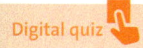 I can describe my neighbourhood.

My town or village

1 Words Places (2)

a) Match pictures a–j to places 1–10. *1b, 2...*

1. a hospital
2. an ice rink
3. a library
4. a supermarket
5. a museum
6. a park
7. a stadium
8. a train station
9. a shopping centre
10. a beach

b) Listen and repeat the places in a).

c) Add the places to your mind map from p. 108.

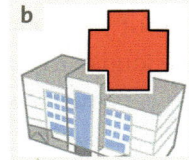
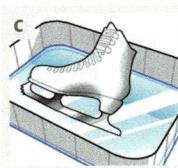

2 Song Kasia's town

Lily's friend Kasia doesn't live in Brighton, she lives in a small town.

a) Close your eyes and listen to Kasia's song. Is Kasia happy with her town or not? Give a 👍 or a 👎.

b) Listen again. What places do you hear? Collect them on the board.

Kasia's town

I think that my town is boring
And I don't like living here.
My town doesn't have a (1) ...
It doesn't have a (2) ... or pier
There isn't anything for me
No (3) ..., no (4) ...
The only thing here that is good
Are my friends in the neighbourhood!

▶ Workbook, p. 60

3 SPEAKING Different places

a) **Partner B:** Look at p. 128.
   Partner A: Look at your picture.
   Take turns to ask and answer questions about your town. You start.

   You My town has a hospital.
         Does your town have a hospital too?
   B   Yes, it does. / No, it doesn't. That's the same. / That's different. My town has a …

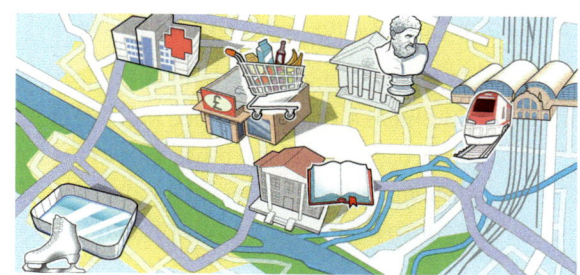

b) Now ask and answer questions about your town or village.

   – Do you like your town or village? – Yes, I do. / No, I don't.
   – Do you have a favourite place? What is it? – Yes, I do. It's …

   ▶ Wordbank 11, p. 192

4 LOOKING AT LANGUAGE Simple present: questions and short answers

Erklär-
film

a) Read and pick A or B.

   Fragen im *simple present* stellst du mit *Do* oder *Does*.

   Mit *I, you, we, they* verwendest du:
   A Do + Verb (for example: go, put, like).
   B Does + Verb.

   Mit *he, she, it* verwendest du:
   A Do + Verb.
   B Does + Verb.

▶ Language file 13, p. 180

b) Complete these short answers with *do, does, don't* or *doesn't*.

   1 Yes, I …   2 No, I …   3 Yes, it …   4 No, it …

   ▶ Language file 14, p. 181

5 In town with Kasia and Bella

Lily interviews her friend Kasia for some homework. Kasia is blind. Write Lily's questions.

1 Lily   Does / with you / go everywhere / Bella / ?
   Kasia Yes, she does. She comes to school too.
2 Lily   you / Do / know / the town well / ?
   Kasia Yes, I do. I have a map of it in my head.
3 Lily   have problems / with Bella / you / in shops / Do / ?
   Kasia No, I don't. Guide dogs can go everywhere.
4 Lily   you and Bella / the bus / use / Do / ?
   Kasia Yes, we do. Everybody on the bus knows Bella!

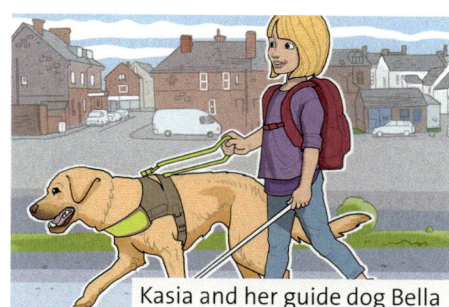
Kasia and her guide dog Bella

▶ Workbook, pages 60–61

6 Towns and visitors

a) Complete the questions with *Do* or *Does*.

1. ... visitors ask you questions in English?
2. ... you have a favourite place in a different country?
3. ... your town or village have a lot of visitors?
4. ... you visit other places in Germany?
5. ... your town have a visitor information centre?

b) Listen and check the questions in a).

Do you visit other places in England?

No, I don't. I never visit other places. I love Brighton!

▶ More practice 7, p. 131   ▶ More practice 8, p. 132

7 LISTENING Questions from visitors

a) Listen to dialogues 1–6 and match them to pictures a–f. *1d, 2...*

b) Does Lily answer *yes* or *no*? Write 1–6, then listen again and tick (✓) or cross (✗).

1. Does bus 12A go to the beach?
2. Do you know a good fish and chip shop?
3. Does the Brighton Museum open on Monday?
4. Do you have the time?
5. Does Brighton have a visitor information centre?
6. Does the sea get warm in summer?

c) ROLE-PLAY Ask the questions in b) and give short answers.

Yes, I do. / No, I don't.
Yes, it does. / No, it doesn't.

Be polite. Use "Excuse me", "Thank you" and "You're welcome."

▶ Workbook, p. 62

112   one hundred and twelve

8 Mediation Welcome to the pier!

Your family wants to go to Brighton. You find a good website about the pier.
Answer your family's questions about it.

1 Wann hat die Seebrücke auf?
2 Muss man dafür Eintritt zahlen?
3 Ich sehe eine Achterbahn und ein Karussell. Was gibt es außerdem?
4 Was kann man dort essen? Gibt es etwas Warmes zu essen?
5 Was sind die roten Stangen auf dem Bild?

We're open from 10 to 6 every day. The pier is free!
There's so much to do! We have great rides and fun trampolines. Play games and win prizes.
Are you hungry? There's so much to eat! You can choose from fish and chips, hot dogs, pizza, crepes, salads and ice cream.
Do you like sweets? Don't miss Brighton Rock! It's hard, it's red, it's sweet, it's bad for your teeth – but it's part of Brighton!

My task

9 Five questions about places

a) Work in teams. Each team chooses a place from their mind map (p. 108, 6b).

b) Team 1 asks *yes/no*-questions to guess the place. Team 2 gives short answers.
Team 1 can ask five questions about the place. They get one point for the correct place.

– *Does this place sell food?* – *Yes, it does.*
– *Is it the supermarket?* – *Yes, it is.*

Does this place	sell	clothes / drinks / food / something / …?
	have	books / films / football matches / games / old things / table tennis / trains / trees / water / …?
Is it the		beach / cinema / library / museum / park / shopping centre / sports centre / stadium / swimming pool / train station / youth club / …?

c) The teams swap roles.   ▶ Digital help

I can talk about my town or village.

Brighton in all weathers

1 LISTENING A walking tour

a) BEFORE YOU LISTEN Find the right picture.

1 It's rainy.
2 It's sunny.
3 It's snowy.
4 It's cloudy.
5 It's windy.

b) Lily's aunt and uncle from Russia are in Brighton for a holiday and Lily is with them on a walking tour. Listen and put the weather pictures in the correct order.

▶ More practice 9+10, p. 132

2 LOOKING AT LANGUAGE Simple present: *wh*-questions

Erklär-film

a) Match the English question words 1–5 to German a–e.

1 What?   a Wie?
2 Where?   b Wann?
3 When?   c Was? Welche?
4 Why?   d Warum?
5 How?   e Wo? Wohin?

b) Some people on the tour have questions. Read questions 1–6 and match them to the guide's answers a–f. *1d, 2…*

1 When does the tour start?   a You can buy them from me.
2 How do I buy tickets for the tour?   b I love Brighton Rock.
3 Why do you love Brighton?   c A ticket costs £15.
4 Where does the tour end?   d In 15 minutes.
5 How much does a ticket cost?   e At the i360 Tower.
6 What food do you like to eat in Brighton? f Because it's a great city!

▶ Language file 15, p. 181
▶ Workbook, p. 63

3 The Upside Down House

Lily's aunt and uncle want to visit the Upside Down House.
Partner B: Look at p. 128.

a) **Partner A:** Look at the online review. Answer partner B's questions.

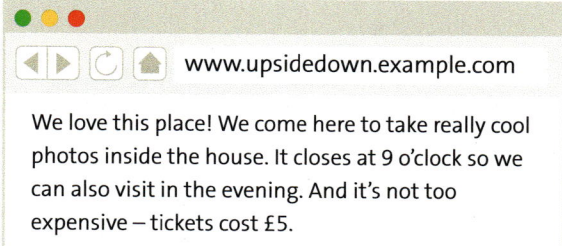

We love this place! We come here to take really cool photos inside the house. It closes at 9 o'clock so we can also visit in the evening. And it's not too expensive – tickets cost £5.

b) **Partner A:** Ask partner B these questions. Add *do* or *does*.

1. When ... the Upside Down House open?
2. Where ... I buy tickets?
3. How ... we take funny photos?

▶ More practice 11, p. 133

My task

4 Quiz-quiz-swap

a) Write one question about your town or village and weather on a card. Use the notes in the table to help you.

What do you do Where do you go How do you travel	when it's	sunny / rainy / snowy / cloudy / windy / hot / cold / warm?

What do you do when it's snowy?

b) **WALK AROUND** Find a partner and ask your question. Answer your partner's question about your town.

When it's sunny / rainy / snowy / windy / hot / cold,	I	have a picnic / stay at home / visit my friends / go skiing / go swimming / ...
	I go to	the beach / the park / the shops / ...
	I travel by ...	bus / bike / car / train / ...
	I walk.	

When it's hot, I go swimming.

c) Swap cards and walk around again. Find a new partner and ask your new question.

▶ Digital help
▶ Workbook, p. 64

Digital quiz   **I can** talk about sights in Brighton and the weather.

4   Story

Lily's idea

1 BEFORE YOU READ   Where Lily lives

a) What can you remember about Lily's neighbourhood? Check on p. 106.

She lives on Whitehawk Estate.
The neighbours are …
The neighbourhood is …
There's a lot of …

b) Look at Lily's poster.
What's her idea for her neighbourhood?
Lily wants to:

1. have a party.
2. have a clean-up day.
3. swap things.

2 READING   Clean-up day

a) Now read the story. Say what Buddy finds in the ground.

It's 9 o'clock on a Sunday morning and there's a big group in front of the youth centre.
"It's a great idea to have a clean-up day,
5   Lily!" says her sister Chloe.
"Look at all these people!"
Mr Davies is there. He lives on the estate too.
He sees Lily and Chloe's mum, Olga, and
10   speaks to her.
"Mrs Hall, who are these people?" asks Mr Davies. "They're too loud. It's Sunday! Today is a quiet day."
"Hello, Mr Davies. Today is the clean-up
15   day. A lot of people are angry about the rubbish everywhere," says Olga. "They want to live on a clean estate."
"I'm angry about this noise! I want to live on a quiet estate," says Mr Davies. He walks
20   away.

Olga looks at Chloe and Lily.
"It's OK, Mum. We can be quiet!" says Lily.
"Yeah! No problem," says Zane.

"OK, let's start! Hello, everybody. Welcome
25 to clean-up day!" says Lily's mum.
"We have a lot of big rubbish bags."
"What about things for the Swap Place?"
asks Lily's neighbour Liz.
"Then other people can use them."
30 "Ah, yes," says Olga. "Let's put good things over there. And let's meet here at 12 o'clock for lunch. Also, some neighbours want to have a quiet day today. Let's remember that."
35 Lily, Chloe and Noah work together.
Buddy wants to help too.
First, he finds a dead mouse.
"Yuk," says Noah.
Next, Buddy brings an old shoe to Lily.
40 "Thanks, Buddy," says Lily.
Then Buddy digs in the ground for a long time. He barks.

"What do you have now?" asks Noah.
"Wow! Good dog! Hey, Lily, look at this."
45 It's a gold ring. "It has 'Jack and Maria' in it," Lily finds out.
"So Jack and Maria are married," says Chloe. "The ring looks old. But who are Jack and Maria? How do we find them?"
50 The neighbours meet at the youth centre at 12 o'clock. They have over fifty bags of rubbish! They also have some old tables and chairs, a bike, shoes and a lot of other things for the Swap Place.
55 They take them to the Swap Place.
They eat lunch and Lily tells the others about the ring.
"Why don't you put a note in the youth centre?" asks Zane.
60 "Maybe somebody knows Jack and Maria."
"Good idea, Zane," Lily answers.
"I can put a note in our building too."

b) What do you think – who are Jack and Maria? Listen to the end of the story.

3 Why, what and how?

Match the questions and answers.

1 Why is Mr Davies angry?
2 When do the neighbours meet for lunch?
3 How many bags of rubbish do they collect?
4 How do the kids find Jack and Maria?
5 How does Mr Davies say "thank you"?

a They put a note in the youth centre.
b He gives money to the youth centre.
c It's too loud.
d Over fifty.
e At 12 o'clock.

4 Words in the story

Find words in the story with these meanings.

1 the meal after breakfast (line 32)
2 the opposite of alone (line 35)
3 (to) find something in the ground (line 41)
4 when a dog "speaks" (line 42)
5 a paper or a card with information (line 58)

5 The Whitehawk Swap Place

True or false?

1 Olga asks about the Swap Place.
2 Things for the Swap Place are things that other people can use.
3 *(To) swap* means to give something to somebody and take a different thing.
4 The neighbours don't have many bags of rubbish.
5 They don't find many things for the Swap Place.

6 LIFE SKILLS Go green!

a) You can organize a Swap Place in your class or at your school. Think of ten things for a Swap Place. Then compare your ideas with the class.

books, toys …

b) Make a poster for your Swap Place with information about it.

c) Choose the best poster.

d) Start to swap!

▶ Workbook, p. 65

I can understand a story about green activities.

| Topic 1 | Topic 2 | Topic 3 | Story | **Viewing** | Study skills | Unit task | **4** |

The Brighton dares: In town

1 Before you watch Places in Brighton

Which places in Brighton are interesting for tourists?
How many places can you name?

2 Viewing In town

a) Watch the video. What are Daisy's and Emir's dares?

1. Go swimming at the beach with a tourist.
2. Give a free tour of Brighton to a tourist.
3. Change[1] the time on the Queen's Park Clock.
4. Sleep in the Queen's Park Clock Tower[2].

b) Watch the video again. Match the people A–F to sentences 1–6.

1. It's always correct!
2. Yes, there's so much to see in Brighton!
3. Do you work here?
4. Does the tour go down to the beach?
5. Don't look at me. I don't know.
6. Sorry, Daisy. I have to go now. Good luck!

A Mara

B Daisy

C Emir

D Gloria

E Joe

F Man

3 Do Emir's trick

a) Write the name of a place in Brighton.
Look in a mirror and copy it. Or use these mirror letters.

b) Read your partner's place!
Use the mirror letters.

ABCDEFGHIJKLM
NOPQRSTUVWXYZ

᙭ᗷƆᗡƎᖴGHIJKLM
NOPQRSTUVWXYZ

[1] (to) **change** *verändern*   [2] **tower** *der Turm*

4 Study skills

Give a short talk

1 Collect ideas

Scout wants to give a short talk about her favourite place in Brighton: the beach. Collect ideas in a mind map or a table.

2 Find photos and make slides

Read Scout's slide and the tips. What's wrong with her slide?

My favourite place in Brighton is the beach because a lot of people come here and they often eat fish and chips or sandwiches. And I love fish and chips too!

Write a big title. Write only short notes. Choose big pictures.

3 Find a good structure

Look at Scout's talk. Put parts A–D in the correct order.

A Explain why it is my favourite place.
B Say hello and what the short talk is about.
C Ask for questions and say thank you.
D Say my favourite place.

4 Make notes

Use the information from 2 and 3 and make short notes on cards.

5 Practise your talk

a) Use good phrases. Copy the table. Put the phrases in the correct place.

> In this photo, you can see … • I want to talk about … • Finally … • Do you have any questions? • Let's look at this picture of … • My short talk is about … • Thank you for listening.

Start the talk	Talk about pictures	End the talk
I want to talk about …	…	…

b) Give Scout's short talk on her favourite place to your partner. Use your notes from 4 and talk freely. Don't just read your text.

▶ Skills file 5, p. 171

I can **plan and practise a short talk.**

| Topic 1 | Topic 2 | Topic 3 | Story | Viewing | Study skills | Unit task | 4 |

Present your top three places for kids

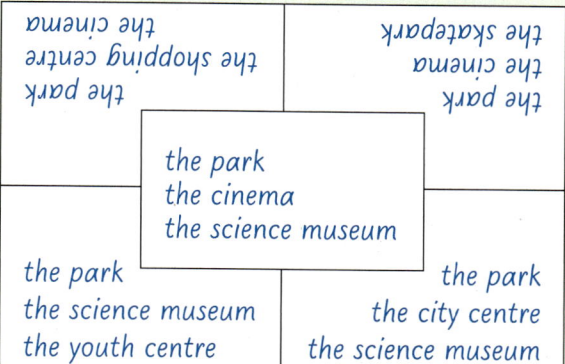

Step 1

Use a placemat in a group.
First draw a placemat on a big piece of paper.
Everybody thinks of three places in your town or village and writes them in one part of the placemat. Talk about the ideas. Agree on three places and write them in the middle of your placemat.

▶ Wordbank 11, p. 192

▶ Digital help

the park the shopping centre the cinema	the park the cinema the skatepark
the park the cinema the science museum	
the park the science museum the youth centre	the park the city centre the science museum

Step 2

Find your top three places on an online map. Make a slide: Show where your places are.

Step 3

Make a slide for each place. Add a photo. Write short notes:

park: play football, cycle
cinema: good on rainy days
science museum: fun, free

▶ Digital help

Step 4

Practise your group talk.
Use good phrases.
Then give feedback.

Please speak more loudly.

Please look at me.

Don't speak so fast, please.

▶ Digital help

Step 5

Give your talk to another group or the class.
Ask the other group 2–3 questions.
Give the other group feedback.

▶ Skills file 5, p. 171

Digital quiz | **I can** give a short talk to a group.

4 Checkpoint   Digital checkpoint

1 Mediation   Jack's favourite place

I can understand information about Brighton.

a) Read the message from your British friend Jack and tell your family about it.
Choose the best description A, B or C.

A Jack will, dass wir ihn und seine Familie in Brighton besuchen.
B Jacks Familie ist oft im Hove Skatepark.
C Jack meint, dass wir den Hove Skatepark in Brighton besuchen sollten.

> Hi!
> Your family wants to visit Brighton? Cool! You must visit Hove Skatepark. It's my favourite place. I often go skateboarding there. It isn't in the town centre, but Portslade train station and Wish Road South bus stop are near the park. And what's best: The park is next to the beach. It's free to get in and it's always open! Have fun!
> Jack

b) Answer your family's questions in German.

1 Ist der Skatepark im Zentrum?
2 Wie kommt man dorthin?
3 Muss man Eintritt zahlen?
4 Bis wann ist der Skatepark geöffnet?

2 Language   We live in Hove

I can describe my neighbourhood *(simple present: negative)*.

Read about Sunita's neighbourhood. Fill in the gaps. Use *don't* or *doesn't*.

I live with my family in Hove. Our neighbourhood has nice shops and parks, but it (1) … have a cinema. There's a great beach in Hove. Nish and I often go there after school, but we (2) … go there at the weekend because it's really busy. There's a museum too, but I (3) … go there very often. I (4) … like museums! I like my neighbourhood, but Nish (5) … like it. He wants to live in London, but my mum (6) … want to live there!

3 Writing   Lea's neighbourhood

Read Lea's notes about her neighbourhood. Then write Lea's message to Sunita.

Hi, Sunita! I live in a …

- small village
- clean
- three shops, nice cinema ☺
- no youth centre ☹
- no stadium ☹

Check

Die Übungen kannst du auch digital machen

4 A tour of Chester

I can talk about my town or village *(simple present: questions and short answers)*.

a) LANGUAGE   Zane visits his cousin Sophie and asks questions about her town.
Fill in the gaps with *do, does, don't* or *doesn't*.

Zane   (1) ... you like your town?
Sophie   Yes, I (2) ... It's a nice place.
Zane   (3) ... your town have a good park?
Sophie   Yes, it (4) ... I often go cycling there.
Zane   (5) ... your town have a beach?
Sophie   No, it (6) ... It's a shame!

b) WORDS   Write the names of the places a–f.

c) LISTENING   Listen to the tour. Where do Zane and Sophie go?
Write the letters a–f from **4b)** in the correct order.

1c, 2...

5 Photos of Brighton

I can talk about sights in Brighton and the weather *(simple present: wh-questions)*.

a) LANGUAGE   Write the words in the correct order.

1. see / in the picture / what / you / can / ?
2. like / the weather / what's / ?
3. do / like / why / you / the picture / ?

b) SPEAKING   Choose your favourite photo (A or B). Your partner asks you the questions from **5a)**.
Answer the questions. Then swap roles.

I can see ...
There's / There are ...

The weather is ...
I like picture A / B because ...

Check

4 Checkpoint Digital checkpoint

6 Reading At the Swap Place

I can understand a story about green activities.

a) BEFORE YOU READ Look at the title and the pictures. What's the story about? Choose the correct answer.

The story is about A Zane's family B Zane's day at school C Zane's things.

At the Swap Place

It's Saturday morning and Zane wants to meet his friends at the park. "Dad, where's my scooter?" asks Zane. "I can't find it. It's not in the flat and it's not outside."

5 "It's at the Swap Place, Zane," says Eno. "We have too many things. And you don't need those old toys."
"But Dad! It's my scooter and I still use it sometimes!" says Zane.
"Ah, I'm really sorry, Zane. Go to the Swap Place now.
10 Maybe it's still there."

"Excuse me," says Zane when he gets there.
"I think my dad …"
The woman in the Swap Place doesn't say hello. She looks sad.
15 "Are you OK? What's wrong?" asks Zane.
"Oh yes, I'm OK," says the woman. "But we have so many things here. The place is really messy. I want to tidy it, but I don't know where to start."
"I can help you with that!"

20 Two hours later, Zane goes home.
"Hi, Dad. Sorry, I'm late. I don't have my scooter, but I have some other things! Two footballs, a console, a book and a jigsaw puzzle. The Swap Place is great."
"Hi, Zane. More things! That's … erm … great."

b) **Read the story: true or false?**

1 Zane's scooter isn't in the flat.
2 Eno finds the scooter outside.
3 The Swap Place is very tidy.
4 Zane helps the woman in the Swap Place.
5 Zane finds a lot of things in the Swap Place.

c) **Find words in the story with these meanings.**

1 the day after Friday (line 1)
2 kids play with them (line 6)
3 not tidy (line 17)
4 where someone lives (line 20)
5 a game with a lot of parts (line 23)

Die Übungen kannst du auch digital machen

7 STUDY SKILLS Buddy's favourite places   I can **plan and practise a short talk.**

a) Look at Noah's slides. Which slide is the best? Why?

1. The first place is the Pavilion Gardens. It's a nice place for a picnic. I go there with my mum and dad.

2. **Brighton Beach**

we walk by the sea

3.
Buddy loves our garden too, because all his toys are there.

Which slide has …

– a big title?
– short notes?
– a big picture?

b) Copy and complete Noah's sentences with words from the box.

1. My … is about Buddy's favourite places.
2. In this … you can see the Pavilion Gardens.
3. In the … photo, we have the beach.
4. Let's … at these pictures of Buddy's toys in the garden.
5. Thank you for …
6. Do you have any …?

> listening • look • next • photo • short talk • questions

8 SPEAKING Ideas for a rainy day   I can **give a short talk to a group.**

Look at Philipp's slides and give his short talk about places to go on a rainy day.

Ideas for a rainy day
– hello
– my presentation

the sports centre
– a lot of activities
– not expensive

the ice rink
– costs 10 euros
– fun

the cinema
– interesting films
– nice cafe

Questions?
– thank you
– any questions

Check

VARNDEAN Teen Zine

This month's topic: Brighton

Our school magazine: by students for students

Questions and answers: The Real Junk Food Project

What is it?
It's a cafe in Brighton.

Why is it different?
The cafe uses waste[1] food and there are no prices[2].

Where does the food come from?
When shops in Brighton have too much food at the end of the day, they don't put it in the bin – they give it to the cafe!

How much do meals cost?
People pay what they can. People with more money pay more and homeless[3] people eat for free. And everybody sits together!

Joke time

What's orange and sounds like a parrot?
A carrot.

What do you call it when it's rainy for two days in Brighton? The weekend!

---

[1] **waste** überschüssig; hier: Lebensmittel, die weggeworfen werden sollten   [2] **price** Preis   [3] **homeless** obdachlos

A postcard from Brighton

Dear Annie,

*Brighton is great!
My favourite place here is Snooper's Paradise.
It's a really cool shop and it has ... everything[1]!
Hats, skateboards, photos, guitars, clocks, toys, books, posters ...*

Leena xx

What's your favourite shop?

The International Birdman[2] competition

Each year in a small town near Brighton there's a special competition: People jump off[3] the pier and try to[4] fly!

They often wear funny clothes too. They get money for charity[5] and have great fun!

I'm a bird!

Oh-oh ...

**Don't try this at home!
But why not draw your own Birdman costume?
Or think of a cool competition for your school?**

---

[1] **something** *etwas* [2] **birdman** *Vogelmensch* [3] **jump off sth.** *von etwas herunterspringen*
[4] **try to do sth.** *versuchen, etwas zu tun* [5] **charity** *wohltätige Organisation*

4 Partner page

Partner page

▶ Page 111

3 SPEAKING Different places

Partner B

a) Look at your picture. Take turns to ask and answer questions about your town. Partner A starts.

Partner A	My town has a hospital. Does your town have a hospital too?
You	Yes, it does. / No, it doesn't. That's the same. / That's different. My town has a … Does your …?

▶ Page 115

3 The Upside Down House

Partner B

a) Ask partner A these questions. Add *do* or *does*.

1 What … people do inside the house?
2 When … the Upside Down House close?
3 How much … the tickets cost?

b) Look at the online review. Answer partner A's questions.

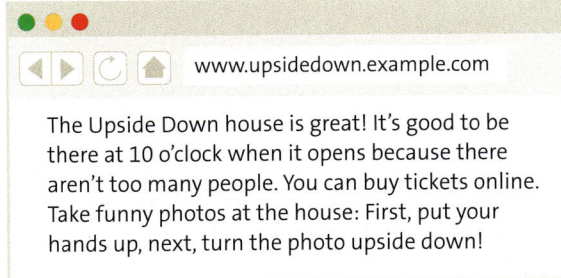

www.upsidedown.example.com

The Upside Down house is great! It's good to be there at 10 o'clock when it opens because there aren't too many people. You can buy tickets online. Take funny photos at the house: First, put your hands up, next, turn the photo upside down!

Diff bank 4

▶ **Page 105**

More practice 1 **I like Brighton**

Which places in Brighton do you like? Why?

| I like | Brighton Marina
Brighton Beach
Brighton Palace Pier
the Duke of York's Cinema
the Hove Skatepark
North Laine
the Pavilion Gardens | because | it's
they're
there's
there are
you can | nice / cool / different / old / …
a skatepark / a lot of cafes / shops /
music / an old cinema / …
have a picnic / listen to music /
watch films / go bowling /
eat fish and chips / play games / … |

▶ **Page 106**

More help **1 From Lily's window**

a) Look at the photo and listen. You're Lily. What can you see and hear?

I can see …
I can hear …

> babies • bikes • buildings • buses • cars • dogs • flats • kids •
> loud / nice music • my neighbour's TV • roads • trees

Parallel exercise **2 Reading Lily's homework**

b) Read Lily's text. Say which words Lily uses for:

1 her neighbours: unfriendly / friendly
2 the shop: small / big
3 activities at the youth centre: great / horrible
4 the park: small / big
5 some places on the estate: dirty / clean
6 the cars: quiet / loud

▶ **Page 107**

More practice 2 **I don't like …**

a) Draw something that you don't like.

b) Take turns to show your pictures. One student says what the picture shows.

You don't like fish.

c) Tell the class about your group.

Otto doesn't like fish, Mariam doesn't like pizza, …

4 Diff bank

▶ **Page 107**

More practice 3 **That's wrong!**

Correct the sentences. Use *don't* or *doesn't*.

1. Noah likes loud music. *That's wrong! Noah doesn't …*
2. Noah has a cat.
3. Noah walks to school.
4. Noah lives in a flat.
5. Noah and Zane live in London.
6. They go to King's School.
7. Zane has two brothers.
8. Zane's dad uses a wheelchair.

▶ **Page 108**

More practice 4 **New activities for the youth centre**

a) The youth centre wants to plan new activities. Look at the questionnaire and Lily's answers. Then complete the sentences. Put in *likes* or *doesn't like*.

1. Lily … singing.
   Lily doesn't like singing.
2. She … dancing.
3. She … cricket.
4. She … trampolining.
5. She … jigsaw puzzles.
6. She … reading.

> Help us plan new activities!
> Write ☺ or ☹ for each activity.
> Name: *Lily Hall*
> singing ☹
> dancing ☹
> cricket ☹
> trampolining ☺
> jigsaw puzzles ☹
> reading ☺

b) What about you? Write your answers in your exercise book.

I like acting. I don't like dancing.

130 one hundred and thirty

More practice 5 WORDS **Great places in Brighton**

Lily tells a new boy at the youth centre about her neighbourhood and Brighton. Complete her sentences with the correct places from the box.

| beach • cafe • cinema • pier • ~~shop~~ • skatepark • sports centre |

You can buy things at the (1) *shop* in the neighbourhood. There's a small (2) … next to it. They have great hot chocolate! There's a (3) … here too – you can play basketball or football there. But the best place to go skateboarding is at the (4) … in Hove.
It's fun to go to the (5) … My sister likes swimming in the water, but I think it's too cold! I like to go to the (6) … because you can play games and eat fish and chips there. And I like to watch films at home, but there's a great (7) … at Brighton Marina.

More practice 6 **Places game**

a) Make a table with nine places.

b) When the teacher explains a place:
Put up your hand and say the correct place. When you have three words ⇨ or ⇩ or ⇧ or ⇘ or ⇙ say "Here!"

shop	…	…
…	…	…
…	pool	…

▶ **Page 112**

More practice 7 **Towns and visitors**

Take turns to ask the questions in 6a). Answer with short answers. Give extra information.

4 Diff bank

▶ Page 112

More practice 8 **A lost visitor**

A visitor asks Lily for help. Complete the questions in the conversation.

Visitor Excuse me, (1 you / come) … from here?
Lily Yes, I do. (2 you / need) … help?
Visitor Yes, I do. I'm lost. I want to go to the visitor information centre. Is it in this road?
Lily Yes, it is. (3 your phone / have) … a map?
Visitor No, it doesn't. I don't have internet now.
Lily OK, Let's look on my phone. (4 you / see) … this place? We're here. And here's the visitor information centre in this building.
Visitor (5 the building / have) … a name?
Lily Yes it does. It's the Brighton Centre. It's not far down there, on the right. (6 that / help) …?
Visitor Yes, it does. Thank you very much.
Lily You're welcome.

▶ Page 114

More practice 9 **The weather in Brighton**

Lily looks at the weather for next week on her phone. British weather changes a lot! Complete the sentences with the words from the box. Use each word once.

cloudy • cold • rainy • snowy • sunny • warm • windy

1 On Monday, it's … and …
2 On Tuesday, it's … and …
3 On Wednesday, it's …
4 On Thursday, it's … and …

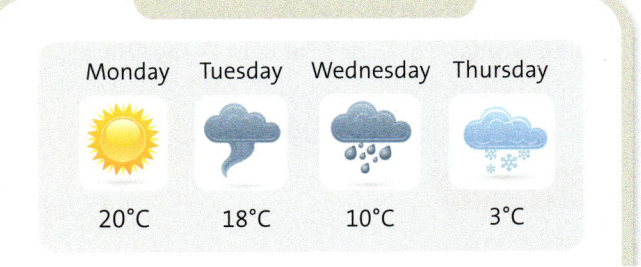

More practice 10 **The next day**

Listen to Eli's tour from the next day. Choose the correct words.

1 Eli says the Pavilion is very new / old.
2 He says you can have a party / picnic outside the Pavilion.
3 Today on the beach it isn't cold / warm.
4 On the pier it's very sunny / windy.
5 The wind takes a person's hat / sandwich.
6 At the end the visitors can / can't visit the i360.

132 one hundred and thirty-two

▶ Page 115

More practice 11 **All about Scout**

Read the questions and Scout's answers.
Put in the correct word from the box.

> How • What • When • Where • Why

1 … do you live?

I live in Brighton. That's great!

2 … do you like Brighton?

Because I love the sea! And the food at the beach.

3 … do you eat?

I eat fish. A lot of fish.

4 … do you find them?

I see them swimming — and I'm fast.

5 … do you sleep?

After I eat!

Unit 5
Enjoy!

My favourite dessert is cake. My dad makes a great birthday cake. He puts fruit and cream in it. A lot of people make it with strawberries, but I'm allergic to strawberries.

Noah's birthday dessert

1 Words Food

a) Look at Noah and Sunita's pages in 7C's class recipe book. Which words in blue do you understand?
Use the photos, words from German and other languages.

I think 'fruit' is 'Obst'. It's like 'Frucht' in German and 'frukty' (фрукты) in Russian.

b) Listen and repeat the food words in blue.

▶ More practice 1, p. 157

Nach dieser Unit kann ich ...

○ über Essen sprechen
○ über Geburtstage und Feste sprechen
○ mein Lieblingsgericht beschreiben
○ über Unterschiede sprechen
○ unbekannte Wörter erklären

Unit task

○ ein Rezeptbuch erstellen

We eat a lot of Indian food at home, but no meat because my family is vegetarian. This is my favourite dish – mattar paneer. It's Indian cheese and peas in a tomato sauce with a lot of spices. We eat it with bread or rice.

vegetables · bread · rice · tomato sauce · peas · cheese

Sunita's favourite dish

2 SPEAKING Our food

a) Read Noah and Sunita's pages again. Complete the sentences.

1. Noah always eats the cake on his ...
2. Noah is allergic to ...
3. Sunita doesn't eat ...   She's a ...
4. You make mattar paneer with ...

b) What about you? Talk about the food on these pages.

I love ...   I don't like ...   I often / never eat ... (because ...)   I'm allergic to ...   ▶ Wordbank 12, p. 193

▶ Workbook, p. 70

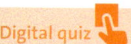 I can **talk about food.**

5 Topic 1

Time for a party

1 READING Noah's invitation

a) BEFORE YOU READ What do you do on your birthday? Tell a partner.

*I have a birthday party.
We eat birthday cake.
We often go bowling.
– What about you?*

▶ More help, p. 157

b) Read Noah's invitation. Answer the questions.

1. How old is Noah on his birthday? – *He's ...*
2. What day of the week is his birthday party? – *It's on ...*
3. What time does the party start? – *It starts at ...*
4. Where's the party? – *It's at ...*
5. What activities are there? – *There are ...*
6. What food is there? – *There's ...*
7. How can Noah's friends answer the invitation? – *They can ... or ... him.*

▶ More practice 2, p. 157

2 WORDS Months

a) SONG Listen and sing. Then listen again and stand up for your birthday month.

b) WALK AROUND Talk to five people. Find out what their birthday month is and tell the class.

January, February, March, April, May, June, July, August, September, October, November, December

When's your birthday?

It's in March. When's your birthday?

It's in December.

▶ Workbook, p. 71

136 one hundred and thirty-six

3 Birthday dates

a) Look at the list of numbers on p. 258.
Listen and repeat the numbers from 1st to 31st.

the first (1st), the second (2nd), the third (3rd), the fourth (4th), the fifth (5th), ...

b) Look how Scout says and writes her birthday. Then listen to eight students. Write their birthdays.

1	Noah: 30th May	5	Theo: ... February
2	Lily: ... April	6	Ivy: ... January
3	Zane: ... August	7	Tareq: ... July
4	Sunita: ... March	8	Marta: ... October

My birthday is **on the first of** April.

My birthday is on 1st April.

c) Check your answers with a partner.

Lily's birthday is on the ... of ... – That's right. / That's wrong. I think it's on ...

 ▶ Numbers, p. 258   ▶ More practice 3+4, p. 158

4 SPEAKING My birthday

a) Make two groups.
Make a line in your group in order of your birthdays.
Which group is quicker?

b) Check: Are you in the right place in the line?
Take turns: Say your birthday.

When's your birthday?

It's on the 21st of August. What about you?

It's on the 10th of March. So I'm before you in the line.

5 WRITING My birthday invitation

a) Look at Noah's invitation in 1 again. Change the parts in blue and write an invitation to your birthday party. Use different colours and add pictures to make it look good!

▶ More help, p. 158

b) GALLERY WALK Look at all the invitations. What do you think? Make notes.

Which invitation ...
1 looks the best (colours, photos)?
2 has the best place?
3 has the best activity?
4 has the best food?

▶ Workbook, p. 72

6 Zane phones Noah

Look at the picture and read the dialogue.
What are Noah and Buddy doing?

1 Noah is playing with Buddy / juggling.
2 Buddy is sleeping / watching Noah.

Zane	Hi, Noah! What are you doing?
Noah	Hi, Zane. Erm, I'm not telling you. I'm learning something new. It's a secret.
Zane	Oh, interesting … I'm phoning to ask: Do you need help with your party?
Noah	Erm, thanks a lot, but no. What are you doing?
Zane	I'm not busy. I'm listening to music at the moment.
Noah	OK. Sorry, I must go, Zane! See you!

7 LOOKING AT LANGUAGE Present progressive

Erklärfilm

a) Complete the box. The sentences are all in ex. 6.

Buddy is	…	Noah.
What are you	…	?
I'm not	…	you.
I'm	…	something new.

I'm	= I am
you're	= you are
she's	= she is
we're	= we are
they're	= they are

b) Read the box. Find the missing part for the question mark.

Du bildest das *present progressive* mit	I'm he's she's it's we're you're they're	+ Verb (play, learn, do, …)	+ **?**

c) Read and pick two correct answers.

Mit dem *present progressive* sagst du …

A was in diesem Moment (*now, at the moment*) gerade geschieht.
B was gestern passiert ist.
C was auf Bildern gerade passiert.

▶ Language file 16, p. 182
▶ More practice 5, p. 158

8 A birthday photo   ▶ Parallel exercise, p. 159

Zane is showing his mum a photo of his friend's birthday party. Complete his sentences with the *ing*-form of the words in the box.

> draw • ~~eat~~ • listen • open • play • sing • sit • take

The spelling of some verbs with *-ing* is different:
sit – si**tt**ing
tak**e** – taking

1. I'm *eating* birthday cake. It's chocolate, my favourite!
2. Sunita and Ruby **are** ... to music.
3. This is Ju. She **is** ... her birthday presents.
4. Noah **is** ... on a chair with a cat.
5. He**'s** ... photos with his phone.
6. Max and Albie have balloons. They**'re** ... with them.
7. Lily is at the table. She**'s** ... a picture.
8. Amina and Vicky **are** ... Happy Birthday.

▶ More practice 6, p. 159; More practice 7, p. 160

---

9 SPEAKING Find the differences

Partner B: Look at p. 156.
Partner A: Look at this picture.
Take turns and find six differences.

> In my picture, the dog is sleeping.

> In my picture the dog isn't sleeping. It's ...
> In my picture, a boy and a girl in blue T-shirts are ...

> In my picture, ...

My task

10 My party photos

Show photos of parties to your partner. Describe them. Or describe the photos on p. 156.

This is my birthday. It's the 26th of February. I'm wearing ... We're playing ...

▶ Digital help   ▶ More help, p. 160

▶ Workbook, pages 73–74

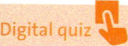 **I can** talk about birthdays and parties.

5 Topic 2

Party shopping

1 Listening A present for Noah

a) Before you listen Can you remember – what does Noah like?   *He likes ... He doesn't like ...*

1. animals (check on p. 32)
2. circus tricks (check on p. 136, p. 138)
3. strawberries (check on p. 134)

b) Sunita and Lily are looking online for a birthday present for Noah. Look at the website. Then listen. Say what they choose.

c) Phrases 1–6 mean "It's a good idea" or "It's a bad idea". Write ☺ or ☹. Listen again and check.

1. That's perfect!
2. I'm not sure.
3. Noah already has bike lights.
4. It's a great present.
5. That's a good idea.
6. It's too expensive.

2 Speaking Find a present

a) Collect a list of cool birthday presents in class.

b) Find a birthday present for each student in your group. Use the presents above and the phrases from 1c). The "birthday kid" listens.

Let's find a present for Samir. – OK. Why don't we buy ...

c) The "birthday kid" says thank you and comments on the present.

| Thanks for the ... | It's a great present. | I'm learning to ... |
| Thanks very much. | I really like it! | ... is my favourite sport / free time activity / game. |

▶ Workbook, p. 75

3 LISTENING Party food and drinks

a) BEFORE YOU LISTEN Can you remember?

What kind of party is Noah's birthday party?
Where's the party?
What's his birthday dessert?

b) Look at Noah's party food.
Listen to Noah and his parents.
What two things are wrong?

Noah's party food

Food
ham sandwiches, cheese and tomato sandwiches, sausages, pasta salad, carrots, cake, melon

Drinks
cola, lemonade

4 READING The shopping list

a) Read the dialogue. Write Noah's shopping list for the party.

Noah	I'm writing the shopping list. How much bread do we need?
Dad	For the sandwiches? A lot of bread! Two packets.
Noah	OK. And how many tomatoes?
Dad	Let's get six.
Noah	How much pasta?
Dad	A big bag of pasta.
Noah	And how many carrots do we need? One bag?
Dad	Yes, we don't need many. And one big melon.
Noah	OK. How many lemons do we need for the lemonade? And how much sugar?
Dad	Let's get twelve lemons. We already have sugar.

bread: 2 packets
tomatoes:
…

b) Compare your list with your partner. Then listen and check.

5 How much? How many?

Erklärfilm

Complete the table with food and drinks from **4a)**.

How much …?	How many …?
bread	tomatoes
…	…

▶ Language file 17, p. 183   ▶ More practice 8, p. 160
▶ Workbook, p. 76

6 Reading A recipe

a) **Noah is looking at recipes online. Read the first part of the recipe and answer the questions:**

What does the sandwich look like?
Who likes to eat them?

www.recipes.example.com

Here is my recipe for clown sandwiches! Everybody loves them because they're fun.
For the sandwiches:

- bread
- butter
- ham or (vegetarian) sausage
- cheese
- vegetables (You can use your favourite vegetables: salad, carrots tomatoes, and more!)

1. First clean and cut the vegetables.
2. Next put butter on the bread.
3. Add salad.
4. Put cheese ham or sausage on the bread.
5. Make a clown with the vegetables. Put them on your sandwich.
6. Enjoy your sandwich!

b) Match pictures A–E to steps 1–6.

7 MEDIATION — A party game

It's your friend's birthday soon. He sends you a message with a link to a party game description.
Write back and tell him in German how the game works.

> www.partygames.example.com
>
> Ich habe hier ein Spiel für meine Geburtstagsparty gefunden, aber ich verstehe nicht alles. Wie funktioniert es genau?

 www.partygames.example.com

A guessing game
Here's a great party game for your birthday! It's really easy to play and it's a lot of fun! You only need a playlist with a lot of popular songs.

To play:
Play a song. Everybody guesses the name of the song and the name of the singer. The first right answer gets 10 points. The first person with 70 points wins!

My task

8 Our party

a) Plan a party for your class. Work in groups. In your group, decide on a kind of party (a dance / garden / film / magic party, ...).

What about ...?

b) In your group, make notes about these things:

your party food
your party music / playlist
games and activities

▶ Digital help   ▶ Wordbank 12, p. 193

c) Tell the class about your party. The class chooses the best party plan.

This is our party food: ...

This is our music playlist. First ... by ...

We want to watch a film / ...

Digital quiz   I can talk about party food and activities.

5   Topic 3

Let's cook!

1 BEFORE YOU WATCH   What are you cooking?

Read Zane's shopping list. What kind of cake is he making?

I think it's a … cake.

> Hey, Zane! What are you doing?

> Hi, Lily. I'm watching a cooking video. I want to make this for Noah's birthday party.

shopping list
- chocolate
- eggs
- cocoa powder
- butter

2 VIEWING   A cooking video

a) Watch the video. Put the photos in the correct order.

b) Watch again and check.

A He's putting the cake in the oven.

B He's adding the eggs.

C He's putting the icing on the cake.

D He's mixing the flour and the cocoa.

E He's adding the vanilla to the eggs.

F He's making the icing with butter and sugar.

c) Do you like chocolate cake? Do you want to make this recipe? Tell a partner.

> I like chocolate cake. It's really good!

> I think this recipe is too hard.

If you want to make this recipe, look on p. 161!

▶ More practice 9, p. 161

▶ Workbook, p. 77

3 Reading Zane's favourite dish

Read Zane's blog post. Write if these sentences are true (T) or false (F).

1. Zane's favourite dish is from India.
2. Jollof rice is a main course.
3. It's a vegetarian dish.
4. Zane's family eats jollof rice with chips.
5. They eat it a lot.
6. Zane thinks that his dad cooks it best.

www.cooking-with-zane.example.net

We eat it with plantain – it's a kind of banana. We fry it in a frying pan. Everybody in my family likes this dish and my dad often cooks it on Sundays. Sometimes I cook it – don't tell him, but I think I cook it best! 😊

This is my favourite dish.
It's called jollof rice and it's from Nigeria.
It's a main course.
You make it with rice, tomatoes, vegetables, chicken – and a lot of spices!
It's delicious and I love it!

My task

4 My favourite dish

Write about your favourite dish. Use Zane's blog post in 3 and these questions to help you.

- What kind of dish is it?
  A main course? A dessert? Is it sweet?
- What country does it come from?
- What's in the dish?
- When do you eat it? Who cooks it?
- Do you eat it with your family?
- What do you drink with it?

▶ Digital help   ▶ More help, p. 161   ▶ Wordbank 12, p. 193

Good to know

Food and drinks in Britain
- Fish and chips is very British, but in Britain you can eat food from everywhere!
- A lot of people drink tea (often with milk and sugar), but a lot of people drink coffee too.

▶ Workbook, p. 78

I can describe my favourite dish.

A different kind of party

1 READING **What's happening in the story?**

a) BEFORE YOU READ Look at the first picture and choose the correct word.

1. Lily, Zane and Sunita are / aren't meeting Noah.
2. Zane is / isn't bringing a drink.
3. Noah and his family are / aren't sitting in the park.
4. Buddy is / isn't running in the park.
5. It is / isn't raining.
6. The kids are / aren't wearing school uniforms.

b) Read the story and find out: What's Noah's secret?

Lily	This is the park and it's 2 o'clock ..., but where are Noah and his family?
5 Zane	Look, there they are! Noah's waving. Oh, and here's Sunita!
Sunita	Hi! What are you bringing to the party, Zane?
10	
Zane	It's my special chocolate cake. It's for Noah's party.
15 Lily	It looks really good!

Zane	Happy birthday, Noah! Here's a dessert for you!
Noah	Thanks! Mum and Dad, my friends are here.
Mum	Hello! Nice to meet you.
20 Lily	And here are some strawberries, Noah.
Noah	Thanks, but I'm allergic to strawberries, remember?
Lily	Oh no, I'm sorry ...
Dad	That's OK, Lily – it's very kind of you to bring them. And I love strawberries!
25	

	Sunita	Zane, are you OK? You're very quiet.
	Zane	Erm, this is a very different kind of party. I mean, it's just us and Noah's family here. And we're just sitting and talking. There's no music, people aren't dancing ... It's not the kind of party I like!
30		
	Sunita	It's different. But Noah doesn't like loud music or dancing. So I think this is the kind of party he likes.

35	**Dad**	Do you want to open your presents now, Noah?
	Noah	No, let's eat my birthday cake first!
	Dad	OK, it's in my bag ... Oh no! Stop, Buddy!
	Noah	Is Buddy OK?
40	**Mum**	Yes, he's OK. There's no chocolate in the cake. But we can't eat it now! I'm sorry, Noah.
	Noah	That's no problem. We can eat Zane's chocolate cake.

45	**Lily**	It's a shame about your birthday cake, Noah. But you look happy. Are you having fun?
	Noah	Yes, I am. This is the best birthday party ever! I'm having a picnic with my family and my best friends and my dog. It isn't too loud, so I'm feeling good. It's sunny, I have presents and we can eat Zane's chocolate cake. It's the perfect party for me!
50		
	Lily	That's great! I'm happy for you.

	Noah	And now – my secret: Watch this!
	Sunita	Wow! Noah, that's amazing!
55	**Zane**	You're really good at juggling!
	Dad	Well done, Noah! When you want to learn something, you work really hard.
	Noah	Ta-dah! This is a circus birthday party, right? Now it's your turn – I can show you how to juggle too!
60		
	Zane	Wow, this is a great party! It's a new kind of party for me, but it's great fun. Thanks, Noah!

2 Who is it?

Complete the sentences with a name or names.

1. ... makes some food for the party.
2. ... can't eat strawberries.
3. ... loves eating strawberries.
4. ... and ... think the party is too quiet at first.
5. ... eats the birthday cake.
6. ... thinks the party is perfect.
7. ... thinks something different about the party at the end.

3 Words in the story

Find the words in the story for the descriptions.

1. When you put your hand up to say hello. (line 6)
2. When you can't eat a kind of food. (line 21)
3. When you eat in the park with friends. (line 47)
4. When something is really great. (line 54)
5. When you do tricks with three or more balls. (line 55)

4 LIFE SKILLS People are different

a) Read the sentences about Noah and his friends. Write how you are the same or different.

1. Noah likes quiet parties. *I like quiet parties too. / I don't like quiet parties.*
2. Zane likes loud music and dancing.
3. Noah's dad likes strawberries.
4. Sunita doesn't eat meat.

b) Talk to your partner. What's the same and what's different?

I don't eat pork. What about you?

I eat pork, so that's different. I like skateboarding.

Cool! I like skateboarding too. That's the same.

c) Tell the class one thing that is the same for you and your partner. Then say one thing that's different.

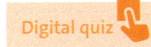 I **can** understand and talk about differences.

Viewing

The Brighton dares: Birthday

1 Before you watch Birthday words

Daisy and Emir do two new dares this week. Can you guess them? Say the numbers.

1 Dance in a library
2 Sing in a supermarket
3 Take¹ your imaginary² friend to a party.
4 Tell a teacher about your imaginary friend.

2 Viewing The dares

a) Watch the video and check your guesses in 1. Which dares are in the video?

b) Choose the correct answers A or B.

		A	B
1	Gloria's party is on …	Saturday.	Wednesday.
2	Emir has to do his dare …	at the party.	in the supermarket.
3	For his dare, Emir has to …	juggle.	sing.
4	People near him are are …	surprised but happy.	angry.
5	The video is …	for the internet.	a present for Gloria.
6	The toy dog is a present from …	Sota (Daisy's friend).	Emir.

c) Watch the video again and answer the questions.

1 Which birthday things can you see in the video?
2 What's everybody doing when the video finishes?

3 All the dares

There are ten dares in this book. Talk about them with a partner.

I think	Daisy's Emir's	school family sports and hobbies town birthday	dare is	the best. cool. funny. great. horrible. interesting. mean. stupid. weird.

---

¹ (to) **take somebody** *jemanden mitnehmen*   ² **imaginary** *Fantasie-, eingebildet*

▶ Workbook, p. 79

5 Study skills

Explaining words

1 What kind is it?

a) Match sentences a–f to the food and drinks.

1e, 2 …

1	melon	a	It's a kind of dessert.
2	chicken	b	It's a kind of British food.
3	tomato	c	It's a kind of meat.
4	fish and chips	d	It's a kind of drink.
5	cake	e	It's a kind of fruit.
6	milk	f	It's a kind of vegetable.

Chips are a kind of potato. Potatoes are a kind of vegetable. Vegetables are good for you. So chips are good for you, right?

b) Now describe these food and drinks with umbrella words.

1 ham   2 banana   3 carrot   4 water   5 lemon   6 ice cream

2 What's it like?

Match the food and drinks to the words in the box.

1 cola   4 sugar
2 carrot   5 mattar paneer
3 pea   6 orange

> big • brown • cold • green • hot • long • orange • red • small • spicy • sweet • white

3 Now you

Describe these food and drinks. Can you add more information?

Example: tomato – It's a kind of vegetable. It's red. It can be big or small. You can eat it in a salad.

1 lemon   4 fish and chips
2 strawberry   5 cake
3 lemonade   6 ham

4 GAME Explain it!

Start in groups of three. Each student writes two words (foods, drinks, dishes) on a piece of paper. Swap words with another group, but don't show them. In each group, a student takes a piece of paper and explains the word. The group has one minute to guess it.

▶ Skills file 6, p. 173

 Digital quiz   I can **explain words**.

Topic 1 Topic 2 Topic 3 Story Viewing Study skills **Unit task** **5**

Write a recipe for a sandwich

Step 1

Do you have a favourite sandwich?
You can use your own recipe or find new ideas on the internet.
What food do you need?

> sandwich
> bread
> vegetables (salad, tomatoes, …)
> cheese
> butter

▶ Wordbank 12, p. 193

Step 2

Write the steps how to make your sandwich. You can use the words in the box.

| first • next • clean • cut • put … on the … • add |

▶ Wordbank 13, p. 194

Step 3

Add pictures to your recipe. Draw pictures or use photos of your sandwich.
You can also show how you make the sandwich or how you eat it.

Step 4

Collect all the recipes for a book.
Look at another student's recipe and write a note with your feedback. Put it on the page.

> Your sandwich looks really good.

> I want to make this!

> Your recipe is easy to make.

▶ Skills file 5, p. 171

Digital quiz   I can research and write a recipe.

one hundred and fifty-one **151**

5 Checkpoint Digital checkpoint

1 A film night

I can talk about food.

a) WORDS Look at the food and drinks. What things can you see? Write the correct word.

b) SPEAKING You and your partner are having a film night. You talk about what you want to buy for food and drinks. Choose three things from a).

> Let's buy some … / I want to buy …
> I love … / I often eat / drink …
> Do you like …?

> Yes, that's a good idea. /
> No, I don't want to buy …, but let's buy …
> I don't like … / I never eat / drink … /
> I'm allergic to …

2 LANGUAGE A very bad picnic

I can talk about birthdays and parties *(present progressive)*.

Sunita shows her friends a photo of a bad family party. Complete her sentences with the *ing*-form of the words in the box.

> bark • eat • listen • play •
> put • sit • text • wear

1 Willow's birthday is in August, so we're … T-shirts, but it's cold and rainy.
2 Mum is … balloons on a tree, but it's very windy.
3 We're … on the grass because there are no chairs.
4 A dog is … because it wants our food.
5 Nish is on his phone. He's … his friends.
6 A seagull is … my sandwich.
7 Ben is … the guitar.
8 But just one person is … to Ben's music!

Check

152   one hundred and fifty-two

Die Übungen kannst du auch digital machen

3 LANGUAGE After the party

I can talk about party food *(much, many, a lot of)*.

Lily is at a family party. Her sister messages her about the food. Look at the picture and complete her answer with the words in the box.

How much food and drink is there?

a lot of • aren't • carrots • isn't • sausages

1 There … much lemonade.
2 There … many sandwiches.
3 There's … salad.
4 There are a lot of …
5 There aren't many …

4 READING Zane's dream party

a) Look at the title of the website and the pictures. Where's Zane's dream party?

 www.stadium-birthday-party.example.net

The stadium: The perfect place for your birthday party

Why?
- The stadium is a special and interesting place.

Party activities:
- A tour of the stadium.
- A football skills lesson with our trainers.
- You and your friends play a football match.

When?
- Sunday mornings: 10 a.m. – 12 p.m.

What about food?
- Enjoy a delicious lunch of sandwiches, fruit and birthday cake.

b) Read the website. Answer the questions. Write in sentences.

1 Why is the stadium a good place for a party?
2 What activities are there?
3 What day of the week are the parties?
4 How long are the parties?
5 What food is there?

c) Where's your dream party? Why? You can use the ideas in the boxes.

cinema • ice rink • park • skatepark • zoo

I like animals / films / skateboarding / skating / sports.

Check

5 Checkpoint Digital checkpoint

5 MEDIATION My favourite dish

I can describe my favourite dish.

You want to tell your mum about your new favourite dish. You find the recipe on the internet and show it to her. Answer your mum's questions:

1. Isst man das zum Frühstück oder zu Abend?
2. Welche Zutaten braucht man dafür?
3. Wie lange wird es im Ofen gebacken?

 www.delicious-dinners.example.net

Toad in the hole

Today I want to tell you about my favourite evening meal: toad in the hole.
I often eat it in winter. The name sounds weird, but the ingredients aren't weird!

You need:
- 3 eggs
- 300 ml milk
- 8 sausages
- 175 g flour
- oil

How to make it:
1. Mix the eggs, milk and flour.
2. Cook the sausages in a frying pan with oil.
3. Put the sausages and the mixture in an oven dish.
4. Cook in the oven for 30 minutes.

6 LISTENING Dinner at Sunita's house

I can understand and talk about differences.

a) Zane is at Sunita's house. Listen. Which picture is Sunita's dining room?

A   B

b) Listen again. Write 'Zane's family' or 'Sunita's family'.

1. … eats dinner in a big dining room.
2. … has a small dining room.
3. … eats dinner in the living room.
4. … doesn't eat meat.
5. … has no animals.

Check

7 STUDY SKILLS Explaining new words   I can explain words.

a) Daniel is explaining some new words, but there are some mistakes. Find the mistake in each sentence.

1 carrot: It's a kind of fruit.
2 chicken: It's a kind of cake.
3 dessert: It's the meal before dinner.
4 milk: It's a kind of food.
5 cornflakes: You eat them with water.
6 tea: It's a cold drink.
7 shopping list: You need it at school.
8 vegetables: They're bad for you.

b) Write the correct sentences (1–8).

1 carrot: It's a kind of …

8 WRITING A banana and chocolate crepe   I can research and write a recipe.

Luisa wants to write a blog post about her favourite dessert recipe: a banana and chocolate crepe. Look at the pictures and read her notes. Then complete her post with the words in the box.

add • fry • eggs • minutes • mix • pan

You make it with flour, sugar, milk, chocolate sauce, a banana and two …

You also need a spoon and a frying …

First … the flour, eggs, milk and sugar.

Then … the mixture for two minutes.

Next turn over the crepe and fry it for two more …

… chocolate sauce and the banana.

5 Partner page

Partner page

▶ Page 139

9 SPEAKING Find the differences

Partner B: Look at this picture.
Take turns and find six differences:

> In my picture, a boy and a girl in blue T-shirts are …

> In my picture they're talking.

> In my picture, they aren't … They're …

10 MY TASK My party photos

Describe these photos to your partner.

This is my birthday. It's the 26th July. We're wearing sunglasses. … We're eating … and drinking …

Diff bank

▶ **Page 134**

More practice 1 **Food words**

a) Start a page in your VOCAB FILE. Make lists or a mind map for vegetables, fruit, meat and other food words. You can draw pictures and add words in other languages.
Add more new words later in the unit.

b) What am I? Choose the correct word from the box.

> cream • pea • strawberry • tomato

1 I'm a very small, green vegetable.
2 People eat me in salads and on burgers.
3 I'm a sweet red fruit.
4 People eat me with cake or fruit or in a dessert.

▶ **Page 136**

More help **1** READING **Noah's invitation**

a) BEFORE YOU READ What do you do on your birthday? Tell a partner.

We often	go swimming. go to the cinema. watch a film at home. play party games. sing *Happy Birthday*. take photos. play games online.		We eat	burgers. ice cream. fruit. kebabs. pizza. sandwiches. sausages.

More practice 2 **Messages to Noah**

Sunita and Noah's cousin Ryan write messages to Noah. Put Sunita's and Ryan's messages in the correct order. Start like this: *Sunita: b, …*

a Bye – see you on Saturday!

b Hello, Noah! I'd love to come to your party – thanks!

c Love, Sunita
xoxo

d I love picnics!

e Bye and happy birthday from Ryan!

f I'm sorry, but I can't come. I'm busy on Saturday.

g Hi, Noah. Thanks for the invitation.

h I have a basketball game.

5 Diff bank

▶ Page 137

 More practice 3 A calendar quiz

Look at the calendar. Take turns to ask and answer the questions.

1 What day of the week is 3rd July? – It's …
2 What date is the second Thursday in July?
3 What date is the fifth Thursday in July?
4 Today is 13th July. What date is the next Saturday?
5 What day and date is Ezra's birthday? (Look at the red circle.) – It's on …

JULY						
Mon	Tue	Wed	Thur	Fri	Sat	Sun
	1	2	3	4	5	6
7	8	9	10	11	12	13
14	15	16	17	18	19	20
21	22	23	24	25	26	27
28	29	30	31			

More practice 4 Your favourite dates

a) What dates so you always remember? Write five dates in your exercise book.

13th December: my dog's birthday

 b) Tell your partner about your dates.

My dog's birthday is on the thirteenth of December.

More help WRITING 5 My birthday invitation

Where?	What?
the cinema • the pool • the skatepark • my house	watch a film • go swimming • go skateboarding • play music • play games • make pizzas • eat cake

▶ Page 138

More practice 5 DOUBLE CIRCLE What are you doing?

Talk to different partners. Choose from the ideas in the box.

A Hi, Anna. What are you doing?
B Hi, Deniz. I'm … What are you doing?
A I'm … OK – see you!

eating a kebab • playing with my pet snake • coding • cleaning my room • playing bingo • standing on my head • teaching my parrot to sing • writing a post • watching a film

▶ Page 139

Parallel exercise 8 **A birthday photo**

Zane is showing his mum a photo of his friend's birthday party. Complete his sentences with the *ing*-form.

1. I'm (eat) … birthday cake. It's chocolate, my favourite!
   I'm eating birthday cake.
2. Sunita and Ruby are (listen) … to music.
3. This is Ju. She's (open) … her birthday presents.
4. Noah is (sit) … on a chair with a cat.
5. He's (take) … photos of the cat with his phone.
6. Max and Albie have balloons. They're (play) … with them.
7. Lily is at the table. She's (draw) … a picture.
8. Amina and Vicky are (sing) … Happy Birthday.

The spelling of some verbs with *-ing* is different:
sit – si**tt**ing
tak**e** – taking

More practice 6 **What are they doing?**

a) It's one o'clock in Germany. What are the people in the pictures doing now?
Use the verbs in the box with the *ing*-form.

go • make • sleep • get up • cycle • eat

The girl in Mexico is …

The boy in New York is …

In London they are … lunch.

The boy in Berlin is …

In Tokyo they are … dinner.

In Sydney they are … to bed.

b) Write what you're doing now. Write what people in your family are doing now.

*I'm sitting in the classroom. I'm …
My little brother is playing at home. …*

5 Diff bank

▶ Page 139

More practice 7 **What's happening?**

🔊 a) Listen to the sounds. What's happening?
Write a sentence. Choose words from the box.

> box • drink tea • eat •
> close a door • play table tennis •
> send a message

Somebody is … / Two people are …

👥 b) Compare your ideas.

In number 1, I think somebody is …

🔊 c) Listen again and check.

More help **10** MY TASK **My party photos**

This is my birthday party.	
This is my dad's / grandma's / little sister's / … party.	
I'm with my mum and dad / my friends / …	
I'm / We're wearing	a party hat / funny glasses / new clothes / a blue dress / new trainers / …
I'm / We're eating	birthday cake / cupcakes / pizza / …
I'm / We're playing	a party game / in the garden / with balloons / …

▶ Page 141

More practice 8 **Making dinner**

Zane and his dad are making dinner.
Complete the dialogue with the words in the box.

> hungry • many • much • pasta •
> tomatoes • two • water

Dad   Let's make dinner!
Zane How many (1) … do we need?
Dad   Five or six.
Zane And how much meat?
Dad   You can use all of it. There isn't (2) … meat in there.
Zane And how many carrots?
Dad   Just, (3) … that's OK. They're big carrots, so you don't need (4) …
Zane How much water do I need for the (5) …?
Dad   You need to cook it in a lot of (6) …
Zane And how much pasta do we need?
Dad   A lot – we're all very (7) …!

What dish are they making?

> Spaghetti Bolognese (upside down)

▶ Page 144

More practice 9 **A recipe**

Do you want to make the cake on p. 144? Here's the recipe:

For the cake:
250 g flour
120 g sugar
50 g cocoa powder
2 teaspoons baking powder
¼ teaspoon salt

2 eggs
60 ml oil
30 ml milk
½ teaspoon vanilla

For the icing:
200 g butter
100 g chocolate
400 g icing sugar

1 Mix the flour, sugar, cocoa powder, baking powder and salt in a bowl.
2 Break the eggs into a different bowl. Add the oil, vanilla and milk. Mix everything a lot.
3 Add the flour mixture to the egg mixture. Be careful: Don't mix too much.
4 Put the mixture in the oven (180 °C for 50 minutes).
5 Mix the butter and icing sugar. Warm the chocolate and add it. Mix everything a lot.
6 Put the icing on the cake and enjoy!

▶ Page 145

More help **4 MY TASK** **My favourite dish**

My favourite dish is	a dessert / a main course / a cake / a drink / …
It's	cold / delicious / hot / spicy / sweet / …
It comes from	my dad's / mum's / family's culture / … China / Germany / India / Italy / Poland / Turkey / …
You make it with	cheese / chocolate / meat / pasta / rice / sugar / tomatoes / …
I eat it My family eats it My dad / mum cooks it I cook it	every day / every week / every Friday / at parties / …

Skills file

Skills file – Übersicht

Auf den **Skills file**-Seiten findest du Methoden und Tipps, die dir helfen, z. B. Wortschatz zu lernen, Informationen zu sammeln, Wörter zu umschreiben oder kleine Vorträge zu halten.

Inhalt	Seite			
SF 1 Wörter lernen	163	SF 4	Arbeit mit dem Wörterbuch	169
SF 2 Mindmaps	166	SF 5	Einen Kurzvortrag halten	171
SF 3 Buchstabieren	168	SF 6	Wörter umschreiben	173

Die mit diesem Symbol gekennzeichneten Abschnitte enthalten Hinweise und Tipps, die dir dabei helfen, elektronische Medien beim Englischlernen einzusetzen.

Dieses Symbol zeigt dir, dass du einen Erklärfilm zu diesem Thema in der App findest.
Erklär-film

Lösungen der Merkaufgaben:

SF 2, Merkaufgabe:
a) *Thema: animals* • *Oberbegriffe: farm animals, wild animals, pets* • *Unterbegriffe: chicken, snake, dog*

SF 3, Merkaufgabe:
- *Sea:* [es] – [i:] – [eɪ]
- *Lanes:* [el] – [eɪ] – [en] – [i:] – [es]
- *BN2 1PS:* [bi:] – [en] – two – one – [pi:] – [es]
- *Brighton:* [bi:] – [ɑ:] – [aɪ] – [dʒi:] – [eɪtʃ] – [ti:] – [əʊ] – [en]

SF 4, Merkaufgabe 1:
beach, because, bed

SF 4, Merkaufgabe 2:
a) *Haupteintrag: opinion*
b) *Haupteintrag: colour*
c) *Haupteintrag: shopping*

SF 4, Merkaufgabe 3:
a) *question:* b) *mouse: mice*
c) *potato: potatoes*

SF 4, Merkaufgabe 4:
a) *drink:* 1. *das Getränk;* 2. *trinken*
b) *love:* 1. *die Liebe;* 2. *lieben, sehr mögen*
c) *mean:* 1. *gemein, fies;* 2. *bedeuten;* 3. *meinen (sagen wollen)*

SF 5, Merkaufgabe 1:
a) *Karteikarte Nr. 3* b) *That's the end of my presentation. Thank you for listening. Do you have any questions?*

SF 5, Merkaufgabe 2:
b) *I like your presentation. Your pictures are very nice. Please don't speak so fast.*

SF 6, Merkaufgabe 1:
a) *room* b) *fruit*

SF 6, Merkaufgabe 2:
It's a place at school. You do sports there.

SF 1

Wörter lernen leichtgemacht

▶ Unit 1 | p. 34

Alle neuen Wörter und Wendungen des Buches findest du im *Vocabulary*, S. 202–235.
Alle fett gedruckten Wörter aus der linken und der rechten Spalte musst du lernen.

Wie kann ich Wörter lernen?

Es gibt viele Möglichkeiten, wie du Wörter lernen kannst.

Hier stellen wir dir einige vor. Probiere sie aus und finde heraus, welche Methoden am besten zu dir passen.

Lerne immer nur fünf bis zehn Wörter auf einmal.

1 Wörter lernen mit dem *Vocabulary*

Auf S. 201 kannst du sehen, wie das *Vocabulary* aufgebaut ist und welche Symbole und Abkürzungen dort verwendet werden. Hier ist ein Beispiel von S. 205:

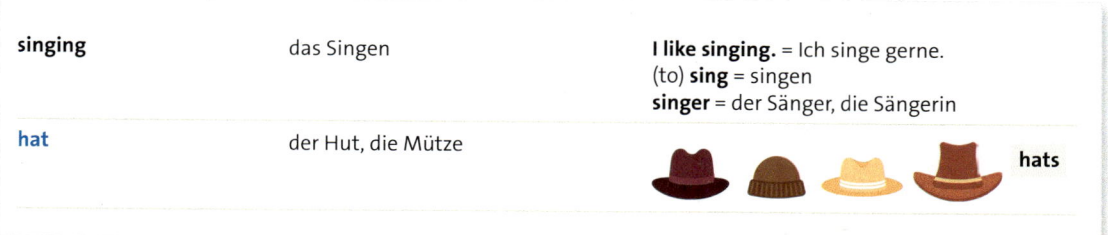

- Lies dir zunächst das englische Wort laut vor.
- Lies dann die deutsche Übersetzung und die Beispiele und Hinweise in der rechten Spalte.
- Schreibe das englische Wort auf und präge dir so die Schreibweise ein.
- Wiederhole diese Schritte mehrfach hintereinander, um dir die Wörter gut zu merken. Wechsle dabei auch die Leserichtung: Beginne mit der deutschen Übersetzung, sage dann das englische Wort.
- Teste dich nun selbst: Decke die deutsche Übersetzung ab, lies das englische Wort. Weißt du noch, was es auf Deutsch bedeutet? Kannst du auch die englischen Beispiele nennen?
- Du kannst auch jemanden bitten dich abzufragen.

Merkaufgabe 1

Probiere das gleich einmal aus: Wähle fünf bis zehn Wörter aus deinem *Vocabulary* und lerne sie wie oben beschrieben. Lasse dich von deinem Partner oder deiner Partnerin abfragen.

Skills file

 2 Wörter lernen mit digitalen Medien

Vokabeln kannst du auch digital auf deinem Smartphone, Tablet oder PC üben.

Am Ende kannst du dich oft mit einem Quiz testen und bekommst ein Feedback zu deinem Lernergebnis.

Oft kannst du die Wörter auch anhören. So lernst du die richtige Aussprache gleich mit!

Wie kann ich mir Wörter besser merken?

Manche Wörter wollen einfach nicht im Gedächtnis bleiben! Dann können dir Merktechniken helfen:

- Schreibe das Wort auf einen Klebezettel und bringe ihn an einer Stelle an, wo du oft hinschaust.

- Male ein **Bild** zum Wort.

- Verbinde das Wort mit einer passenden **Geste** oder **Bewegung**.

- Suche passende **Reimwörter**: *house – mouse*

- Finde Wörter aus der gleichen **Wortfamilie**:
  dance → dancing
  swim → swimmer

- Erfinde **Bildwörter**.

- Verwende das Wort in einem Satz oder einer typischen **Redewendung**:
  how → How are you?
  ride → ride a bike

- Finde **Gegensatzpaare**:
  big – small
  sunny – rainy

- Finde **Oberbegriffe** *(umbrella words)*:
  football → sport
  monkey → animal

> **Merkaufgabe 2**
>
> Wähle aus deinem *Vocabulary* drei Wörter, die du dir bisher noch nicht merken konntest. Wende drei verschiedene Merktechniken an.

 Denke daran, dass du mit deinen Eltern sprichst, bevor du eine kostenpflichtige App herunterlädst.

 Das *Vocabulary* (S. 202–235) enthält in der dritten Spalte viele Merkhilfen, die du beim Lernen nutzen kannst.

ein Bild zum Wort

ein Bildwort

ein Gegensatzpaar

Wörter sammeln und ordnen in einem *Vocab file*

In einem Vokabelordner *(Vocab file)* kannst du Wörter sammeln und in Listen, Mindmaps und Tabellen ordnen.

Dadurch kannst du sie nicht nur besser lernen und behalten, sondern auch noch später nutzen, z. B. wenn du über ein Thema sprechen oder schreiben möchtest.

Zudem kannst du neue Wörter und Seiten an jeder Stelle beliebig ergänzen.

So gestaltest du die Seiten deines *Vocab files*:

- Lege Mindmaps zu bestimmten Themen an, wie z. B. zu *food*. Schreibe das Thema in die Mitte.
- Ergänze Oberbegriffe *(umbrella words)* und suche passende Wörter oder auch Unterbegriffe dazu (z. B. *lunch: fish and chips, sandwich, salad, …*).
- Erstelle nach und nach weitere Listen, Mindmaps und Tabellen und hefte sie in deinen Ordner. Ergänze deine Listen, wenn du neue Wörter lernst.

Wenn deine Sammlung umfangreicher wird, kannst du ein farbiges Register einfügen, um den Überblick zu behalten.

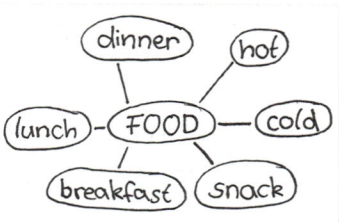

Merkaufgabe 3

Besorge dir einen Schnellhefter oder Ordner. Lege deine erste Wortliste an und suche im *Vocabulary* passende Wörter dazu, z. B.:

- Reimwörter *(rhyme words)*
- Gegensatzpaare *(opposites)*
- schwierige Wörter *(difficult words)*
- Lieblingswörter *(my favourite words)*

In den *Wordbanks* auf S. 184–194 findest du viele nützliche Wörter, Sätze und Ausdrücke zu bestimmten Themen wie z. B. Schule, Tiere oder Freizeitaktivitäten.

Skills file

SF 2

Sammeln und ordnen – Mindmaps

▶ Unit 1 | p. 34

Wobei kann mir eine Mindmap helfen?

Eine Mindmap (englisch *mind map*) hilft dir beim Sammeln und Ordnen von Ideen. Du kannst sie bei der Planung von Projekten oder Präsentationen, beim Wörterlernen, bei der Strukturierung von eigenen Texten oder auch bei der Erarbeitung von Lesetexten verwenden.

Wie erstelle ich eine Mindmap?

1 Das Thema

Nimm dir ein leeres Blatt und schreibe das Thema in Großbuchstaben in die Mitte. Umrahme das Thema mit einem Kreis oder einer Wolke.

2 Oberbegriffe

Finde Oberbegriffe zu deinem Thema. Verwende für jeden Oberbegriff eine neue Farbe. Jetzt hat deine Mindmap Hauptäste.

3 Unterbegriffe

Ergänze nun weitere Ideen zu den Oberbegriffen als Unterbegriffe. Verwende dieselbe Farbe wie für den Oberbegriff.

Deine Hauptäste haben nun Nebenäste. An diese kannst du noch weitere Ideen als Unteräste anhängen.

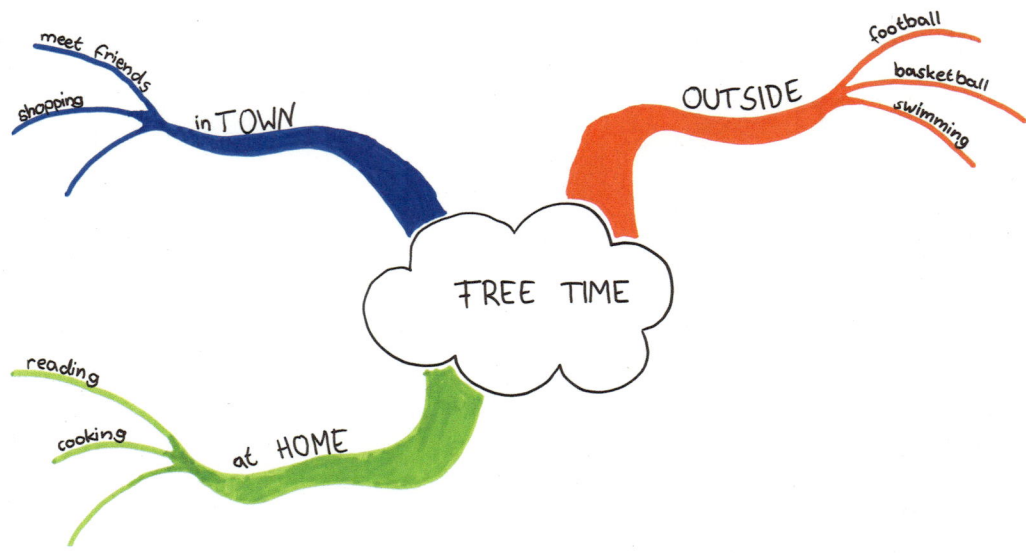

4 Überarbeiten

Gehe alles noch einmal durch und mache deine Mindmap noch anschaulicher: Lassen sich vielleicht Verbindungen zwischen den einzelnen Hauptästen oder den Nebenästen herstellen? Mit Zeichnungen und Symbolen kannst du die Ideen deiner Mindmap weiter verdeutlichen.

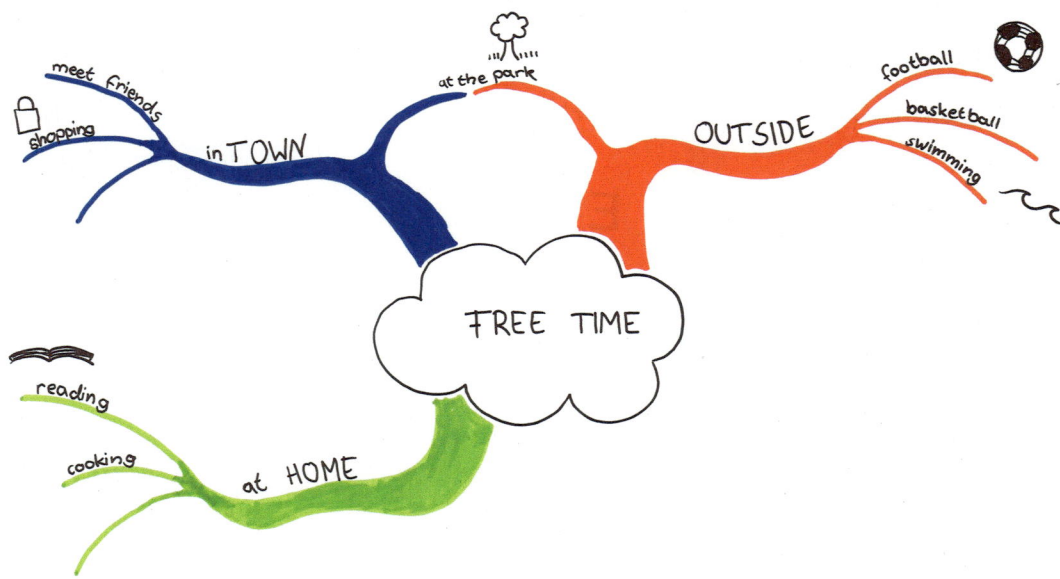

Merkaufgabe

a) Sortiere die folgenden Begriffe:

> dog • farm animals • pets • wild animals • snake • animals • chicken

- Was ist das Thema?
- Was sind die Oberbegriffe?
- Welches sind mögliche Unterbegriffe?

(Die Lösung findest du auf S. 162.)

b) Erstelle eine Mindmap zu diesem Thema. Gehe wie oben beschrieben (1–4) vor.

Skills file

SF 3

Buchstabieren

▶ Unit 2 | p. 60

Oft spricht man Wörter oder auch Namen auf Englisch ganz anders aus, als man sie schreibt. Um sie nicht falsch zu schreiben, bittet man darum, sie zu buchstabieren.

Dazu brauchst du das englische Alphabet:

Can you spell your name, please?

My name is Scout. That's S–C–O–U–T.

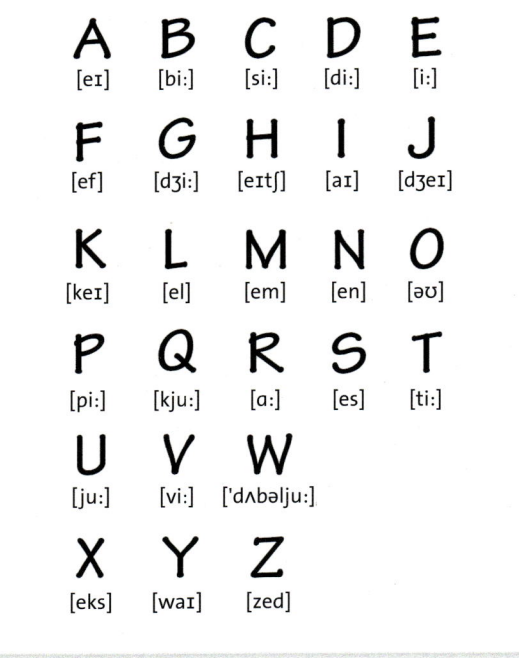

💡 Einige Laute haben in der Lautschrift besondere Zeichen, z. B.
- [ʃ] sprichst du wie „sch".
- [ʤ] sprichst du wie „dsch" (z. B. in „Dschungel").
- [:] Dieses Zeichen sieht wie ein Doppelpunkt aus. Es soll dir sagen, dass der Laut davor lang gesprochen wird.

▶ English sounds, p. 257

Wie übe ich buchstabieren auf Englisch?

🔊
- Höre dir das Alphabet in der App an und lies jeden Buchstaben laut mit, z. B. oben oder auf S. 257.
- Versuche danach, das Alphabet alleine zu sprechen. Die Lautschrift in eckigen Klammern kann dir helfen, dich an die Aussprache zu erinnern.

Merkaufgabe

Buchstabiere Scouts Adresse: *Sea Lanes, BN2 1PS, Brighton*

(Die Lösung findest du auf S. 162.)

💡 Wenn dir jemand etwas buchstabiert, schreibe zuerst die einzelnen Buchstaben auf. Danach lies das ganze Wort oder den ganzen Namen.

SF 4

Arbeit mit dem Wörterbuch

▶ Unit 3 | p. 92

Wenn du die Bedeutung eines englischen Wortes nicht weißt, kannst du das *English-German Dictionary* deines Englischbuchs (S. 236–246) oder ein Online-Wörterbuch zu Hilfe nehmen.

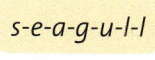

Wie finde ich Wörter und Ausdrücke im *Dictionary*?

1 In deinem *English-German Dictionary* (und in anderen Wörterbüchern) sind die Wörter alphabetisch geordnet:

e kommt vor f
fa kommt vor fe
fac kommt vor fal

> **Merkaufgabe 1**
>
> Schreibe die folgenden Wörter in der richtigen alphabetischen Reihenfolge untereinander auf:
>
> **1** *because*   **2** *beach*   **3** *bed*
>
> Suche die Wörter anschließend in deinem *English-German Dictionary* (S. 236–246). Überprüfe, ob sie in der gleichen Reihenfolge erscheinen wie deine Wörter.
>
> (Die Lösung findest du auch auf S. 162.)

> **explanation** [ɛksplə'neɪʃn] die Erklärung 4 (108)
> °**eye** [aɪ] das Auge
>
> **F**
>
> °**fact** [fækt] die Tatsache
> °**false** [fɔːls] falsch, unrichtig
> **family** ['fæməli] die Familie 2 (44/45)
> **fan** [fæn] der Fan 2 (47)
> °**far** [fɑː] weit (entfernt)
> **fast** [fɑːst] schnell 2 (48)
> **favourite** ['feɪvərɪt]:
>   1. der Liebling, der Favorit, die Favoritin (14)
>   2. Lieblings- (14)
>   °**my favourite thing to do** das, was ich am liebsten tue
> **February** ['februəri] der Februar 5 (136)
> °**feed** [fiːd] füttern **Don't feed the seagulls.** Füttert / Füttern Sie nicht die Möwen.

2 Zusammengesetzte Wörter und längere Ausdrücke findest du bei einem Haupteintrag. Der Haupteintrag steht farbig oder **fett** am Anfang, Untereinträge kommen nach dem Haupteintrag. Schaue dir rechts den Eintrag für *name* an.

> **name** [neɪm] der Name (10/11)
> **What's your name?** Wie heißt du? (10/11)

> **Merkaufgabe 2**
>
> Finde den Haupteintrag zu folgenden Redewendungen:
>
> **a)** *in my opinion*   **b)** *What colour is ...?*   **c)** *go shopping*
>
> (Die Lösung findest du auf S. 162.)

Skills file

Was erfahre ich alles aus dem *Dictionary*?

- Im *English-German Dictionary* findest du die deutsche Übersetzung zu den englischen Wörtern aus deinem Buch.
- Außerdem kannst du die richtige Schreibweise eines Wortes überprüfen.
- Du erfährst auch, wie das Wort ausgesprochen wird. Schaue dir dafür die Lautschrift hinter dem Wort an.
- Und du kannst herausfinden, ob ein Wort einen unregelmäßigen Plural hat. Ist die Pluralform regelmäßig, findest du keinen Zusatz.

> **share** [ʃeə] teilen 3 (90)
> **sharpener** [ˈʃɑːpnə] Anspitzer 1 (21)
> **she** [ʃiː] sie *(weibliche Person)* 1 (24) **she's** (= she is) sie ist 1 (24)
> **shelf** [ʃelf], *pl* **shelves** das Regal 2 (52)
> **shelves** [ʃelvz] *Plural von* shelf
> **shoe** [ʃuː] der Schuh 2 (52)
> **shop** [ʃɒp] das Geschäft, der Laden 4 (104/105) **be at the shops** Einkäufe erledigen 4 (104/105)

Merkaufgabe 3

Finde den Plural von **a)** *question* **b)** *mouse* **c)** *potato*

(Die Lösung findest du auf S. 162.)

- An den Ziffern 1., 2., ... kannst du sehen, dass ein Wort mehrere Bedeutungen hat. Lies daher immer den ganzen Eintrag und entscheide dann, welche Bedeutung in deinem Fall die richtige ist.

> **text** [tekst]:
> 1. der Text 3 (79)
> 2. die SMS 5 (136)
> 3. **text sb.** jm. eine SMS schicken 5 (136)

Merkaufgabe 4

Diese Wörter können unterschiedliche Bedeutungen haben:

a) *drink* **b)** *love* **c)** *mean*

Schlage im *English-German Dictionary* nach, was sie bedeuten.

(Die Lösung findest du auf S. 162.)

Wie finde ich Wörter in einem Online-Wörterbuch?

Es gibt sehr viele Online-Wörterbücher im Internet oder als App. Frage deine Lehrkraft, welches Online-Wörterbuch sie dir empfehlen kann. Mit einem Online-Wörterbuch kannst du Wörter sehr schnell finden. So gehst du vor:

Zunächst musst du die Sprachen und die Suchrichtung eingeben (Englisch – Deutsch oder Deutsch – Englisch) und dann das Wort in das Suchfeld tippen. Gibt es ein Lautsprechersymbol, kannst du dir das gesuchte Wort auch anhören.

Manchmal kannst du das Wort direkt per Spracheingabe suchen. Vielleicht findest du dazu ein Mikrofonsymbol?

SF 5

Einen Kurzvortrag halten

▶ Unit 4 | p. 120

Ab und zu sollst du vor deiner Klasse etwas vortragen oder präsentieren. Hier erfährst du, wie du dich darauf gut vorbereiten kannst.

Wie bereite ich einen Kurzvortrag vor?

1 Sammeln und aufschreiben

Sammle Ideen und Informationen zu deinem Thema als Stichpunkte und ordne sie, z. B. mithilfe einer Mindmap (SF 2, S. 166–167) oder in einer Tabelle.

2 Veranschaulichen

Überlege, welche Bilder du zeigen kannst und wie du sie präsentieren möchtest, z. B. als Poster oder am Computer.

Bei einer Präsentation am Computer:

- Wähle ein einfaches Layout.
- Wähle eine gut lesbare Schrift und verwende eine Schriftgröße von mindestens 16 Punkt.
- Schreibe nur wenig Text.
- Wähle nur ein Bild pro Folie. Schreibe dazu, woher du dein Bild hast, z. B. den Namen der Internetseite.

3 Ordnen

Ein Kurzvortrag sollte folgendermaßen aufgebaut sein:

- **Einleitung:** Nenne das Thema.
- **Hauptteil:** Nenne deine Hauptpunkte. Erzähle dann mehr zu jedem Punkt.
- **Abschluss:** Bedanke dich fürs Zuhören. Erkundige dich, ob jemand eine Frage hat.

I'd like to talk about …

First I'd like to talk about …
Then I'd like to tell you about …
I'd also like to talk about …
This picture shows …

That's the end of my presentation.
Thank you for listening.
Do you have any questions?

4 Notizen auf Karteikarten

Mache dir kurze Notizen auf Karteikarten. Du kannst dabei auch Symbole benutzen (z. B. „?" bedeutet: *Do you have any questions?*).

Skills file

Nummeriere die Karteikarten, damit du beim Vortragen den Überblick behältst.

Merkaufgabe 1

Schaue dir die drei Karteikarten rechts an.

a) Welche Nummer hat die Karte, deren Text du hier lesen kannst? 1, 2 oder 3?

b) Formuliere aus den Notizen vollständige Sätze.

(Die Lösungen findest du auf S. 162.)

 5 Üben

Übe deinen Vortrag mithilfe deiner Notizen vor dem Spiegel oder mit einem Partner oder einer Partnerin. Du kannst dich auch selbst mit einem Smartphone aufnehmen. Achte auf die Zeit.

Worauf muss ich beim Vortragen achten?

Überprüfe zu Beginn, ob alles vorbereitet ist: Ist das Poster aufgehängt? Ist der Computer bereit? Liegen die Vortragskarten richtig sortiert? Dann beginne deinen Vortrag:

- Schaue dein Publikum an und warte, bis es ruhig ist.
- Sprich langsam, laut und deutlich.
- Zeige während deines Vortrags auf Bilder oder dein Poster.

Feedback

Hole dir eine Rückmeldung darüber, wie deine Präsentation bei anderen ankommt. Vielleicht ist ein guter Tipp dabei, wie du dich verbessern kannst.

Can you give me some feedback, please?

Bitten dich andere um ein Feedback, sei respektvoll:

- Nenne zuerst Gelungenes, denn Lob tut gut und spornt an! Sage, was dir besonders gefallen hat.
- Dann mache Verbesserungsvorschläge.

Merkaufgabe 2

Die Präsentation eines Mitschülers hat dir gut gefallen. Seine Zeichnungen sind besonders schön, aber er hat etwas zu schnell gesprochen. Welches Feedback ist besser?

a) *Please don't speak so fast. Your pictures are very nice.*

b) *I like your presentation. Your pictures are very nice. Please don't speak so fast.*

SF 6

Wörter umschreiben

▶ Unit 5 | p. 150

Gerade beim Sprechen kommt es häufig vor, dass dir ein englisches Wort fehlt oder nicht einfällt.
Dann kannst du versuchen, es zu umschreiben.

It's a thing. It helps me in the rain.

It's an umbrella, Scout!

Wie umschreibe ich etwas?

1 Erkläre das Wort, indem du zunächst einen passenden Oberbegriff *(umbrella word)* auswählst. In dieser Tabelle findest du besonders häufige Oberbegriffe:

	umbrella words
Personen	boy • child • girl • man • person • woman • ...
Orte	building • country • place • room • ...
Dinge	drink • food • fruit • game • musical instrument • sport • thing • vegetable • ...

Hier ein Beispiel:
- gesuchtes Wort: *student*
- passende Oberbegriffe: *person, school*

Merkaufgabe 1

Finde unter den vier Wörtern den Oberbegriff *(umbrella word)*:

a) *kitchen • hall • room • bedroom*

b) *apple • orange • fruit • banana*

(Die Lösungen findest du auf S. 162.)

2 Nenne dann nähere Details:

It's a person. He or she is at school.

	umbrella word	Umschreibung
student	It's a <u>person</u>.	He or she is at school.
kitchen	It's a <u>room</u> in the house.	You make food there.
banana	It's a kind of <u>fruit</u>.	It's long and yellow.

 Das sind Redewendungen, die du zum Umschreiben nutzen kannst:

It's a kind of ...
It's a person ...
It's a place ...
It's a thing ...

Merkaufgabe 2

Finde eine passende Umschreibung für *sports hall*.

(Die Lösung findest du auf S. 162.)

Language file

Auf den **Language file**-Seiten findest du ...

Inhalt	Seite			Seite
LF 1	Der *s*-Genitiv und die *of*-Fügung 174	LF 9	*There is ... / There are ...* 178
LF 2	Der Artikel 175	LF 10	Gegenwart – einfache Form:
LF 3	Der Plural der Nomen 175		a) Bejahte Aussagesätze 179
LF 4	Die Personalpronomen 176	LF 11	b) Die Wortstellung 179
LF 5	Die Possessivbegleiter 176	LF 12	c) Verneinte Aussagesätze 180
LF 6	Das Verb *be*	LF 13	d) Fragen mit *do/does* 180
	a) Bejahte Aussagesätze 177	LF 14	e) Kurzantworten 181
LF 7	b) Verneinte Aussagesätze 177	LF 15	f) Fragen mit Fragewörtern 181
LF 8	c) Fragen und Kurzantworten 178	LF 16	Gegenwart – Verlaufsform 182
		LF 17	*Much – many – a lot of* 183
		Grammatical terms 183

LF 1

Der *s*-Genitiv und die *of*-Fügung *(The possessive form and the of-phrase)*

▶ Hello! + Unit 1

Der *s*-Genitiv *(The possessive form)*

Noah's phone
Noahs Handy

Scout's hat
Scouts Hut

the dog's colour
die Farbe des Hundes

the girls' bikes
die Fahrräder der Mädchen

Die *of*-Fügung *(The of-phrase)*

the end of the game
das Ende des Spiels

a kilo of apples
ein Kilo Äpfel

Mit dem *s*-Genitiv drückst du aus, dass etwas jemandem oder zu jemandem gehört.

Anders als im Deutschen wird im Englischen **bei Personen und Tieren** im Singular das s mit einem Apostroph (') angehängt.

Im Plural enden viele Hauptwörter bereits auf s, dann hängst du kein zweites s, sondern nur einen Apostroph (') an.

Wenn zwei **Sachen** zusammengehören, verwendest du die *of*-Fügung.
Man gebraucht sie auch bei Mengenbezeichnungen.

174 one hundred and seventy-four

LF 2

Der Artikel *(The article)* ▶ Unit 1 | p. 21

Der unbestimmte Artikel *(The indefinite article)*

a bag
a girl

an apple
an elephant

an hour [ən ˈaʊə]
a uniform [eɪ ˈjuːnɪfɔːm]

> Der unbestimmte Artikel (ein, eine) heißt im Englischen *a* oder *an*.
> Du verwendest
> - *a*, wenn das folgende Wort mit einem Konsonanten (b, c, d, ..., z) beginnt,
> - *an*, wenn das folgende Wort mit einem Vokal (a, e, i, o, u) beginnt.
>
> **!** Entscheidend ist die Aussprache des Wortes, nicht die Schreibung.

Der bestimmte Artikel *(The definite article)*

the [ðə] ruler
the [ðə] classroom

the [ði] elephant
the [ði] English book

> Der bestimmte Artikel (der, die das) heißt im Englischen immer nur *the*.
> Du sprichst
> - [ðə], wenn das folgende Wort mit einem Konsonanten beginnt,
> - [ði], wenn das folgende Wort mit einem Vokal beginnt.

LF 3

Der Plural der Nomen *(The plural of nouns)* ▶ Unit 1 | p. 22

a book	two books
a table	two tables
a bus	two buses
a beach	two beaches
a story	two stories
a pony	three ponies
man	men
woman	women
child	children
jeans	Jeans
trousers	Hose
clothes	Kleidung

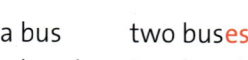

> Bei den meisten Nomen wird im Plural die Endung *-s* angehängt.
>
> Nach *-s*, *-x*, *-ch* oder *-sh* wird *-es* angehängt.
>
> Bei Nomen, die auf Konsonant + *y* enden, wird *y* zu *-ies*.
>
> Einige Pluralformen sind unregelmäßig. Diese musst du lernen.
>
> Einige Nomen haben keine Singularform und werden nur im Plural gebraucht:
> *The trousers are new.* Die Hose ist neu.

Language file

LF 4

Die Personalpronomen (The personal pronouns) ▶ Unit 1 | p. 24

I *(ich)* **you** *(du)* **he** *(er)*

she *(sie)* **it** *(er, sie, es)* **we** *(wir)*

you *(ihr)* **they** *(sie)*

Personalpronomen ersetzen Nomen *(table ⇨ it)* oder Eigennamen *(Ben ⇨ he)*.

Das Pronomen *I* (ich) wird im Englischen immer großgeschrieben.

Das Pronomen *it* steht für Dinge und Tiere und entspricht „er", „sie" oder „es":

   *It's short.*   **Er** ist kurz.

   *It's blue.*   **Sie** ist blau.

   *It's new.*   **Es** ist neu.

Bei Tieren, die du nicht kennst, verwendest du *it*: *It's a dog.*
Über Haustiere, deren Namen du kennst, sprichst du mit *he* oder *she*: *She's my dog*.

LF 5

Die Possessivbegleiter (The possessive determiners) ▶ Units 1–2

Is this **your** book?
Ist das dein Buch?

I	**my** room	*mein Zimmer*
you	**your** bike	*dein Fahrrad*
he	**his** drink	*sein Getränk*
she	**her** ball	*ihr Ball*
it	**its** name	*sein/ihr Name*
we	**our** dog	*unser Hund*
you	**your** teacher	*euer Lehrer*
they	**their** class	*ihre Klasse*

Possessivbegleiter zeigen an, wem etwas gehört.

This is **my** favourite hat.

❗ Nicht verwechseln:
their = ihr/e
they're = sie sind

LF 6

Das Verb *be* *(The verb be)*

a) **Bejahte Aussagesätze** *(Positive statements)* ▶ Unit 1 | p. 24

Kurzform	Langform
I'm eleven.	I am eleven.
You're ten.	You are ten.
He's nice.	He is nice.
She's in my class.	She is in my class.
It's a dog.	It is a dog.
We're here.	We are here.
You're from London.	You are from London.
They're from Hove.	They are from Hove.

Es gibt Kurz- und Langformen. Bei den Kurzformen ist ein Buchstabe weggefallen. Dafür steht ein Apostroph (').

Kurzform	
I'm	
You're	
He's / She's / It's	from Brighton.
We're	
You're	
They're	

Langform	
Zane is	from Brighton.
Sunita and Noah are	

Kurzformen werden eher beim Sprechen und in persönlichen E-Mails oder Chats verwendet.
Sie stehen meist nach Pronomen *(I, you, he, she, it, we, you, they)*.

Langformen benutzt du meist nach Eigennamen *(Zane, Sunita)* oder Nomen *(bike, teachers)*. Man verwendet sie außerdem bei offiziellen Schreiben.

LF 7

b) **Verneinte Aussagesätze** *(Negative statements)* ▶ Unit 1 | p. 29

Kurzform	Langform
I'm not old.	I am not old.
You aren't old.	You are not old.
He isn't old.	He is not old.
She isn't old.	She is not old.
It isn't old.	It is not old.
We aren't old.	We are not old.
You aren't old.	You are not old.
They aren't old.	They are not old.

Bei der Verneinung benutzt du fast immer die Kurzformen.

I'm not mean, I'm nice!

Language file

LF 8

Das Verb *be* (The verb be)

Erklärfilm

c) Fragen und Kurzantworten *(Questions and short answers)* ▶ Unit 2 | p. 47

Are you eleven? — Yes, I am. / No, I'm not.
Bist du elf? — Ja. / Nein.

Is your room OK? — Yes, it is. / No, it isn't.
Ist dein Zimmer OK? — Ja. / Nein.

Fragen	Kurzantworten
Are you here, Ali?	Yes, I am. No, I'm not.
Are you all OK?	Yes, we are. No, we aren't.
Is Timo at home?	Yes, he is. No, he isn't.
Is Mum tired?	Yes, she is. No, she isn't.
Is your room nice?	Yes, it is. No, it isn't.
Are the cats here?	Yes, they are. No, they aren't.

Antworte auf eine Frage im Englischen nicht einfach mit *yes* oder *no*. Das klingt meist unhöflich. Verwende Kurzantworten.

Are you hungry? — Yes, I am.

LF 9

There is … / There are … ▶ Unit 2 | p. 50

There's a beach in Brighton.
Es gibt einen Strand in Brighton.

There are two girls in the pool.
Da sind zwei Mädchen im Pool.

There's	a man. a bike.
There are	two boys. three dogs.

Mit *there is* (= *there's*) oder *there are* sagst du, dass etwas vorhanden ist.

Im Deutschen heißt es meist:
Es gibt …
Da sind …
Es stehen …
Da liegen …

LF 10

Die einfache Form der Gegenwart *(The simple present)*

Erklärfilm

a) **Bejahte Aussagesätze** *(Positive statements)* ▶ Unit 3 | p. 80

I often **get up** at 7 o'clock.
Ich stehe oft um 7 Uhr auf.

Dad always **makes** breakfast.
Papa macht immer das Frühstück.

I / You / We / They	start.
He / She / It	start**s**.

Mit dem *simple present* sagst du, was oft oder jeden Tag passiert oder auch selten oder nie geschieht.

Diese Signalwörter findest du oft in Sätzen im *simple present*:
always, often, sometimes, rarely, never.

Mit *he, she* und *it* musst du immer ein *-s* ans Verb anhängen.

He, she, it – ein *-s* muss mit!

❗ Achte auf diese Formen:
have – ha**s**
do [duː] – doe**s** [dʌz]
go – goe**s**
watch [wɒtʃ] – watch**es** [wɒtʃɪz]
wash – wash**es**
tidy – tid**ies**

LF 11

Erklärfilm

b) **Die Wortstellung** *(Word order)* ▶ Unit 3 | p. 83

s	v	o
Deniz	loves	old cars.

s	a	v	o
Mia	always	walks	to school.
Yusuf	sometimes	goes	by bike.

In Aussagesätzen ist die Wortstellung wie im Deutschen: *subject – verb – object*.

Mit Häufigkeitsadverbien *(always, often, sometimes, rarely, never)* kannst du sagen, wie oft etwas geschieht.

Anders als im Deutschen stehen sie im Englischen meist direkt vor dem Hauptverb.

Dad   always   makes   breakfast.

Papa   *macht*   immer   das Frühstück.

Language file

LF 12

Erklär-film

Die einfache Form der Gegenwart *(The simple present)*

c) Verneinte Aussagesätze *(Negative statements)* ▶ Unit 4 | p. 107

We **don't** live in town.
Wir wohnen nicht in der Stadt.

My dad **doesn't** like snakes.
Mein Papa mag keine Schlangen.

I / You / We / They	**don't** start.

He / She / It	**doesn't** start.

Aussagen im *simple present* kannst du mit *don't* oder *doesn't* verneinen.

Bei *I, you, we, they* verwendest du *don't*.

I don't like cats.

Bei *he, she, it* verwendest du *doesn't*.

LF 13

d) Fragen mit *do / does (Do / Does-questions)* ▶ Unit 4 | p. 111

Do you like this game?
Magst du dieses Spiel?

Does your sister play football?
Spielt deine Schwester Fußball?

Fragen

Do	I / you / we / they / your parents	like music?

Does	he / your dad / she / Lily / it	like music?

Fragen, auf die man mit „ja" oder „nein" antworten kann, heißen Entscheidungsfragen. Sie beginnen mit *Do* oder *Does*.

Mit *I, you, we, they* verwendest du *Do*.
Mit *he, she, it* verwendest du *Does*.

LF 14

Die einfache Form der Gegenwart *(The simple present)*

e) **Kurzantworten** *(Short answers)* ▶ Unit 4 | p. 111

Kurzantworten	
Yes, I **do**.	No, I **don't**.
Yes, he **does**.	No, he **doesn't**.
Yes, she **does**.	No, she **doesn't**.
Yes, it **does**.	No, it **doesn't**.
Yes, you **do**.	No, you **don't**.
Yes, we **do**.	No, we **don't**.
Yes, they **do**.	No, they **don't**.

Es ist unhöflich, auf Entscheidungsfragen nur mit *yes* oder *no* zu antworten. Besser ist eine Kurzantwort.

LF 15

f) **Fragen mit Fragewörtern** *(Questions with question words)* ▶ Unit 4 | p. 114

Where **does** your pet sleep?
Wo schläft dein Haustier?

What **do** snakes eat?
Was fressen Schlangen?

Auch Fragen mit Fragewörtern stellst du mit *do* oder *does*. Das Fragewort steht wie im Deutschen am Anfang.

How? — Wie?
What? — Was?
When? — Wann?
Why? — Warum?

Who **cooks** lunch?
Wer kocht das Mittagessen?

What **makes** you sad?
Was macht dich traurig?

Wenn mit *Who* oder *What* nach dem Subjekt des Satzes gefragt wird, bildest du die Frage ohne *do* oder *does*.

Language file

LF 16

Erklär-film

Die Verlaufsform der Gegenwart *(The present progressive)* ▶ Unit 5 | p. 138

I'**m** reading a comic.
Ich lese gerade einen Comic.

Dad **is** cooking dinner.
Papa macht gerade das Abendessen.

What **are** you doing at the moment?
Was machst du jetzt gerade?

Aussagesätze — Yes
I'**m**
You'**re**
He'**s**
She'**s**   working.
It'**s**
We'**re**
They'**re**

verneinte Sätze — No
I'**m not**
You **aren't**
He **isn't**
She **isn't**   working.
It **isn't**
We **aren't**
They **aren't**

Fragen — ?
Am I
Are you
Is he
Is she   working?
Is it
Are we
Are they

Mit dem *present progressive* sagst du, was jemand jetzt gerade tut. Damit beschreibst du auch, was auf Bildern passiert.

Diese Zeitangaben findest du oft in Sätzen im *present progressive*:
now, at the moment, today.

Das *present progressive* besteht aus zwei Teilen:

| 'm oder 're oder 's | + | Verb + -ing |

I'm having lunch now.

Bei Verben, die auf *-e* enden, fällt das *-e* bei der *ing*-Form weg:

hav**e** – having
mak**e** – making
rid**e** – riding

Bei einigen Verben wird der letzte Buchstabe verdoppelt:

plan – plan**n**ing
stop – stop**p**ing
sit – sit**t**ing

LF 17

Much – many – a lot of

▶ Unit 5 | p. 141

zählbar　　　nicht zählbar

Bejahte Aussagesätze
We've got a lot of apples.
I eat a lot of fruit.

Verneinte Aussagesätze
My dad doesn't watch many films.
I don't like much sugar in my tea.

Fragen
How many apples do we need?
How much money do you have?

Mit *much*, *many* oder *a lot of* kannst du über unbestimmte, größere Mengen sprechen.

Dabei ist es wichtig, ob es sich um zählbare oder nicht zählbare Nomen handelt.

Zählbare Nomen haben eine Pluralform: *one apple – two apples*.

Nicht zählbare Nomen kannst du nicht in die Mehrzahl setzen: *cheese, fruit, music, love*.

In bejahten Sätzen verwende *a lot of* – bei zählbaren und nicht zählbaren Nomen.

In verneinten Sätzen und Fragen verwendest du
– *many* bei zählbaren Nomen (viele),
– *much* bei nicht zählbaren Nomen (viel).

Lassen sich die Nomen zählen, musst du eher *many* wählen.

Grammatical terms *(Grammatische Fachbegriffe in diesem Buch)*

adjective	das Adjektiv: *good, old*		positive	die positive Form: *do, can*
adverb (of frequency)	das (Häufigkeits-)Adverb: *often, always*		possessive determiner	Possessivbegleiter: *my, your, his, her*
article	der Artikel: *a / the* book		present progressive	die Verlaufsform der Gegenwart: *I'm speaking*
form	die Form		short answer	die Kurzantwort: *Yes, I do. / No, I'm not.*
long form	die Langform: *I am, do not, you are*		short form	die Kurzform: *I'm, don't*
negative	die negative Form: *don't go*		simple present	die einfache Gegenwart: *I speak English, he likes it*
noun	das Nomen/Substantiv: *friend, car*		statement	Aussage(satz)
object	das Objekt: *I like cats.*		subject	das Subjekt: *They eat dinner.*
personal pronoun	Personalpronomen: *I, you*		verb	das Verb: *(to) go, (to) do*
plural	Plural, Mehrzahlform: *books*		wh-question	die Frage mit Fragewort: *What's this? Who are you?*

Wordbank

Wordbank 1: Numbers

▶ Hello! | p. 10

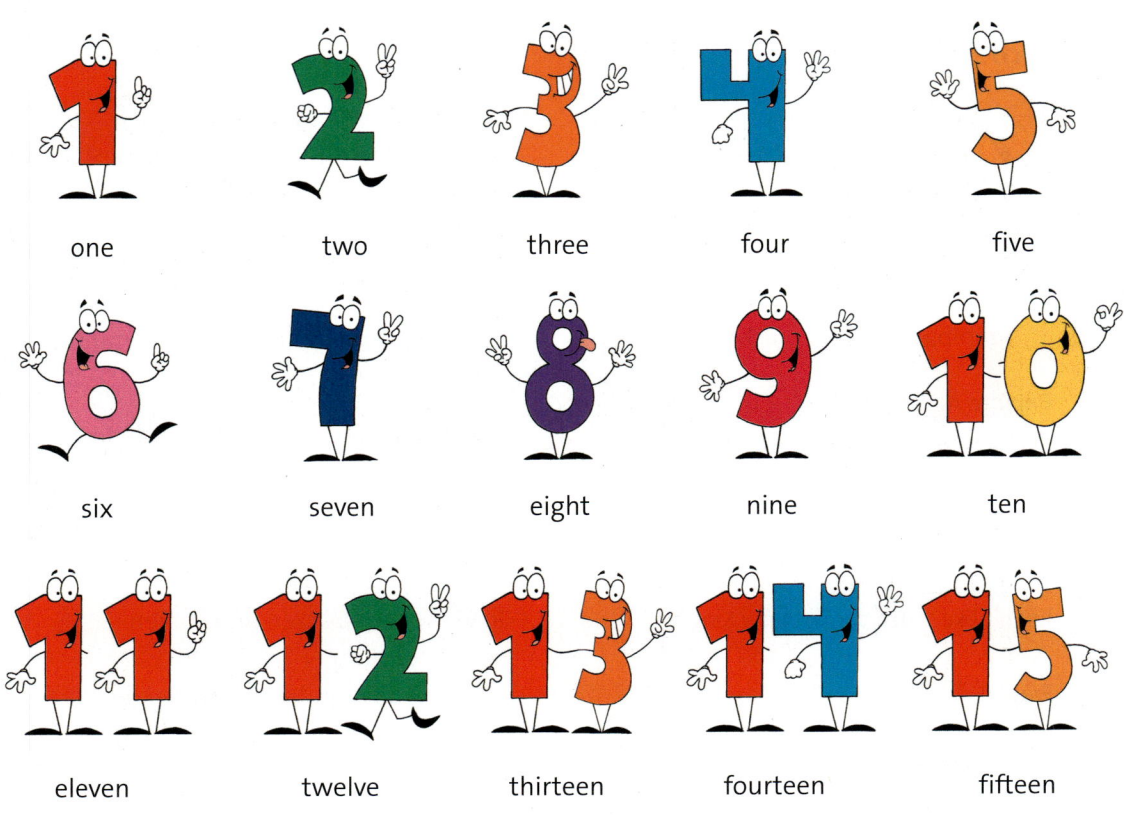

one, two, three, four, five
six, seven, eight, nine, ten
eleven, twelve, thirteen, fourteen, fifteen

Wordbank 2: Colours

▶ Hello! | p. 12

orange, purple, red, yellow, white, black, green, blue, brown

Wordbank 3: Animals

▶ Hello! | p. 14

cat, dog, elephant, fish, horse, lion, monkey, parrot, seagull, snake, …

a bear

a butterfly

a crocodile

a dolphin

a duck

a llama

a meerkat [1]

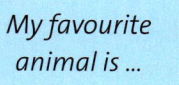
My favourite animal is …

an owl

a panda

a penguin

a rhino

a spider

a tiger

a whale

[1] **meerkat** *das Erdmännchen*

Wordbank

Wordbank 4: Free time

▶ Hello! | p. 15

dancing, drawing, football, listening to music, taking photos, swimming, ...

baking

basketball

boxing

climbing

coding

cycling

nail art

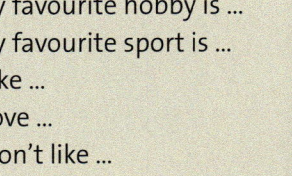
My favourite hobby is ...
My favourite sport is ...
I like ...
I love ...
I don't like ...

gaming

gymnastics

hanging out with friends

judo

kayaking

horse riding

reading

Wordbank 5: School subjects

▶ Unit 1 | p. 27

art, computing, design and technology, English, French, maths, music, PE, ...

German (Deutsch)

media studies (Medienkompetenz)

school club (AG)

business and employment studies: technology, economics, home economics (Arbeitslehre: Technik, Wirtschaft, Hauswirtschaft)

science: biology, chemistry, physics (Naturwissenschaften: Biologie, Chemie, Physik)

social studies: history, geography, politics (Gesellschaftswissenschaften: Geschichte, Geografie, Politik)

ethics (Ethik)

RE: religious education (Religionslehre)

philosophy (Philosophie)

special needs support (Förderunterricht)

study time (Arbeitsstunde, Eigenarbeit, Hausaufgaben)

tutor time (Klassenlehrkraftstunde/Verfügungsstunde)

Wordbank

Wordbank 6: Places at school

▶ Unit 1 | p. 29

art room, canteen, classroom, computer room, corridor, sports hall, …

cinema

dance studio

drama room

games room

library

music room

office

playground

science lab

sports field

staff room

swimming pool

Wordbank 7: Family

▶ Unit 2 | p. 45

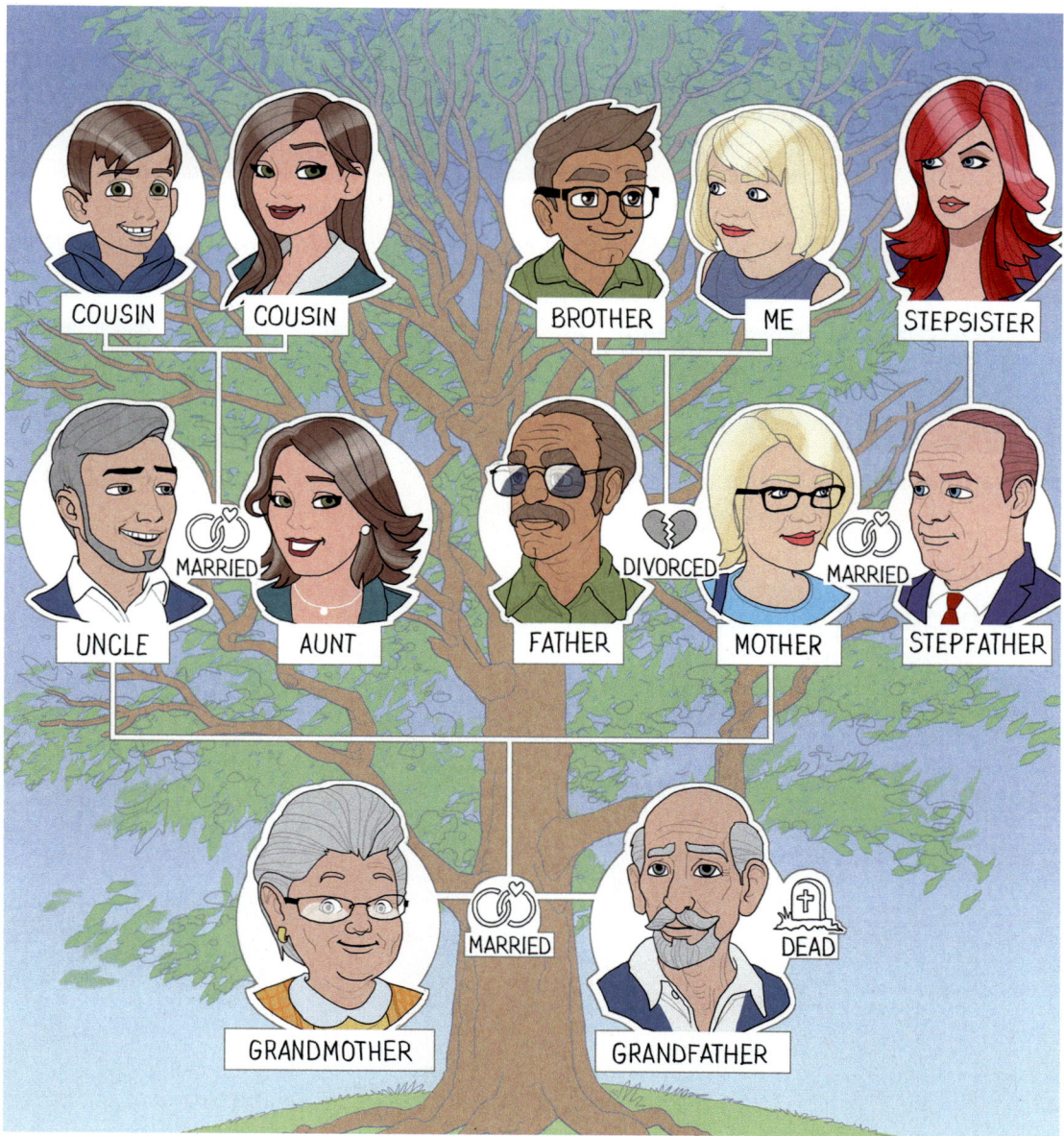

parents / grandparents	die Eltern / die Großeltern
child / children	das Kind / die Kinder
son / daughter	der Sohn / die Tochter
grandson / granddaughter	der Enkel / die Enkelin
blended family	die Patchworkfamilie
separated	getrennt
husband / wife	der Ehemann / die Ehefrau
single	alleinstehend
niece / nephew	die Nichte / der Neffe

Wordbank

Wordbank 8: Pets
▶ Unit 2 | p. 49

cat, dog, fish, hamster, horse, parrot, rabbit, snake

budgie (der Wellensittich) | chicken (das Huhn) | ferret (das Frettchen) | guinea pig (das Meerschweinchen) | kitten (das Kätzchen)

lizard (die Echse) | mouse (die Maus) | puppy (der Welpe) | rabbit (das Kaninchen) | rat (die Ratte)

Wordbank 9: Things in my room
▶ Unit 2 | p. 55+61

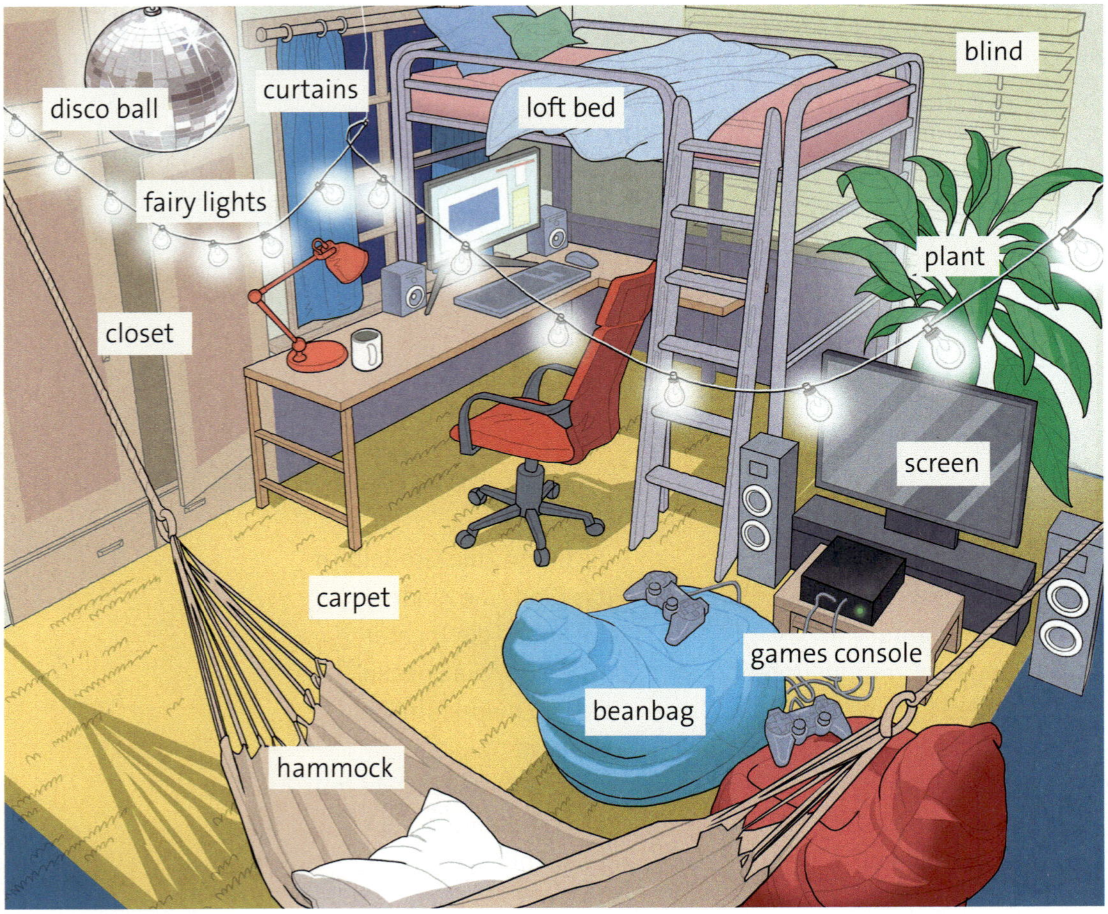

disco ball, curtains, loft bed, blind, fairy lights, closet, plant, screen, carpet, beanbag, games console, hammock

Wordbank 10: The times of the day

▶ Unit 3 | p. 81

Wordbank

Wordbank 11: Places in my town or village
▶ Unit 4 | p. 111

Wordbank 12: Food

▶ Unit 5 | p. 143

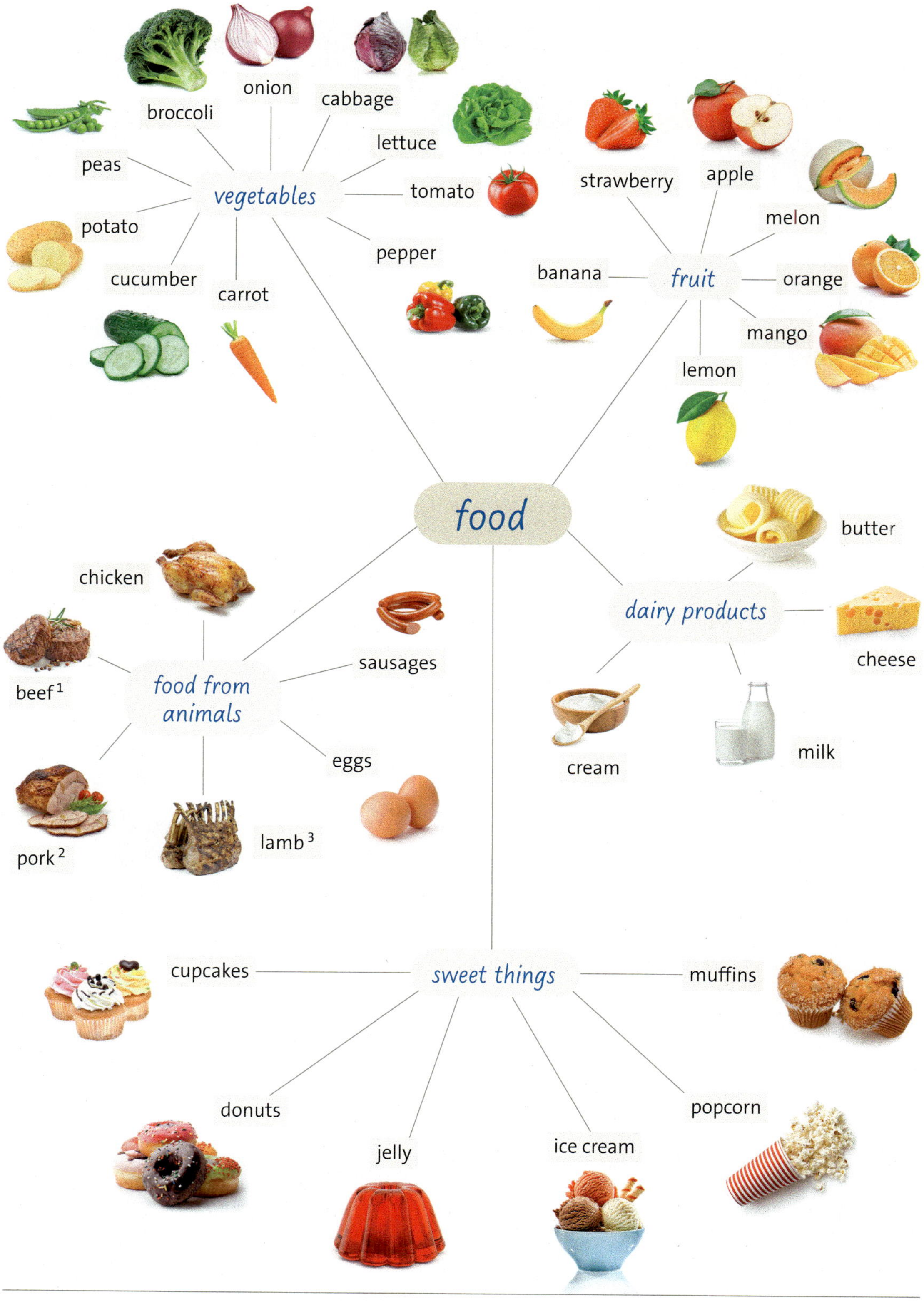

vegetables
- broccoli
- onion
- cabbage
- lettuce
- peas
- tomato
- potato
- pepper
- cucumber
- carrot

fruit
- strawberry
- apple
- melon
- banana
- orange
- mango
- lemon

food

food from animals
- chicken
- beef [1]
- sausages
- pork [2]
- eggs
- lamb [3]

dairy products
- butter
- cheese
- cream
- milk

sweet things
- cupcakes
- muffins
- donuts
- popcorn
- jelly
- ice cream

[1] **beef** Rindfleisch   [2] **pork** Schweinefleisch   [3] **lamb** Lammfleisch

one hundred and ninety-three

Wordbank

Wordbank 13: Cooking

▶ Unit 5 | p. 144

(to) add

(to) bake

(to) boil

(to) cut

(to) fry

(to) mix

(to) pour

(to) roll out

(to) stir

saucepan

frying pan

oven, baking tray

plate

bowl

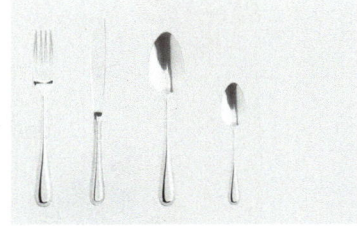
fork, knife, spoon, tablespoon

194　one hundred and ninety-four

Let's talk

Hier findest du englische Sätze mit ihrer deutschen Übersetzung. Höre sie dir in der App an. Da jede Sprache anders funktioniert, ist eine wortwörtliche Übersetzung oft nicht möglich: Achte daher auf die kleinen Unterschiede.

1 Sich und andere vorstellen

Über den Namen und das Alter sprechen

Hello!	Hello, I'm … / Hi! I'm …	Hallo, ich bin …
	What's your name?	Wie heißt du?
Unit 1	Sunita is 12 years old.	Sunita ist 12 Jahre alt.
	I'm 12 too.	Ich bin auch 12.
Unit 5	When's your birthday?	Wann hast du Geburtstag?
	My birthday is on the first of May.	Mein Geburtstag ist am ersten Mai.

Sich begrüßen und verabschieden

Hello!	Hi! / Hello!	Hi! / Hallo!
	Bye!	Tschüs!
	Goodbye.	Auf Wiedersehen. / Tschüs.
	Nice to meet you.	Freut mich, dich / euch / Sie kennenzulernen.
	Nice to meet you too.	Freut mich auch.
Unit 1	See you.	Bis dann. / Tschüs.
Unit 2	Speak later.	Tschüs. / Bis später.
Unit 3	Hello, everybody!	Hallo allerseits!
	See you later.	Bis später.

Über die Familie und Freunde sprechen ▸ Wordbank 7, p. 189

Unit 1	This is my best friend.	Das ist meine beste Freundin / mein bester Freund.
	We are / aren't friends.	Wir sind / sind keine Freunde.
	These are my new friends.	Das sind meine neuen Freunde.
	A good friend is helpful.	Ein guter Freund ist hilfsbereit.
Unit 2	That's me.	Das bin ich.
	That's my family.	Das ist meine Familie.
	That's me and my sister.	Das bin ich mit meiner Schwester.
	Next to me is my brother.	Neben mir ist mein Bruder.
	These are my parents.	Das sind meine Eltern.
	Grandma and grandpa live in the neighbourhood.	Oma und Opa wohnen in der Nachbarschaft.
	My uncle and my aunt are from Russia.	Mein Onkel und meine Tante sind aus Russland.
	I have three cousins.	Ich habe drei Cousinen und Cousins.

one hundred and ninety-five

Let's talk

Unit 3	My dad often works long days.	Mein Papa arbeitet oft lange.
	I have a lot of friends now.	Ich habe jetzt viele Freunde.
	My sister doesn't live with us.	Meine Schwester lebt nicht bei uns.

Über Hobbys, Vorlieben und Abneigungen sprechen ▶ Wordbank 4, p. 186

Hello!	I like sandwiches.	Ich mag Sandwiches.
	My favourite animal is a fish.	Meine Lieblingstiere sind Fische.
	What's your favourite …?	Was ist dein Lieblings…?
	My favourite hobby is … What about you?	Mein Lieblingshobby ist … Und deins?
	I like dancing.	Ich mag Tanzen.
	I don't like football.	Ich mag Fußball nicht. / Ich mag keinen Fußball.
Unit 1	Let's go to the beach!	Lass uns / Lasst uns an den Strand gehen!
Unit 2	My dream pet is a dog.	Mein Traum-Haustier ist ein Hund.
Unit 3	I often go cycling.	Ich fahre oft Fahrrad.
	I never go swimming.	Ich gehe nie schwimmen.
Unit 4	Which places / things do you like?	Welche Orte / Dinge magst du?
	I like the sports centre.	Ich mag das Sportzentrum.
	I don't like the rubbish.	Ich mag den Müll nicht.
	We love this place!	Wir lieben diesen Ort!
	I like living here.	Ich lebe gern hier.

Das eigene Zuhause beschreiben ▶ Wordbank 9, p. 190

Unit 2	This is my home.	Das ist mein Zuhause.
	I live in a flat / house.	Ich wohne in einer Wohnung / in einem Haus.
	Our house has a garden / balcony.	Unser Haus hat einen Garten / Balkon.
	Where is your room?	Wo ist dein Zimmer?
	It's on the second floor.	Es ist im zweiten Stock.
	What's in your room?	Was ist / gibt es in deinem Zimmer?
	There's a bed and there are two chairs.	Da ist / Es gibt ein Bett und da sind zwei Stühle.
	I have my own room.	Ich habe ein eigenes Zimmer.
	Is your room messy or tidy?	Ist dein Zimmer unordentlich oder aufgeräumt?
	Are you at home?	Bist du zu Hause?
	I'm at home.	Ich bin zu Hause.
	My room is small, but it's perfect for me.	Mein Zimmer ist klein, aber es ist perfekt für mich.
	I live with my parents and my brother.	Ich lebe zusammen mit meinen Eltern und meinem Bruder.
	We live in a small house near Bremen.	Wir leben in einem kleinen Haus bei Bremen.
	There's a kitchen, a living room, two bedrooms and a bathroom.	Es gibt eine Küche, ein Wohnzimmer, zwei Schlafzimmer und ein Bad.

Unit 5	Do you often clean your room?	Machst du dein Zimmer oft sauber?
	Yes, I do – but it's always messy.	Ja – aber es ist immer unordentlich.

Über den Wohnort und die Nachbarschaft sprechen

Hello!	Where are you from?	Wo kommst du her?
	I'm from …	Ich bin / komme aus …
Unit 2	I live in …	Ich wohne in …
	I live with my mum and dad.	Ich wohne zusammen mit meiner Mutter und meinem Vater.
	We live in a flat / a house in …	Wir wohnen in einer Wohnung / einem Haus in …
	Tell me about your home!	Erzähl mir was über dein Zuhause.
	Where's your home?	Wo bist du zu Hause?
	Who are your neighbours?	Wer sind eure Nachbarn?
Unit 3	Where's your house?	Wo ist dein / euer Haus?
	Our house isn't near my school.	Unser Haus ist nicht in der Nähe meiner Schule.
Unit 4	Where do you live?	Wo wohnst du?
	I live in a village / town / city / in the country.	Ich wohne in einem Dorf / einer Stadt / einer Großstadt / auf dem Land.
	What's your neighbourhood like?	Wie sieht deine Nachbarschaft aus?
	It's busy, but nice.	Es ist ziemlich viel los, aber es ist nett.
	I like our neighbours, they're really friendly.	Ich mag unsere Nachbarn. Sie sind wirklich freundlich.
	My neighbourhood has some problems.	Es gibt einige Probleme in meiner Nachbarschaft.

2 Über Gefühle, Wünsche und Empfindungen sprechen

Unit 1	I'm happy / sad.	Ich bin glücklich / traurig.
	I'm in trouble.	Ich bin in Schwierigkeiten.
	That's horrible.	Das ist schrecklich.
	I'm not happy about that.	Darüber bin ich nicht froh.
Unit 2	Are you OK?	Bist du in Ordnung?
	Are you scared of snakes?	Hast du Angst vor Schlangen?
	I'm alone.	Ich bin allein.
	That's great.	Das ist großartig.
Unit 3	I love you.	Ich liebe dich.
	I'm really surprised.	Ich bin echt überrascht.
	Don't be sorry for her.	Sie muss euch nicht leidtun.
Unit 4	I don't like the rubbish.	Ich mag den Müll nicht.
	I'm angry about this noise.	Ich ärgere mich über diesen Lärm.
Unit 5	I feel sad / great.	Ich bin traurig / Ich fühle mich toll.

Let's talk

3 Über den Schulalltag sprechen ▶ Wordbanks 5+6, pages 187–188

Unit 1	We're in the same class.	Wir sind in der gleichen Klasse.
	Mr Lee is my class teacher and English teacher.	Herr Lee ist mein Klassenlehrer und Englischlehrer.
	I'm at a new school.	Ich bin an einer neuen Schule.
	What about your new school?	Wie ist es an der neuen Schule?
	I'm lucky. The students in my class are really nice.	Ich habe Glück. Die Schülerinnen/Schüler in meiner Klasse sind echt nett.
	Where are your English lessons?	Wo finden deine/eure Englischstunden statt?
	They're in room 2.	Die sind in Raum 2.
	On Monday morning I have maths.	Montagmorgen habe ich Mathematik.
	The next lesson is …	Die nächste Stunde ist …
	I'm in class 7B.	Ich bin in Klasse 7b.
	Where's the canteen?	Wo ist die Kantine?
	The name of my school is …	Meine Schule heißt …
	I'm at … school.	Ich bin auf der … Schule.
	My timetable is great.	Mein Stundenplan ist super.
	The classrooms aren't near the canteen.	Die Klassenräume sind nicht in der Nähe der Kantine.
Unit 2	Is it hard to do your homework?	Fällt es dir schwer deine Hausaufgaben zu machen?
	Then he does his homework.	Dann macht er seine Hausaufgaben.
Unit 3	Lesson 1 is at …	Die erste Stunde fängt um … an.
	I go to school by bus/bike/car/train.	Ich fahre mit dem Bus/Rad/Auto/Zug zur Schule.
	Me too.	Ich auch.
	I walk to school.	Ich gehe zu Fuß zur Schule.
	My school journey is short.	Mein Schulweg ist kurz.
	School starts at 9 o'clock.	Die Schule fängt um 9 Uhr an.
	I come home from school at 4 o'clock.	Ich komme um 4 Uhr von der Schule nach Hause.
	My homework takes 30 minutes.	Ich brauche 30 Minuten für die Hausaufgaben.
Unit 5	Are you good at …?	Bist du gut in …?

4 Über den Tagesablauf sprechen, sich verabreden

Unit 3	My parents work long days.	Meine Eltern arbeiten sehr lang.
	In the morning I get up at 7 o'clock, have a shower and get dressed.	Morgens stehe ich um 7 Uhr auf, dusche und ziehe mich an.
	Sometimes I meet my friends in the afternoon.	Am Nachmittag treffe ich mich manchmal mit meinen Freunden.
	We meet every Friday afternoon at 3.30.	Wir treffen uns jeden Freitagnachmittag um halb vier.
	In the evening I often play computer games.	Abends spiele ich oft Computerspiele.

		On weekdays I always go to bed at 9 o'clock.	An Wochentagen gehe ich immer um 9 Uhr ins Bett.
		Are you free on Saturday?	Hast du am Samstag Zeit?
		Sorry, I'm busy on Saturday.	Tut mir leid, am Samstag bin ich beschäftigt.
		Let's meet in the afternoon.	Lass uns nachmittags / am Nachmittag treffen.
		Let's meet on Sunday!	Lass uns am Sonntag treffen!
		I'd love to. / Yes, please!	Sehr gern!
		Good idea!	Gute Idee!
		Sorry, I can't.	Tut mit leid, ich kann nicht.
		Can we meet on Sunday at 3 o'clock?	Können wir uns am Sonntag um 3 Uhr treffen?
	Unit 4	I practise the guitar every day.	Ich übe jeden Tag (auf der) Gitarre.
		On Saturday mornings I always look after my little sister.	Samstagvormittags passe ich immer auf meine kleine Schwester auf.
	Unit 5	What are you doing?	Was machst du gerade?
		What do you usually do at the weekend?	Was machst du / macht ihr normalerweise am Wochenende?
		We usually stay at home.	Normalerweise bleiben wir zu Hause.
		Where's the party?	Wo findet die Party statt?
		Thanks for the invitation.	Danke für die Einladung.
		Send me a message if you can come or not.	Sende mir eine Nachricht, ob du kommen kannst oder nicht.

5 Seine Meinung äußern und diskutieren

Unit 1	Can you say that again, please?	Kannst du das bitte noch einmal sagen?
	Listen, please.	Bitte hör zu.
	You're welcome.	Bitte, gern geschehen. / Nichts zu danken.
	I think …	Ich denke / glaube …
	I don't know.	Das weiß ich nicht.
Unit 2	Good / Great / Clever idea!	Gute / Tolle / Schlaue Idee!
	We can talk about problems.	Wir können über Probleme reden.
Unit 3	Yes, that's right.	Ja, das stimmt.
	No, that's wrong.	Nein, das ist falsch.
	I think you're right / wrong.	Ich glaube, da hast du recht / unrecht.
Unit 4	Do you think it's interesting?	Denkst du, es ist interessant?
	Why do you think it's interesting?	Warum denkst du, es ist interessant?
	Do you have any questions?	Hast du / Habt ihr Fragen?
Unit 5	What do you think?	Was denkst du?
	What do you mean?	Was meinst du?

Let's talk

6 Über Essen und Lebensmittel sprechen ▶ Wordbank 12, p. 193

Unit 1	I'm really hungry.	Ich habe echt Hunger. / Ich bin echt hungrig.
	We're always hungry.	Wir haben immer Hunger.
Unit 4	Try the pizza.	Probier mal die Pizza.
	No, I'm not hungry.	Nein, ich habe keinen Hunger.
	Where do you buy your food?	Wo kaufst du / kauft ihr Essen / Lebensmittel ein?
	We buy our food in the supermarket / at the market.	Wir kaufen unser Essen im Supermarkt / auf dem Markt.
Unit 5	What food do you eat?	Was isst du so?
	We eat a lot of fruit and vegetables.	Wir essen viel Obst und Gemüse.
	I'm not vegan, but I eat vegan food sometimes.	Ich bin kein Veganer / keine Veganerin, aber ich esse manchmal vegan.
	I like vegetarian food because it's healthy.	Ich mag vegetarisches Essen, weil es gesund ist.
	Eating too much meat is not healthy.	Zu viel Fleisch ist ungesund.
	My favourite dish is pizza.	Mein Lieblingsgericht ist Pizza.
	I'm allergic to …	Ich bin allergisch gegen …
	It's a main course / dessert.	Es ist ein Hauptgericht / Dessert.
	It's a kind of meat / vegetable / fruit.	Es ist eine Art Fleisch / Gemüse / Obst.
	It's sweet / spicy / …	Es ist süß / würzig / …
	Enjoy your food.	Guten Appetit. / Lass es dir schmecken.

7 Feedback geben

Unit 1	I like the photos.	Ich mag die Fotos.
	The colours are nice.	Die Farben sind schön.
Unit 2	Your short talk is cool / very nice.	Dein Kurzvortrag ist cool / sehr schön.
	I like the posters.	Ich mag die Poster.
Unit 3	Your video is funny / interesting / cool / …	Dein Video ist witzig / interessant / cool / …
	You speak clearly.	Du sprichst deutlich.
	You have good ideas / scenes.	Du hast gute Ideen / Szenen.
	I like the start / the scene with … / the end.	Ich mag den Anfang / die Szene mit … / das Ende.
	Well done!	Gut gemacht!
Unit 4	That was useful information.	Das waren nützliche Informationen.
	Please check that again.	Überprüfe das bitte noch einmal.
	Remember to make notes.	Denk daran, Notizen zu machen.
	Your notes are helpful.	Deine Notizen sind hilfreich.
Unit 5	I'd like to see more pictures.	Ich würde gerne mehr Bilder sehen.
	The instructions are very clear.	Die Anweisungen sind sehr klar.

Vocabulary

Im *Vocabulary* findest du alle neuen Wörter und Wendungen, die du lernen musst. Sie stehen in der Reihenfolge, in der sie im Buch zum ersten Mal vorkommen. Höre dir in der App jedes Wort beim Lernen genau an und sprich es nach.

Symbole und Abkürzungen

▶ p. 12 ▶ pp. 18/19	Die Seitenzahl in der linken Spalte zeigt dir, wo das Wort zum ersten Mal in diesem Buch vorkommt (*p.* = *page*, Seite; *pp.* = *pages*, Seiten).
▶▶ Hello	Die doppelten Pfeile weisen auf ein Wort mit gleicher Bedeutung hin, das du gelernt hast. Blaue Wörter kennst du aus der Grundschule.
(to) close ◀ ▶ (to) open	Das „Gegenteil"-Zeichen bedeutet: *(to) close* ist das Gegenteil von *(to) open*.
❗ *English:* I'm **at** school. *German:* Ich bin **in** der Schule.	Das ❗ zeigt: Vorsicht, hier keinen Fehler machen!
a – an a **d**og an **e**lephant a **n**ice picture an **o**ld picture	In den Merkboxen findest du wichtige Hinweise zu den neuen Wörtern und Wendungen.
sb.	*somebody* (jemand)
sth.	*something* (etwas)
infml.	*informal* (informell, umgangssprachlich)
pl.	*plural* (Plural, Mehrzahlform)

Hinweise

Tipps zum Vokabellernen findest du im **Skills file** auf S. 163–165.
Die **Wordbanks** (S. 184–194) bieten dir nach wichtigen Themen gesammelte Stichwörter.
Let's talk (S. 195–200) enthält Wendungen für wichtige Situationen, z.B.: seine Meinung äußern und diskutieren.
Im **English-German Dictionary** (S. 236–246) kannst du englische Wörter nachschlagen. Wenn du wissen möchtest, was ein deutsches Wort auf Englisch heißt, dann kannst du im **German-English Dictionary** (S. 247–256) suchen.

Hello! Vocabulary

🔊 Hello!

▶ pp. 10/11

Hello.	Hallo. / Servus.	
Nice to meet you.	Freut mich, dich/euch/Sie kennenzulernen.	
nice	nett, schön	
(to) meet	kennenlernen; (sich) treffen	
you	du; dich; dir; ihr; euch; Sie; Ihnen	
I	ich	❗ „I" wird immer großgeschrieben – auch wenn es nicht am Satzanfang steht.
I'm (= I am)	ich bin	
hungry	hungrig	**I'm hungry.** = Ich habe Hunger.
careful	vorsichtig	**Careful,** Leo! = Vorsicht, Leo! (*wörtlich*: (Sei) vorsichtig!)
seagull	die Möwe	a **seagull** – **seagulls**
a seagull	eine Möwe	**a** computer — **ein** Computer **a** show — **eine** Show **a** baby — **ein** Baby
it's (= it is)	es ist *(bei Dingen und Tieren auch)* er ist; sie ist	**it** = es *(bei Sachen und Tieren auch:* er; sie*)* **is** = ist
the	der, die, das	**the** computer — **der** Computer **the** show — **die** Show **the** baby — **das** Baby
What's your name?	Wie heißt du? (*wörtlich:* Was ist dein Name?)	
What …?	Was …?	
your	dein/e; euer/eure; Ihr/e	
you / your	du, dir *(Dativ)*, dich *(Akkusativ)* / dein, deine	ihr, euch *(Dativ)*, euch *(Akkusativ)* / euer, eure
name	der Name	
Hi.	Hallo.	▶▶ Hello.
too	auch	❗ *English:* I'm hungry **too**. *German:* Ich habe **auch** Hunger.
(to) like	mögen	
What about you?	Und du? / Was ist mit dir?	
football	der Fußball	
thank you, thanks	danke (schön)	
colour	die Farbe	❗ *English:* What colour **is** …? *German:* Welche Farbe **hat** …?

Hello!

colours

black schwarz	**blue** blau	**brown** braun	**green** grün	**grey** grau	**pink** pink, rosa
purple violett, lila	**orange** orange; die Orange		**red** rot	**yellow** gelb	**white** weiß

and	und	
right	richtig	
wrong	falsch	**right** ◀ ▶ **wrong**
class	die Klasse; der Unterricht; der Kurs	❗ one **class** – two **class**es

Goodbye, holidays

▶ p. 12

Goodbye.	Auf Wiedersehen! / Servus.	**Hello.** ◀ ▶ **Goodbye.**
holiday(s)	der Urlaub; die Ferien; Urlaubs-	❗ **on** holiday = **im**/**in den** Urlaub
in the picture	auf dem Bild	**picture** = Bild **in** = in; auf
mum	die Mama, die Mutti	
dad	der Papa, der Vati	
Leo's mum	die Mama / die Mutti von Leo	
number	die Zahl, die Ziffer, die Nummer	
1 one **2** two **3** three **4** four **5** five **6** six **7** seven **8** eight **9** nine **10** ten **11** eleven **12** twelve **13** thirteen **14** fourteen		▶ Numbers, p. 258
drink	das Getränk	noun: **drink** – verb: (to) **drink** (trinken)
animal	das Tier	
thing	das Ding, die Sache	
(to) eat	essen; fressen	
things **to** eat	Dinge zum Essen	**to** = (um) zu Nice **to** meet you! = Schön, dich/euch/Sie kennen**zu**lernen!
here	hier; hierher	**Here's** (= **Here is**) Scout.
can	können	
can't (= cannot)	nicht können	
I can see …	ich kann … sehen	*I can see Scout. What about you?* (to) **see** = sehen
(to) remember	sich erinnern an; daran denken, nicht vergessen	Can you **remember** my name? (dich erinnern an) **Remember**, seagulls like sandwiches too! (Denk dran!)
dog	der Hund	

Hello! Vocabulary

About me

▶ p. 14	**about me/you/...**	über mich/dich/...	**me** = **1.** mir; **2.** mich; **3.** *(in bestimmten Wendungen)* ich mich; mir

Hello Mrs Palmer, it's me, Tim.
Hi, Tim.

my	mein/e	**my** name (**mein** Name) / **my** class (**meine** Klasse)
favourite animal	das Lieblingstier	adjective: **favourite** – noun: **favourite** (der Liebling, der Favorit, die Favoritin)
cat	die Katze	
an elephant	ein Elefant	**a – an** / **a d**og **an e**lephant / **a n**ice picture **an o**ld picture
horse	das Pferd	
lion	der Löwe	
monkey	der Affe	
parrot	der Papagei	
snake	die Schlange	
fish, *pl* **fish**	der Fisch, die Fische	❗ one **fish** – two **fish**
▶ p. 15 **hobby**	das Hobby	❗ *English:* one **hobby** – two, three **hobbies** / *German:* ein **Hobby** – zwei, drei **Hobbys**
sport	der Sport; die Sportart	
dancing	das Tanzen	verb: (to) **dance** (tanzen) – noun: **dance** (der Tanz, die Tanzveranstaltung)
drawing	das Zeichnen	verb: (to) **draw** (zeichnen) – noun: **drawing** (die Zeichnung; das Zeichnen)
listening to music	Musik (an)hören	(to) **listen (to)** = (sich etwas) anhören; zuhören **Listen,** Scout! Hör zu, Scout! **Listen to** Leo. Hör(t) Leo zu. **Listen to** the song. Hört euch das Lied an.
music	die Musik	❗ Betonung auf der 1. Silbe: **mu**sic
swimming	das Schwimmen	(to) **swim** = schwimmen **swimmer** = der Schwimmer, die Schwimmerin
photo	das Foto	**in the photo** = auf dem Foto

Hello!

taking photos	das Fotografieren (*Hobby*)	❗ *English:* Can you **take** a **photo** of us? *German:* ... ein **Foto** von uns **machen**?
(to) **love**	lieben, sehr mögen	verb: (to) **love** – noun: **love** (die Liebe)
I don't like football.	Ich mag Fußball nicht. / Ich mag keinen Fußball	
cap	die (Schirm-)Mütze, die Kappe	cap
rucksack	der Rucksack	
phone	das Telefon	noun: **phone** – verb: (to) **phone** (anrufen; telefonieren) **phone number** = die Telefonnummer ❗ "Handy" klingt zwar englisch, aber für das (Mobil-)Telefon heißt es auf Englisch immer **phone**.
bike	das Fahrrad	bike
big	groß	
this	dies; diese(r, s)	**This** is Scout. – Hello, Scout! Nice to meet you.
with	mit; bei	❗ 1. Is Max the kid **with** the red bike? (mit) 2. Where's Scout? – Scout is **with** Leo. (bei)
(to) **put**	(*etwas wohin*) tun, legen, stellen, stecken	**Put** your books in your rucksack.
▶ p. 16 the **top** five hobbies	die fünf besten/ beliebtesten Hobbys	**top** = die Spitze, das obere Ende **at the top (of** sth.**)** = oben; am oberen Ende (von etwas); an der Spitze (von etwas)
singing	das Singen	**I like singing.** = Ich singe gerne. (to) **sing** = singen **singer** = der Sänger, die Sängerin
hat	der Hut, die Mütze	hats

Ready for school

▶ p. 17 ready	fertig, bereit	Here's my cap and my rucksack – I'm **ready**!
for	für	Scout, here's a sandwich **for** you!
school	die Schule	This is my new **school**, and I'm in class 5C.
please	bitte	Sing a song for me, **please**.
(to) **open**	öffnen; aufschlagen (*Buch*)	Please **open** your books. verb: (to) **open** – adjective: **open** (offen, geöffnet)
book	das Buch	

1 Vocabulary

(to) **sit down**	sich hinsetzen	
(to) **put your hand up**	sich melden, aufzeigen	**hand** = die Hand
(to) **look at** sth.	sich etwas anschauen	(to) **look** = sehen, schauen
board	die Tafel	Please look at the **board**.
(to) **stand up**	aufstehen	(to) **stand up** ◄ ► (to) **sit down**
new	neu	I like my **new** school.
English	Englisch; englisch	adjective: **English** – noun/country: **England** ❗ Ländernamen, -adjektive und Sprachen werden im Englischen immer großgeschrieben: **E**ngland, **E**nglish
in English	auf Englisch	

🔊 Unit 1: My new school

▶ pp. 18/19

old	alt	**old** ◄ ► **new**
How old?	Wie alt?	**How** ...? = Wie ...?
coding	das Programmieren (*Computer*)	(to) **code** = programmieren (*Computer*); kodieren
walking	das Wandern	verb: (to) **walk** ((zu Fuß) gehen, wandern) – noun: **walk** (der Spaziergang)
cooking	das Kochen	verb: (to) **cook** (kochen) – noun: **cook** (der Koch, die Köchin)
student	der Schüler, die Schülerin; der Student, die Studentin	❗ Betonung auf der 1. Silbe: **stu**dent
at	an; in; bei; auf	**at** school = **in** der Schule **at** this school = **auf/an** dieser Schule
year	das Jahr; der Jahrgang	Scout the seagull is three **years** old.

Topic 1

▶ p. 20

time	die Zeit; die Uhrzeit	I'm hungry! Is it **time** to eat?
(to) **be busy**	beschäftigt sein, (viel) zu tun haben	**busy** = (viel)beschäftigt (to) **be** = sein
tired	müde	Are you two **tired**?

1

	tie	die Krawatte	
	(school) uniform	die (Schul-)Uniform	
	they're (= they are) **they aren't**	sie sind sie sind nicht	**they** = sie (*Plural*) **you are** = = du bist / ihr seid
	good	gut	I like my new school. It's a **good** school!
	(to) know	wissen; kennen	I have two cats and a parrot. – I **know**! **good to know** = gut zu wissen
	British	britisch	adjective: **British** – noun/country: **(Great) Britain**
	(to) have	haben	Are you hungry? You can **have** my sandwich!
	horrible	schrecklich	I don't like this film. It's **horrible**!
	It's not	Es ist nicht	I'm **not** ten. And I'm **not** a seagull. Ich bin **nicht** zehn. Und ich bin **keine** Möwe.
	great	großartig, toll	**great** ◄ ► **horrible**
▶ p. 21	**desk**	der Schreibtisch	
	glue stick	der Klebestift	**glue** = der Kleber, der Klebstoff
	an exercise book	ein Schulheft, ein Übungsheft	**exercise** = die Übung, die Aufgabe
	pencil case	das Federmäppchen	**case** = das Etui, der Behälter, der Kasten
	pencil	der Bleistift	
	pen	der Kugelschreiber, der Stift; der Füller	
	rubber	das Radiergummi	
	pencil sharpener	der Bleistift(an)spitzer	
	ruler	das Lineal	
	an apple	ein Apfel	
▶ p. 22	**Mr** Lee	Herr Lee	**Mr** Lee **Ms/Mrs** Lee **Ms** = allgemeine Anrede für Frauen **Mrs** = Anrede für verheiratete Frauen
	teacher	der Lehrer, die Lehrerin	**class teacher** = Klassenlehrer/in

two hundred and seven **207**

1 Vocabulary

I'm late.	Ich habe mich verspätet.	**late** = (zu) spät
window	das Fenster	
yes	ja	**yes** ◄ ► **no** (nein)
now	nun, jetzt	Ah, great! I love sport. And **now** I'm hungry!
(to) **take**	(mit)nehmen; bringen	Please **take** your book and read exercise 10. Remember: **Take** your sandwiches with you! Can you **take** the new kids to the toilet?
Let's ..., Let us ...	Lass uns .../ Lasst uns ...	Please listen – **let us** start now.
us	uns	Please look at **us** and listen to **us**.
(to) **start**	beginnen, anfangen (mit)	verb: (to) **start** – noun: **start** (der Anfang, der Start)
first	erste(r, s)	❗ **first = 1.** erste/r/s; **2.** zuerst, als Erstes **at first** = zuerst, am Anfang
of	von	• the colour **of** my bike (... meines Rades) • the names **of** the animals (... der Tiere)
▶ p. 23 **in class**	im Unterricht	Please don't eat your sandwiches **in class**.
What page ...?	Welche Seite ...?	❗ **what? = 1.** welche(r, s)?; **2.** was?
page (= p.)	die (Buch-/Heft-)Seite	**on page 15 / on p. 15** = auf Seite 15 / auf S. 15 but Please open your books **at page** 10. (... auf Seite 10.)
(to) **help**	helfen	verb: (to) **help** – noun: **help** (die Hilfe)
answer	die Antwort	noun: **answer** – verb: (to) **answer** (antworten (auf), beantworten)
the answer **to** the question	die Antwort auf die Frage	❗ **to =** **1.** auf: the answer **to** the question; **2.** (um) zu: things **to** eat
question	die Frage	**answer** ◄ ► **question**
(to) **use**	benutzen, verwenden	**user** = der (Be-)Nutzer, die (Be-)Nutzerin
Here you are.	Bitte schön. / Hier, bitte.	*Can I use your book, please?* *Yes, here you are.*
(to) **ask**	fragen	What page is it? – Don't **ask** me. I don't know. ❗ *English:* Can I **ask** you a **question**? *German:* Kann ich dir eine **Frage stellen**?
You're welcome.	Bitte, gern geschehen. / Nichts zu danken.	❗ **welcome:** **1.** You're **welcome**. (Bitte, gern geschehen. / Nichts zu danken.) **2. Welcome (to ...)!** = Willkommen (in/an ...)!

	"bitte"			
	• in Aufforderungen und Bitten:	please	Open your book, **please**. / What's this in English, **please**? Schlag dein Buch auf, bitte. / Was ist dies auf Englisch, bitte?)	
	• wenn du jemandem etwas gibst:	Here you are.	Can I use your pen, please? – Yes, **here you are**. (Kann ich deinen Stift benutzen? – Hier, bitte)	
	• wenn sich jemand bedankt hat:	You're welcome.	I can help you. – Thanks. – **You're welcome**. (Ich kann dir helfen. – Danke. – Bitte, gern geschehen.)	
	classroom	das Klassenzimmer		
	word	das Wort	What's the English **word** for "Handy"? – The right **word** is "phone".	

Topic 2

▶ p. 24	**timetable**	der Stundenplan	Look at **timetable**, please. Can you see your English **lessons**?	
	lesson	die (Unterrichts-)Stunde	**lessons** *(pl)* = Unterricht(sstunden)	
	room	der Raum, das Zimmer	The English lessons are in **room** number 201.	
	(to) think	denken, meinen, glauben	**I think ...** = Ich denke/meine/glaube/finde, ...	
	he's (= he is) **he isn't** (= is not)	er ist er ist nicht	**he** = er	
	(to) be right	Recht haben	**You're right.** = Du hast Recht. (to) **be right** ◀ ▶ (to) **be wrong** (Unrecht haben)	
	she's (= she is)	sie ist	**she** = sie *(weibliche Person)*	
	's (is) (= ist) **he's** (he is) **she's** (she is)	He**'s** my dad. She**'s** my mum.	it**'s** (it is) / that**'s** (that is) what**'s** (what is)	It**'s**/That**'s** nice. What**'s** your name?	
	we're (= we are)	wir sind		you**'re** (you are) we**'re** (we are) they**'re** (they are)	du **bist**; ihr **seid** wir **sind** sie **sind**
	all	alle(s)	Are **all** your school things in your rucksack?	
	but	aber	I like cooking, **but** I like parkour too.	
	break	die Pause	My favourite time at school is the **break**!	
	minute	die Minute	❗ Betonung auf der 1. Silbe: **min**ute	
▶ p. 25	**girl**	das Mädchen		
	boy	der Junge	girl boy	
	(to) make	machen, herstellen	Let's **make** music! We can sing a song.	
	friend	der Freund, die Freundin	Scout the seagull is Leo's **friend**.	

1 Vocabulary

message	die Nachricht, die Mitteilung	Look at Zane's **message** on my phone: "My new school uniform is great!"
(to) be lucky	Glück haben	**You're lucky.** = Du hast Glück. **lucky** (number) = Glücks-(zahl) my **lucky** colour = meine Glücksfarbe ❗ Sie **hat Glück.** = She's **lucky.** Sie **ist glücklich.** = Sie's **happy.**
See you.	Bis dann. / Tschüs.	**See you soon.** = Bis bald!
day	der Tag	
week	die Woche	School starts this **week**. (diese Woche) **the days of the week** (*pl*) = die Wochentage
on Monday	am Montag	**on Sundays** = an jedem Sonntag, sonntags ❗ **on** = 1. an/am: We don't go to school **on** Sunday.; 2. auf: My books are **on** my desk.

Monday (der) Montag **Thursday** (der) Donnerstag **Sunday** (der) Sonntag	**Tuesday** (der) Dienstag **Friday** (der) Freitag ❗ Die Wochentage werden immer großgeschrieben.	**Wednesday** (der) Mittwoch **Saturday** (der) Samstag

▶ p. 26 **subject**	das (Schul-)Fach	What's your favourite **subject** at school?
assembly	die Schulversammlung	All my days at school start with **assembly**.
history	die Geschichte (*vergangene Zeiten*)	
geography	die Geografie, die Erdkunde	❗ Betonung auf der 2. Silbe: ge**o**graphy
lunch	das Mittagessen	What's **for lunch**? (Was gibt es zum Mittagessen?)
maths	die Mathe(matik)	a **maths** exercise ○ + ○ = 10 ○ × □ + □ = 12 ○ × □ − △ × ○ = 0 △ = ?
art	die Kunst	I like drawing pictures. I love **art** lessons!
science	die Naturwissenschaft	a **science** lesson
French	Französisch; französisch	
design and technology	das Werken, der Werkunterricht	**design** = Gestaltung, Design **technology** = Technik(unterricht); Technologie
computing	die Informatik	
PE (= physical education)	der (Schul-)Sport	

Topic 3

▶ p. 28	place	der Ort, der Platz	Put it here. This is the right **place**.
	canteen	die Kantine, die (Schul-)Mensa	Time for lunch! Where's the **canteen**?
	hall	die Halle, der Saal	**sports hall** = Sporthalle ❗ hall = **1.** die Halle, der Saal; 　　　　**2.** der Flur, die Diele
	bag	die Tasche	bags
	where?	wo? / wohin?	Scout, **where's** (= **where is**) my sandwich?
	toilet	die Toilette	
	map	die Landkarte, der Stadtplan	
	building	das Gebäude	What's this **building**, Mum? – My old school!
	near	nahe (bei), in der Nähe von	Hove is **near** Brighton.
	always	immer	You're a great friend. You're **always** so nice!
▶ p. 29	(to) **be scared (of)**	Angst haben (vor)	Scout, you're my friend! I'm not **scared of** you.
	food	das Essen, das Lebensmittel; das Futter	▶▶ things to eat
	bad	schlecht; schlimm	**bad** ◀ ▶ **good**
	grandma	die Oma	grandpa / grandma
	because	weil	I'm happy **because** now we have PE.

Story

▶ p. 30	**after** lesson 1 / **after** school	nach der ersten Unterrichtsstunde / nach der Schule	preposition (+ noun): **after** school (**nach** der Schule) conjunction (+ sentence): **after** you read (**nachdem** du liest)
	friendly	freundlich, nett	Don't be scared. They're **friendly** dogs.
	helpful	hilfsbereit; hilfreich, nützlich	You always help me. You're so **helpful**! (hilfsbereit) Here are **helpful** tips for this exercise. (hilfreiche/nützliche Tipps)
	mean	gemein, fies	▶▶ not very nice **mean** ◀ ▶ **friendly**

1 Vocabulary

who	wer	**how?** wie? **where?** wo? **what?** was? **who?** wer?
sad	traurig	**sad** ◀ ▶ **happy**
then	dann, danach	Now it's assembly time, **then** we have maths.
(to) go	gehen; fahren	Can I **go** to the toilet, please? (gehen) Let's **go** to Plymouth. (fahren)
that	das (dort)	**that's** (= **that is**) = das (da) ist Is **that** a seagull? – Yes, **that's** Scout.
to	zu, nach	❗ **to** = 1. (um) zu: things **to** eat; 2. zu, nach: I go **to** school.; 3. an (jn.) (z. B. schreiben an jn., eine E-Mail an jn.): an email **to** my friend
beach	der Strand	Let's go **to the beach**. (= zum Strand, an den Strand) ❗ **on** the beach = **am** Strand
Bye.	Tschüs.	**Hello.** ◀ ▶ **Bye.** / **Goodbye.**
slow	langsam	This animal is very **slow**.
too slow	zu langsam	Let's go to the beach. – Sorry, I'm **too** busy.
so weird	so seltsam, so komisch	I have a cat now. I'm **so** happy! **weird** = seltsam, komisch
from	von, aus	Scout is **from** Hove, not **from** Brighton. (Scout kommt aus …)
bully	der Mobber, die Mobberin; der Tyrann, die Tyrannin	noun: **bully** – verb: (to) **bully** (tyrannisieren, mobben)
our	unser/e	**our** poster (**unser** Poster) **our** class (**unsere** Klasse)
trouble	der Ärger, Schwierigkeiten	He is **in trouble**. (Er hat Ärger. / Er ist in Schwierigkeiten.)
him	ihm, ihn	That's Tom. I know **him** from school. (ihn) I'm in the football team with **him**. (ihm)
▶ p. 31 **still**	(immer) noch	It's 4.30 and Joe **still** isn't here.
(to) stop	(an)halten; stoppen; aufhören (mit)	(to) **start** ◀ ▶ (to) **stop** This is a nice place. Let's **stop** here, sit down and eat our sandwiches. (stoppen, anhalten) Please **stop** singing and listen! (aufhören mit) verb: (to) **stop** – noun: **stop** (der Halt, der Haltepunkt; die Unterbrechung) to = zu, nach
away	weg, fort	(to) **walk/go away** = weggehen
her friends	ihre Freunde/Freundinnen	I – my we – our she – her you – your

212 two hundred and twelve

These are my friends.	Das hier sind meine Freunde/Freundinnen.	
this, that – these, those		
• Wenn etwas naher beim Sprecher / bei der Sprecherin ist, verwendet man eher **this** und **these**.		This **dog** is so nice, and I love these **cats**.
• Wenn etwas weiter entfernt ist, verwendet man eher **that** und **those**.		**That** snake and **those** seagulls ... no, I'm scared.
very friendly	sehr freundlich, sehr nett	Don't be scared. Our dog is **very** friendly.
free	frei; kostenlos	**free time** = Freizeit, freie Zeit Are you **free** after school? = Hast du nach der Schule Zeit?
opposite	das Gegenteil	The **opposite** of 'new' is 'old'.
▶ p. 32 **people** (*pl*)	die Leute, die Menschen	four **people**
best	beste(r, s); am besten	You're my **best** friend!
when	wenn (*zeitlich*)	I eat a sandwich **when** I'm hungry.

Study skills

▶ p. 34 **(to) learn**	lernen	How can I **learn** all these new words?
vocabulary, *infml auch* **vocab**	der Wortschatz, das Vokabular; das Vokabelverzeichnis	Listening to English songs is good for your **vocabulary**. (Wortschatz) Learn the new words on these **vocabulary** pages. (Vokabeln, Vokabelverzeichnis)
mind map	die Gedankenkarte, das Wörternetz, die Mindmap	
file	die Datei; der Ordner, die Liste	I have a **file** on my computer with all the new words from my French lessons.
or	oder; sonst	Do you like cats **or** dogs? – I love cats!

Unit task

▶ p. 35 **step**	die Stufe; der Schritt	Let's sit down on the **steps** and look at the map.
them	sie, ihnen	I – me he – him we – us they – them

2 Vocabulary

Unit 2: My family and home

▶ pp. 44/45

family	die Familie	❗ Betonung auf der 1. Silbe: **fam**ily
home	das Heim, das Zuhause	(to) **go home** = nach Hause gehen **at home** = zu Hause
aunt	die Tante	**aunt** ◀ ▶ **uncle**
uncle	der Onkel	
brother	der Bruder	**brother** ◀ ▶ **sister**
sister	die Schwester	
cousin	der Cousin, die Cousine	❗ Betonung auf der 1. Silbe: **cou**sin
circle	der Kreis	drawing a **circle**
neighbour	der Nachbar, die Nachbarin	**neighbourhood** = die Nachbarschaft, die Gegend, das Viertel There's a bike shop in my **neighbourhood**.

Topic 1

▶ p. 46

pet	das (Haus-)Tier	Are seagulls good **pets?** – No, they aren't!
a lot (of) **lots (of)**	viel/e; sehr viel/e	I have **a lot of** books in my room. (viele) I like the breaks at school **a lot.** (sehr)
rabbit	das Kaninchen	rabbit — hamster
quiet	ruhig, still, leise	It's **quiet** and I can listen to music. Super!
why	warum	**what?** was? **when** wann? **where?** wo(hin)? **why?** warum? **who?** wer? **how?** wie?
vet	der Tierarzt, die Tierärztin	a **vet** with a dog
(to) live	leben, wohnen	Leo **lives** in Hove.
house	das Haus	

weekend	das Wochenende	**at the weekend** = am Wochenende **at weekends** = (immer) an den Wochenenden
loud	laut	Quiet, please. You're too **loud**.
messy	unordentlich	adjective: **messy** – noun: **mess** (das Chaos, die Unordnung)
▶ p. 47 **polite**	höflich	
only	nur, bloß; erst	I **only** have one pet. (nur) My sister is **only** two. (erst)
▶ p. 48 **hard**	schwer, schwierig; hart	This exercise is so **hard**. Help me, please!
homework	die Hausaufgabe(n)	What's for **homework**? = Was haben wir als Hausaufgabe(n) auf? ❗ *English:* (to) **do** your homework *German:* **(deine)** Hausaufgaben **machen** **homework** hat <u>keinen Plural</u>: Homework <u>is</u> horrible. Hausaufgaben <u>sind</u> schrecklich.
(to) **find**	finden	I can't **find** my bag. Where is it?
special	besondere(r, s)	... **is special** = ... ist etwas Besonderes What's **special about** this place? = Was ist das Besondere **an** diesem Ort?
small	klein	**small** ◀ ▶ **big**
lizard	die Eidechse	
fast	schnell	I like my bike, but it isn't very **fast**.
cute	niedlich, süß	Our rabbit is still very small and he's so **cute**!
dream	der Traum	I'm a vet. It's my **dream** job. I love it. noun: **dream** – verb: (to) **dream (of/about sth.)** (träumen (von etwas))
interesting	interessant	Books about animals are very **interesting**.
mouse, *pl* **mice**	die Maus	two **mice**
his room	sein Zimmer *(zu „he")*	Lily and **her** friends ◀ ▶ Noah and **his** friends

Topic 2

▶ p. 50 **different**	verschieden; anders (als)	six **different** colours

2 Vocabulary

tree	der Baum	
garden	der Garten	
ground floor	das Erdgeschoss	**ground** = der (Erd-)Boden **floor** = **1.** die Etage, das Stock(werk); **2.** der Fußboden
there's (= there is) there are	es ist … / es gibt … es sind … / es gibt …	**there** = da, dort; dahin, dorthin
flat	die Wohnung	 flats

▶ p. 51

bathroom	das Bad(ezimmer)	
bedroom	das Schlafzimmer	
dining area	der Essbereich, die Essecke	
area	der Bereich, die Gegend, die Fläche	
living room	das Wohnzimmer	
kitchen	die Küche	
office	das Büro	
(to) tell	erzählen, sagen	**Tell** the class about your hobbies. Please **tell** me how I can help you.

Topic 3

▶ p. 52

bed	das Bett	(to) **go to bed** = ins Bett gehen
cushion	das Kissen	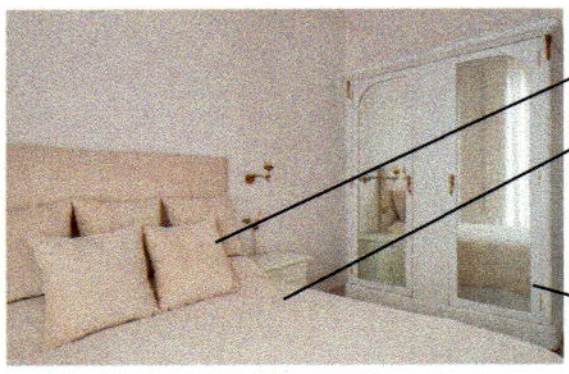
wardrobe	der Kleiderschrank	
clothes (pl)	die Kleidung, die Kleidungsstücke	❗ *English:* **All** her **clothes are** black. *German:* Ihre gesamte **Kleidung ist** schwarz.
lamp	die Lampe	
shelf, *pl* shelves	das Regal	❗ one **shelf** — two **shelves**
robot	der Roboter	Hello, **robot**! 

	chocolate	die Schokolade	❗ Betonung auf der 1. Silbe: **choc**olate
	table	der Tisch	a **table** a **desk**
	shoe	der Schuh	
	chair	der Stuhl	
▶ p. 53	**next to**	neben	
	in front of	vor	There are trees **in front of** the house. = It's a nice house with trees **in front**. (… mit Bäumen davor.)
	behind	Hinter	
	door	die Tür	
	under	unter	**on** the desk ◀ ▶ **under** the desk

	tidy	ordentlich	**tidy** ◀ ▶ **messy**
			• adjective: **tidy**
			  My room is always very **tidy**.
			• verb: (to) **tidy** (aufräumen)
			  I always **tidy** my room.

▶ p. 54	**person**	die Person	❗ Nur selten wird der Plural **persons** benutzt. Normalerweise: one **person** – five **people**
▶ p. 55	**he/she/it has**	er/sie/es hat	I have he has you have she has we have it has they have
	sweets *(pl)*	die Bonbons, die Süßigkeiten	noun: **sweets** – adjective: **sweet** (süß)
	today	heute	What's our first lesson **today**? – French.
	its terrarium	sein Terrarium / ihr Terrarium	❗ I have a pet. **It's** (= **It is**) a cute hamster. **Its** name is Joe. (= the name of the hamster)
	your **own** room	dein/ein eigenes Zimmer	❗ *English:* Do you have your **own** room? *German:* Hast du **ein eigenes** Zimmer?

Story

▶ p. 56	**feeling**	das Gefühl	• noun: **feeling**
			  It's hard for me to talk about my **feelings**.
			• verb: (to) **feel** (fühlen; sich fühlen)
			  It's hard for me to talk about how I **feel**.

	angry	wütend	Scout has my sandwich. I'm so **angry**!
	alone	allein	I often walk **alone** and think.

Vocabulary

parents *(pl)*	die Eltern	▶▶ your mum and dad

work	die Arbeit	• noun: **work** – **at work** = **bei** der Arbeit, **am** Arbeitsplatz
		• verb: (to) **work** =
		    1. arbeiten – **Work** with a partner.
		    2. funktionieren – It's not a great computer, but it **works.**

of course	natürlich, selbstverständlich	Where's my phone? Oh, in my bag, **of course!**
funny	witzig, lustig; seltsam	• All these animals in the house – it's not **funny!** (witzig, lustig) • What's so **funny about** a horse in the living room? (Was ist so lustig **an** …?) • That's **funny** … my phone isn't in my bag … where is it? (seltsam)
guitar	die Gitarre	❗ Beachte die Schreibweise: g**ui**tar
(to) **speak (to)**	sprechen (mit)	I can **speak** English. Can I **speak to** you after the lesson, Mr Lee? **speaking** = das Sprechen
later	später	**Speak later.** = Tschüs. / Bis später.
(to) **talk (to)**	sprechen, reden (mit)	**Talk to** your friends **about** your hobbies.
▶ p. 57 **dinner**	das Abendessen	I'm hungry! **What's for** dinner, dad? (Was gibt es zum Abendessen?) **for** lunch / **for** dinner = **zum** Mittagessen / **zum** Abendessen
(to) **play**	spielen	❗ *English:* (to) **play the** guitar *German:* **Gitarre spielen** **player** = der Spieler, die Spielerin
really	wirklich	Our teachers are **really** nice.
headphones *(pl)*	der Kopfhörer	❗ *English:* These **are** my new **headphones.** *German:* Dies **ist** mein neuer **Kopfhörer.**
problem	das Problem	❗ Betonung auf der 1. Silbe: **prob**lem
game	das Spiel	Let's meet at Jo's and play some nice **games.**

▶ p. 58 **on the phone**	am Telefon	❗ **on** =
		    1. auf: **on** the desk
		    2. an/am: **on** Monday, **on** the phone

idea	die Idee	Let's play badminton in the park. – Great **idea.**
long	lang	**(for) a long time** = lange, (für) eine lange Zeit Sorry, I can't talk to you **for a long time.** Twelve pages? That's a **long** story!

Study skills

▶ p. 60	(to) **spell**	buchstabieren	verb: (to) **spell** – noun: **spelling** (die Schreibweise, die Rechtschreibung)
	alphabet	das Alphabet	❗ Betonung auf der 1. Silbe: **al**phabet
	address	die Adresse	Where do you live? What's your **address?** ❗ Beachte die Schreibweise: a**dd**re**ss**
	road	die Straße *(in oder zwischen Orten)*	Our house is on a quiet **road.**
	(to) **say**	sagen	Be quiet! – Listen, it's nice to **say** "please".
	like this	so, auf diese Art	▶▶ (in) this way Look, it's not hard if you do it **like this**. ❗ 1. it's always **like this** (so) 2. a story **like this** (so/solch eine Geschichte)
	oh	Null *(im gesprochenen Englisch)*	
	(to) **write (to)**	schreiben (an)	**Write to** your friends and tell them about your holidays.
	again	wieder, noch einmal	Stand up.... Thanks, you can sit down **again** now.

Unit task

▶ p. 61	(to) **present** sth. **(to** sb.**)**	(jm.) etwas präsentieren, vorstellen	• verb: (to) **present** sth. **to** sb. – • noun: **presentation** (das Referat, die Präsentation) (to) **give a presentation** = ein Referat halten ❗ *English:* **Present** your idea **to** your friends. *German:* Stelle deinen Freunden deine Idee vor. (*nicht:* ~~Present them your idea~~.)

🔊 Unit 3: My day

▶ pp. 76/77	**their**	ihr/e *(Plural)*	**I** – **my** name **we** – **our** names **you** – **your** name **you** – **your** names **he** – **his** name **they** – **their** names **she** – **her** name **it** – **its** name
	journey	die Reise, die Fahrt; der Weg	It's not a long **journey** from here to Hove. You can walk or take the bus.
	bus	der Bus	❗ *English:* **on** the bus *German:* **im** Bus
	by bike/bus/...	mit dem Fahrrad/Bus/...	Let's not walk there, let's go **by** bus.
	car	das Auto	
	train	der Zug, die Eisenbahn	❗ *English:* **on** the train *German:* **im** Zug
	short	kurz; klein *(Person; Körpergröße)*	**short** ◀ ▶ **long** It's a **short** walk. (= not a long walk) My brother is only 5. He's still **short**. (klein *(Körpergröße)*)

3 Vocabulary

Topic 1

▶ p. 78 **weekday**	der Werktag, der Wochentag	Monday, Tuesday, Wednesday, Thursday and Friday are **weekdays.** weekdays ▶▶ weekend	
hour	die Stunde	❗ Das "h" wird nicht gesprochen. Das Wort klingt genau wie "our"	
clock	die (Wand-, Stand-, Turm-)Uhr		
4 a.m.	4 Uhr (früh)morgens	**9 a.m.** = 9 Uhr vormittags	
4 p.m.	4 Uhr nachmittags, 16 Uhr	**9 p.m.** = 9 Uhr abends, 21 Uhr	
at 8 o'clock	um 8 Uhr	It's **1 o'clock** now.	

15	fifteen	21	twenty-one	40	forty	100	a/one hundred
16	sixteen	22	twenty-two	50	fifty	101	a/one hundred and one
17	seventeen	(…)		60	sixty	102	a/one hundred and two
18	eighteen	30	thirty	70	seventy	103	a/one hundred and three
19	nineteen	31	thirty-one	80	eighty	(…)	
20	twenty	(…)		90	ninety		▶ Numbers, p. 258

end	das Ende, der Schluss	noun: **end** - verb: (to) **end** (enden; beenden)
in the end **at** the end (of)	schließlich; zum Schluss am Ende (von)	Walk or take the bus? **In the end** I often go by bus. **At the end of** a long school day I'm always tired.
▶ p. 79 **before** (school / the lesson)	vor (der Schule / der Unterrichtsstunde)	**before** the lesson ◀ ▶ **after** the lesson

	before		◀ ▶	after	
plus noun:	**before** school	(**vor** der Schule)	◀ ▶	**after** school	(**nach** der Schule)
plus sentence:	**before** you read	(**bevor** du liest)	◀ ▶	**after** you read	(**nachdem** du liest)

(to) **win**	gewinnen	I feel good when my football team **wins.** verb: (to) **win** – noun: **winner** (der Gewinner, die Gewinnerin / der Sieger, die Siegerin)
competition	der Wettbewerb	One of my photos is in an art **competition.**
son	der Sohn	Louise Adebayo has a **son,** Zane.
wheelchair	der Rollstuhl	a **wheelchair**
husband	der Ehemann	Zoe and Carl are our parents. Carl is Zoe's **husband.**
(to) **get up**	aufstehen	On weekdays I **get up** at 7 a.m.

	shower	die Dusche	(to) **have a shower** = (sich) duschen
	breakfast	das Frühstück	

	(to) **take**	dauern, *(Zeit)* brauchen, in Anspruch nehmen	The journey from London to Brighton **takes** an hour by train.
			❗ (to) **take** =
			  1. dauern, *(Zeit)* brauchen, in Anspruch nehmen;
			  2. (to) **take photos** = Fotos machen

	sometimes	manchmal	Do you always walk to school? – No, **sometimes** I go by bus.
	(to) **watch** (sth.)	(sich etwas) anschauen; (etwas) beobachten	(to) **look** • (to) **see** • (to) **watch** • **Look** at the picture. ((an)schauen) • Can you **see** me? (sehen) • Can I **watch** the football game? (anschauen) Let's **watch** the dogs. (beobachten)
▶ p. 80	**often**	oft	I love cooking. I **often** cook nice things to eat.
	shopping	das Einkaufen; die Einkäufe	(to) **do the shopping** = die Einkäufe erledigen, einkaufen gehen (to) **go shopping** = einkaufen gehen
▶ p. 81	**morning**	der Morgen	❗ *English:* **in** the morning *German:* morgens, **am** Morgen
	(to) **get dressed**	sich anziehen	You're late! **Get dressed!** Where are your clothes?
	(to) **brush**	bürsten	verb: (to) **brush** – noun: **brush** (die Bürste)
	tooth, *pl* **teeth**	der Zahn	(to) **brush your teeth** = (sich) die Zähne putzen
	project	das Projekt	❗ Betonung auf der 1. Silbe: **pro**ject
	everybody	jeder; alle	**Hello everybody!** = Hallo/Servus allerseits! Mr Lee is really nice. **Everybody** likes him.
	other	andere(r, s)	the **others** = die anderen
	country	das Land, *(auch:)* die ländliche Gegend	❗ *English:* **in** the country *German:* **auf** dem Land
	afternoon	der Nachmittag	
	evening	der Abend	

• **in** the morning	morgens, am Morgen	• **on** Monday	am Montag
in the afternoon	nachmittags, am Nachmittag	**on** Tuesdays	dienstags, an Dienstagen
in the evening	abends, am Abend	**on** Friday morning	freitagmorgens, am Freitagmorgen

3 Vocabulary

Topic 2

▶ p. 82	**(school) club**	die AG *(in der Schule)*	**club** = **1.** der Klub, der Verein; **2. school club** = die AG
	(to) **be fun**	Spaß machen; lustig sein	• **fun** = Spaß • Swimming is **fun.** = … macht Spaß. • (to) **have fun** = Spaß haben • That's a **funny** story! = Das ist eine lustige Geschichte!
	(to) **run**	rennen, laufen	**running** = das Laufen *(Sport)*
	trampolining	das Trampolinspringen/-turnen	**trampoline** = das Trampolin
	most schools	die meisten Schulen	**Most** students in my class go to school clubs.
	sea	das Meer, die See	❗ *English:* **by** the sea *German:* **am** Meer, **an** der See
▶ p. 83	**never**	nie, niemals	always / often / sometimes / never
	(to) **cycle**	Rad fahren	**cycling** = das Radfahren
▶ p. 85	(to) **want**	wollen	❗ • (to) **want** = etwas (haben) wollen I **want** a new computer. • (to) **want** <u>to do</u> sth. = etwas tun wollen I **want to have** it now.
	activity	die Aktivität, die Tätigkeit	❗ Betonung auf der 2. Silbe: ac**tiv**ity

Topic 3

▶ p. 86	(to) **ask** sb. **to do** sth.	jn. bitten, etwas zu tun	Can I **ask** you **to help** me? = Can I **ask** you **for** some help? ❗ (to) **ask** = **1.** fragen; **2.** (to) **ask** sb. **for** sth. = jn. **um** etwas bitten
	I'd love to. **(= I would love to.)**	Sehr gerne. / Das würde ich sehr gerne.	**Would you like** a drink? – Oh yes, please, **I'd love** a cola! • **I'd like/love …** (= **I would like/love …**) = Ich hätte (liebend) gern … / Ich möchte (liebend gern). • **I'd love/like to meet** Zane. = Ich würde mich (liebend) gern mit Zane treffen.

222 two hundred and twenty-two

Story

▶ p. 88	**newspaper** (*kurz auch:* **paper**)	die (Tages-)Zeitung	**paper** =
			 1. die (Tages-)Zeitung
			   I read the **paper / newspaper** in the morning.
			 2. das Papier
			   I can draw an elephant. Do you have a pen and **paper**?

	surprised	überrascht	This bike for only £150? I'm really **surprised**.
	(to) read	Lesen	**reader** = der Leser, die Leserin
	secret	geheim; das Geheimnis	This is a **secret** message. (geheim) It's our **secret**. (Geheimnis)
	(to) be/feel sorry for sb.	Mitleid haben mit jm.	**I'm** / I **feel sorry for** him. = Ich habe Mitleid mit ihm. / Er tut mir leid.
	her	sie; ihr	❗ **her** = 1. sie; ihr: I can see **her**. (sie) / I can help **her**. (ihr) 2. ihr/e *(wessen?)*: **her** dog, **her** room
▶ p. 89	**prize**	der Preis, der Gewinn	The **prize** for the winner of this competition is a weekend in Paris. **prize show** = die Preisverleihung *(Zeremonie)* **show** = die Show, die Aufführung; die Ausstellung

	Well done.	Gut gemacht!	**well** = gut *(Adverb)*
			 • adjective: **good**
			   Your English is very **good**.
			 • adverb: **well**
			   You speak English very **well**.

	news	Nachrichten	**news** hat <u>keinen Plural</u>: That <u>is</u> good **news**. Das <u>sind</u> gute **Nachrichten**.
	some	einige, ein paar; etwas, ein wenig	There are **some** books in my bag. (einige) I speak **some** French. (etwas, ein wenig)
	money	das Geld	Nice bike ... how much **money** do I have?
	part (of)	der Teil (von)	What **part of** England are you from? (Aus welchem Teil Englands ...?) A pet is always **part of** the family.
	Which part ...?	Welcher Teil ...?	**Which** school club do you like?
▶ p. 90	**(to) pay (for** sth.**)**	(etwas be)zahlen	❗ *English:* Let me **pay for** the pizzas. *German:* Lass mich die Pizzas **bezahlen**.
	cleaner	die Reinigungskraft	
	(to) get	*(sich etwas)* holen/besorgen; bekommen	Where can I **get** help? (bekommen) Let's **get** some sandwiches. (holen/besorgen)

3 Vocabulary

(to) **give**	geben	Can you **give** me that book, please?
pound (£)	das Pfund *(britische Währung)*	❗ you write: **£ 5** – you say: five **pounds**
much	viel; sehr	**How much** time do we have? *(viel)* I like Zane so **much**. *(so sehr)* **Thank you very much.** = Vielen Dank. / Danke vielmals.
euro, *pl* **euros**	der Euro	
kind	nett, freundlich	▶▶ friendly
(to) **send**	senden, schicken	I'd like to **send** my sister a message. = I'd like to **send** a message **to** my sister.
(to) **share**	teilen	I **share** a room **with** my brother. = My brother and I **share** a room. (Wir teilen uns ein Zimmer.)

Study skills

▶ p. 92	(to) **look** sth. **up**	etwas nachschlagen, nachschauen	What's "Möwe" in English? – Sorry, I don't know. Let's **look** it **up**.
	jigsaw (puzzle)	das Puzzle	**puzzle** = das Rätsel
	(to) **collect**	(ein)sammeln	My friend Jamie **collects** old clocks.
	card	die Karte	playing **cards** = die Spielkarten
	group	die Gruppe	Please work in **groups** of 3 or 4 students.

Unit task

▶ p. 93	**recording**	die Aufnahme	noun: **recording** – verb: (to) **record** (aufnehmen, aufzeichnen)
	light	das Licht; die Lampe	I have good **lights** on my bike. I want to see where I'm going in the evening! **car light** = der Autoscheinwerfer
	(to) **speak clearly**	deutlich sprechen	
	scene	die Szene	
	simple	einfach	These exercises are very **simple**. (= they're not very hard)

Unit 4: Where I live

pp. 104/105

cinema	das Kino	**at** the **cinema** = **im** Kino
shop	das Geschäft, der Laden	(to) **be at the shops** = Einkäufe erledigen
marina	der Jachthafen	
boat	das Boot; das Schiff	**boats** in the **marina**
picnic	das Picknick	(to) **have a picnic** = ein Picknick machen
chips *(pl)*	die Pommes frites	**fish and chips** = Fisch mit Pommes frites

Topic 1

▶ p. 106

(to) **hear**	hören	❗ (to) **hear** = hören (können) (to) **listen** (to) = zuhören, horchen **Listen!** Can you **hear** the wind?
clean	sauber	adjective: **clean** – verb: (to) **clean** (sauber machen, putzen)
dirty	schmutzig	**dirty** ◀ ▶ **clean**
youth centre	das Jugendzentrum	**youth** = die Jugend; der Jugendliche **centre** = das Zentrum; die Mitte
estate	die Wohnsiedlung; das Gewerbegebiet	**on** our **estate = in** unserer (Wohn-)Siedlung
rubbish	der (Haus-)Müll, der Abfall	This is the right place for your **rubbish**!

▶ p. 107

rain	der Regen	It's a **rainy** day. = It's **raining**. adjective: **rainy** – noun: **rain** (der Regen) – verb: (to) **rain** (regnen)
ice cream	das (Speise-)Eis	**Ice cream** on a warm day – great!

▶ p. 108

crafts *(pl)*	das Kunsthandwerk, das Basteln	I'm in the **crafts** club at school because I like making things.

two hundred and twenty-five

4 Vocabulary

a girls' class	ein Mädchenkurs, ein Kurs für Mädchen	

Apostroph + s: Etwas gehört (zu) jemandem. Aber beachte die **Stellung des** Apostrophs!

Singular + Apostroph + s: **eine** Person	Plural-s + Apostroph: **mehrere** Personen
the **girl's** dog der Hund **des Mädchens** 	the **girls'** dogs die Hunde **der Mädchen** 

	(to) **explain** sth. **to** sb.	jm. etwas erklären	❗ *English:* Please **explain** it **to me**. *German:* **Erkläre** es **mir** bitte. verb: (to) **explain** — noun: **explanation** (die Erklärung)
	(to) **buy**	kaufen	▶▶ (to) get sth. I'm hungry. Let's **buy** some sandwiches.
▶ p. 109	**town**	die Stadt	**in town** = in der Stadt **town centre** = das Stadtzentrum
	village	das Dorf	a very small town in the country
	many	viele	You have **many** fish in your aquarium! **How many** are there?

much („viel") – **many** („viele")

How much time do we have? **Wie viel** Zeit …?	We don't have **much** time, but we have **a lot of / lots of** work. **nicht viel** Zeit **viel** Arbeit
How many shops are in your village? **Wie viele** Geschäfte …?	There aren't **many** shops, but there are **a lot of / lots of** trees. **nicht viele** Geschäfte **viele** Bäume

Topic 2

▶ p. 110	**hospital**	das Krankenhaus	I have a problem with my hand. I'm going **to hospital** on Tuesday. (ins Krankenhaus) Is he still **in hospital**? (im Krankenhaus)
	ice rink	die Schlittschuhbahn	
	library	die Bücherei, die Bibliothek	I don't always buy books, I often get them from the **library**. **at the library** = in der Bücherei/Bibliothek
	supermarket	der Supermarkt	I buy my food **at the supermarket** (**im** Supermarkt) or **at the market** (**auf** dem Markt). **market** = der Markt
	museum	das Museum	**at** the **museum** = **im** Museum
	stadium	das Stadion	I love football and often watch a game **at the stadium**. (**im** Stadion)
	(**train**) **station**	der Bahnhof	❗ Betonung auf der 1. Silbe: **sta**tion
▶ p. 111	**the same**	gleich; derselbe/dieselbe/dasselbe; dieselben	Sunita and Noah are in **the same** class.
	everywhere	überall	There's rubbish **everywhere** here in the park

	guide dog	der Blindenhund	I have a **guide dog** because I can't see very well, and my dog helps me. noun: **(tour) guide** (der Reiseleiter, die Reiseleiterin / der Fremdenführer, die Fremdenführerin) – verb: (to) **guide** (führen, leiten)
	(to) **come**	(mit)kommen	**Come** to our disco on Saturday! (kommen) Your friends can **come,** too! (mitkommen)
	head	der Kopf	a snake with three **heads**
▶ p. 112	**visitor**	der Besucher, die Besucherin; der Gast	nouns: **visitor** / **visit** (der Besuch) – verb: (to) **visit** (besuchen) Can we **visit** grandpa on Sunday? He loves having **visitors.**
	Germany	Deutschland	noun/country: **Germany** – adjective/language: **German**
	information	die Information(en)	**visitor information centre** = die Touristeninformation, das Fremdenverkehrsbüro **information** hat <u>keinen Plural</u>: That **is** interesting **information**. Das <u>sind</u> interessante **Informationen**.
	warm	warm	(to) **get warm** = warm werden
	summer	der Sommer	**summer** ◀▶ **winter** (der Winter)
	Excuse me, …	Entschuldigung, … / Entschuldigen Sie, …	**Excuse me,** please. Where's the train station?
▶ p. 113	(to) **sell**	verkaufen	(to) **sell** sth. ◀▶ (to) **buy** sth.
	something	etwas	Can I ask you **something**? I'm hungry! Can I have **something** to eat?
	water	das Wasser	

Topic 3

▶ p. 114	**weather**	das Wetter, die Witterung	What's the **weather** like? Can we go to the beach?
	sunny	sonnig	**It's sunny.** = Die Sonne scheint. adjective: **sunny** – noun: **sun** (die Sonne)
	snowy	schneebedeckt; verschneit	adjective: **snowy** – noun: **snow** (der Schnee) – verb: (to) **snow** (schneien)
	cloudy	wolkig, bewölkt	adjective: **cloudy** – noun: **cloud** (die Wolke)

4 Vocabulary

windy	windig	It's **windy**. adjective: **windy** – noun: **wind** (der Wind)
(to) **cost**	kosten	How much does this phone **cost**? verb: (to) **cost** – noun: **cost** (die Kosten; der Preis)
▶ p. 115 **upside down**	verkehrt herum, auf dem Kopf	the **upside down house** = das Haus, das auf dem Kopf steht
inside the house	im Haus	**inside** the house ◀ ▶ **outside** the house (außerhalb des Hauses)
(to) **close**	schließen, zumachen	(to) **close** ◀ ▶ (to) **open**
so	also, daher	It's Sunday, **so** we don't go to school. ❗ **so** = 1. **so** big/cold/… = so groß/kalt/… 2. also, daher
also	auch	I like music, and I **also** like dancing. = I like music and I like dancing, too.
expensive	teuer	£5 for this comic? That's very **expensive**! (= it costs a lot of money)
Next …	Als Nächstes …	**Next** I'd like to look at some photos with you. ❗ **next** = 1. der/die/das nächste; 2. als Nächstes
(to) **turn** sth. **(over)**	etwas umdrehen	**Turn** it upside down. = Dreh/Stell es auf den Kopf. (to) **turn** = (sich) umdrehen

swap	der Tausch	• noun: **swap**
		  My friends and I like to have **clothes swaps**.
		  (der Kleidertausch, die Kleidertauschparty) –
		• verb: (to) **swap** (tauschen)
		  I **swap** clothes with my friends.

Verben und Nomen, die dieselbe Form haben					
answer	1. (be)antworten	2. die Antwort	phone	1. anrufen	2. das Telefon
cook	1. kochen	2. der Koch, die Köchin	rain	1. regnen	2. der Regen
dance	1. tanzen	2. der Tanz	snow	1. schneien	2. der Schnee
drink	1. trinken	2. das Getränk	swap	1. tauschen	2. der Tausch
help	1. helfen	2. die Hilfe	walk	1. (zu Fuß) gehen	2. der Spaziergang
love	1. lieben	2. die Liebe	work	1. arbeiten	2. die Arbeit

(to) **travel**	reisen, fahren	verb: (to) **travel** – noun: **travel** (das Reisen)
hot	heiß, warm	**hot chocolate** = der Kakao, die heiße (Trink-)Schokolade
cold	kalt	**cold** – **warm** – **hot** adjective: **cold** – noun: **cold** (die Kälte; die Erkältung) (to) **be cold** = frieren (to) **have a cold** = erkältet sein

(to) **stay**	bleiben; übernachten	Why can't I **stay** in bed? (bleiben) Come to London and **stay** at my flat! (übernachten) verb: (to) **stay** – noun: **stay** (der Aufenthalt)
(to) **ski**	Ski laufen, Ski fahren	verb: (to) **ski** – noun: **ski** (der Ski) (to) **go skiing** = (zum) Skilaufen gehen

Story

▶ p. 116	(to) **clean** sth. **up**	etwas aufräumen, sauber machen	verb: (to) **clean up** – noun: **clean-up** (die Säuberung) **clean-up day** = der Dreck-weg-Tag *(Aktionstag zum Müllsammeln)*
	noise	das Geräusch; der Lärm	Listen! What's that **noise**? (Geräusch) All that **noise**! I can't do my homework. (Lärm) noun: **noise** – adjective: **noisy**
▶ p. 117	**over there**	da drüben, dort drüben	**over here** ◀ ▶ **over there**
	together	zusammen	Work in groups and find answers to these questions **together.**
	dead	tot	Fish and chips? No, I don't eat **dead** animals.
	(to) **bring**	bringen, mitbringen	Daisy, **bring** me the shoe!
	(to) **dig**	graben	My dog likes **digging** in the sand.
	(to) **bark (at** sb.**)**	(jn. an)bellen	My dog never **barks at** you: he knows you!
	(to) **find out (about)**	herausfinden; sich informieren (über)	Let's **find out** when the show starts. (herausfinden) **Find out about** the cricket club at our school and tell your friends. (sich informieren über)
	married (to)	verheiratet (mit)	Jack is **married to** Jill. = Jack is Jill's husband.
	(to) **look**	aussehen	What does it **look** like? (Wie sieht es aus?)
	Look at the pictures. Sieh dir die Bilder an.	**Look**, Noah. There's a seagull. Schau mal, Noah. Da ist eine Möwe.	Your school uniform **looks** great. Deine Schuluniform sieht toll aus.
	over 50	über / mehr als 50	Seagulls can fly **over** the sea. (über *(räumlich)*) It's a school with **over** 1000 students. (mehr als)
	note	die Notiz; der kurze Brief	(to) **make notes** = (sich) Notizen machen *(zur Vorbereitung)*
	maybe	vielleicht	Let me think – **maybe** this is the answer: …

4 Vocabulary

	somebody someone	jemand	❗ **somebody** *or* **someone** = jemand **everybody** *or* **everyone** = jeder; alle There's **someone / somebody** at the door.
▶ p. 118	meal	die Mahlzeit, das Essen	Do you eat a hot **meal** at lunchtime? *(warme Mahlzeit)*
	line	die Zeile; die Reihe	a **line** of houses
	things **that** people can use	Dinge, die Menschen gebrauchen/benutzen können	Let's take things **that** people can still use to the swap place.
	(to) mean	bedeuten; meinen *(sagen wollen)*	What does this word **mean**? *(bedeuten)* What do you **mean**? *(meinen)* verb: (to) **mean** – noun: **meaning** *(die Bedeutung)*
	(to) go green	grün/umweltfreundlich werden	(to) **go red** = erröten, rot werden
	toy	das Spielzeug	Little Emma likes to play with **toy** cars.

Study skills

▶ p. 120	slide	das Dia; die Folie *(Präsentationssoftware)*	
	title	der Titel, die Überschrift	I like the band and their music, but some of their song **titles** are really weird.
	structure	die Struktur	❗ Betonung auf der 1. Silbe: **struc**ture noun: **structure** – verb: (to) **structure** sth. *(etwas strukturieren, aufbauen)*
	finally	schließlich, endlich	▶▶ in the end
	Do you have any questions?	Habt ihr / Hast du (irgendwelche) Fragen?	**Are there any** cats in your photo? – No, **there aren't any** cats in my photo. There aren't **any** …. / I don't have **any** …. = Es gibt/sind kein/e … / Ich habe kein/e ….

Unit task

▶ p. 121	(to) speak more loudly	lauter sprechen

Ähnliche Wörter im Englischen und Deutschen
Viele englische Wörter ähneln deutschen Wörtern.
Beachte aber: 1) Nomen werden im Deutschen großgeschrieben, im Englischen in der Regel klein.
2) Oft unterscheiden sich die Aussprache und die Schreibweise.

				Auch die Monatsnamen sind ähnlich:	
allergic	cola	perfect	tomato	January	July
ball	melon	playlist	trick	February	August
banana	milk	salad	T-shirt	March	September
butter	mini	sauce	vanilla	April	October
circus	moment	smart	vegetarian	May	November
coffee	pasta	sweatshirt		June	December

Unit 5: Enjoy!

pp. 134/135

(to) **enjoy**	genießen	**enjoy doing sth.** = genießen, etwas zu tun **Enjoy!** = Viel Vergnügen!/Guten Appetit!
birthday	der Geburtstag	**on** my birthday = **an** meinem Geburtstag
		Happy **birthday**! When's your **birthday**? My **birthday** is in April. Herzlichen Glückwunsch zum Geburtstag. Wann hast du Geburtstag? Ich habe im April Geburtstag.
cake	der Kuchen, die Torte	a chocolate **cake**
fruit	das Obst	
cream	die Sahne	**strawberries** and **cream**
strawberry	die Erdbeere	
allergic (to)	allergisch (gegen)	It's sad, but I can't eat strawberries. I'm **allergic to** them.
dessert	die Nachspeise, das Dessert	**for** dessert = **zum/als** Nachtisch ❗ weiches 's' in der Wortmitte: de**s**sert
no	kein, keine; verboten	I have **no** brothers or sisters. Sorry, **no** dogs! (Hunde verboten!) ❗ no = 1. kein/e; verboten; 2. nein
meat	das Fleisch	I don't eat **meat**.
vegetarian, *infml auch:* **veggie**	vegetarisch; der/die Vegetarier/in	I'm a **vegetarian**. I really like **vegetables**. (das Gemüse)
dish	das Gericht *(die Mahlzeit)*	This is my favourite Indian **dish**. ▶▶ meal ❗ **dish** = 1. das Gericht *(die Mahlzeit)*; 2. die Schüssel, die Schale
cheese	der Käse	
pea	die Erbse	**peas**
tomato, *pl* **tomatoes**	die Tomate	**tomato sauce** (die Tomatensoße) **tomato**
spice	das Gewürz	noun: **spice** – adjective: **spicy** (würzig)

noun + -y → adjective				
cloud	→ cloudy	**but:**		
mess	→ messy	fun	→	fu**nn**y
rain	→ rainy	sun	→	su**nn**y
snow	→ snowy	spice	→	spicy

5 Vocabulary

bread	das Brot	**white bread**	**black bread**
rice	der Reis	**rice** with vegetables	

Topic 1

▶ p. 136 **invitation (to)** — die Einladung (zu, nach) — I have an **invitation to** Jill's party.
noun: **invitation** – verb: (to) **invite** (einladen)

twelfth (12th) birthday — der zwölfte Geburtstag

1st	2nd	3rd	4th	5th	8th	9th	12th
first	**second**	**third**	**fourth**	**fifth**	**eighth**	**ninth**	**twelfth**
erste(r, s)	zweite(r, s)	dritte(r, s)	vierte(r, s)	fünfte(r, s)	achte(r, s)	neunte(r, s)	zwölfte(r, s)

▶ **Numbers, p. 258**

The **months** (die Monate)
1 **January** der Januar   4 **April** der April   7 **July** der Juli   10 **October** der Oktober
2 **February** der Februar   5 **May** der Mai   8 **August** der August   11 **November** der November
3 **March** der März   6 **June** der Juni   9 **September** der September   12 **December** der Dezember

(from) 2 o'clock **to** 5 o'clock — (von) 2 Uhr / 14 Uhr bis 5 Uhr / 17 Uhr — We go to school **from** Monday **to** Friday.
❗ **to** =
  1. bis: from Monday **to** Friday;
  2. (um) zu: things **to** eat;
  3. zu, nach: I go **to** school.;
  4. auf: the answer **to** your question

circus — der Zirkus

(to) text sb. — jm. eine SMS schicken — **Text** me when you're back from London, OK?
❗ **text** = 1. Text; 2. SMS;
  3. (to) **text** sb. = jm. eine SMS schicken

if — ob
❗ **if** =
  1. ob: I don't know **if** this is the right answer.
  2. falls: **If** you see our missing cat, please phone us.
  What if …? = Was wäre, wenn …?

▶ p. 137 **date** — das Datum — **birthday date** = das Datum des Geburtstags
the first of April (1st April) — der erste April

▶ p. 138 **(to) juggle** — jonglieren — He's **juggling** with **balls.**

(to) sleep — schlafen — verb: (to) **sleep** – noun: **sleep** (der Schlaf)

	(to) **need** sth. (to) **need to do** sth.	etwas brauchen etwas tun müssen	I **need** money. I **need to buy** a new bike.
	moment	der Moment	❗ Betonung auf der 1. Silbe: **mo**ment **at** the moment = im Moment, zurzeit
	must	müssen	I **must** go. = Ich muss Schluss machen. (am Telefon/ Briefschluss) ❗ kein **-s** bei *he/she/it*: Noah **must** go.
▶ p. 139	**balloon**	der Ballon	
	difference	der Unterschied	noun: **difference** – adjective: **different**
	(to) **wear**	tragen, anhaben *(Kleidung)*	At English schools students **wear** uniforms.
	sunglasses *(pl)*	die Sonnenbrille	**sunglasses** ist ein Pluralwort: Where **are** my **sunglasses**? I can't find **them**.

Topic 2

▶ p. 140	**present**	das Geschenk	a **present**
	perfect	perfekt	❗ Betonung auf der 1. Silbe: **per**fect
	sure	sicher	The next lesson is art. – Are you **sure**? Can you help me? – **Sure.** (Sicher! / Na klar!)

	already	schon	Get up! It's 7 o'clock **already**!
			– Go away! It's Sunday!
			❗ Wortstellung:
			  Noah **already has** bike lights. –
			  Noah **hat schon** Fahrradleuchten.

▶ p. 141	**kind (of)**	die Art (von), die Sorte (von)	What **kind of** food do you eat for lunch? all **kinds of** things (lauter Dinge, alles mögliche)
	ham	der Schinken	
	sausage	das (Brat-, Bock-)Würstchen, die Wurst	
	salad	der Salat *(als Gericht oder Beilage)*	a **salad** with **ham**
	carrot	die Möhre, die Karotte	
	melon	die Melone	❗ Betonung auf der 1. Silbe: **me**lon
	lemonade	die Limonade	**Lemonade** is a sweet cold drink.
	shopping list	die Einkaufsliste	What do we need to buy at the supermarket? Let's make a **shopping list**. noun: **list** (die Liste) – verb: **(to) list** ((auf)listen)
	packet	die Packung, das Päckchen	a **packet of** bread (eine Packung Brot)

5 Vocabulary

	lemon	die Zitrone	
	sugar	der Zucker	There's a lot of **sugar** in these sweets.
▶ p. 142	recipe	das (Koch-)Rezept	**recipe book** = das Kochbuch
	butter	die Butter	You need milk to make **butter** or cream.
	more	mehr, weitere	Please find **three more** words for the mind map. (noch drei Wörter, drei weitere Wörter)
	(to) cut	schneiden	verb: (to) **cut** – noun: **cut** (der Schnitt)
	(to) add	hinzufügen; addieren	When you **add** blue to yellow, you get green.
▶ p. 143	(to) guess	(er)raten	**Guess** how old I am. – 15? – No, I'm 14. a **guessing game** = ein Ratespiel verb: (to) **guess** – noun: **guess** (die Vermutung)

„Stumme" Buchstaben
Manche Buchstaben, die in Wörtern geschrieben werden, sind „stumm" – du sprichst sie nicht aus:

Stummes d	Stummes gh	Stummes h	Stummes k	Stummes u	Stummes w
san**d**wich	ei**gh**t	**h**our	**k**now	g**u**ess	**w**answer
We**d**nesday	nei**gh**bour	w**h**at		g**u**ide	**w**rite
	ri**gh**t	w**h**en		g**u**itar	**w**rong
		w**h**ere			

	easy	einfach, leicht	easy ◀ ▶ hard
	popular	beliebt, populär	Many people love this film. It's very **popular.**
	point	der Punkt	You get one **point** for every right answer.

Topic 3

▶ p. 144	egg	das Ei	
	cocoa	der Kakao	❗ Beachte Aussprache und Schreibung! • Betonung auf der 1. Silbe: **co**coa • *English:* **co**c**oa** – *German:* K**a**k**ao**
	powder	das Pulver	
	oven	der Backofen	Put the cake in the **oven** for 45 minutes.
	icing	die Glasur, der Zuckerguss	**icing sugar** = der Puderzucker
	(to) mix	(ver)mischen	verb: (to) **mix** – noun: **mixture** (die Mischung)
	flour	das Mehl	
	vanilla	die Vanille	I like this dessert with custard or **vanilla** sauce.
▶ p. 145	main course	das Hauptgericht	▶▶ **main dish** **main** = Haupt-, wichtigste(r, s)
	chicken	das Huhn; das (Brat-)Hähnchen	I'm a vegetarian, so I don't eat **chicken**.
	banana	die Banane	I love fruit like **bananas,** strawberries or melons.

	(to) fry	braten; frittieren	**Fry** the vegetables in a **pan** and eat them with a tomato sauce – a great meal!
	pan	die Pfanne	**frying pan** = die Bratpfanne
	tea	der Tee	
	milk	die Milch	**eggs, milk, flour, sugar**
	coffee	der Kaffee	Let's make **tea** or **coffee,** sit down and talk.
	(to) be called	heißen	Our dog **is called** Fido. (= It's name is Fido.)

Story

▶ p. 146	(to) **wave (to** sb.**)**	(jm. zu)winken	Oh, there they are, but they don't see us! **Wave to** them!
▶ p. 147	just	nur, bloß; einfach	It's **just us.** = Es sind nur wir. **Just** listen to me for five minutes, please. Don't **just** sit there! Get up and help me.
	a shame	schade; eine Schande	You're not free this afternoon? **That's a shame!** (Das ist schade!) **What a shame!** (Wie schade!)
	amazing	erstaunlich; großartig	24000000 people live in Shanghai? **Amazing**! (erstaunlich) This museum is so great – really **amazing.** (großartig)
	(to) **be good at** sth. **/ at doing** sth.	etwas gut können; gut in etwas sein	You speak French, English and Russian? You're **good at** learning languages!
	it is sb.**'s turn (to do** sth. **)**	jd. ist dran / an der Reihe (etwas zu tun)	(to) **take turns** (**to do** sth.) = sich abwechseln; sich dabei abwechseln, etwas zu tun
	how to do sth.	wie man etwas tut / tun kann / tun soll	I don't know ... ... **what to do / what to say.** ... **how to answer.** ... **where to go.**
	pork	das Schweinefleisch	**Pork** is the meat from **pigs**. **pig** = das Schwein

Study skills

▶ p. 150	**potato,** pl **potatoes**	die Kartoffel	

Dictionary

English – German

Im *English-German Dictionary* kannst du nachschlagen, was ein englisches Wort bedeutet oder wie es ausgesprochen wird.

Es werden folgende **Abkürzungen und Symbole** verwendet:

infml = *informal* (umgangssprachlich) *pl* = *plural* (Mehrzahl)
sb. = *somebody* (jemand) *sth.* = *something* (etwas)
jd. = jemand jm. = jemandem jn. = jemanden

° Mit diesem Kringel sind Wörter markiert, die nicht zum Lernwortschatz gehören.

Die **Fundstellenangaben** zeigen, wo ein Wort zum ersten Mal vorkommt. Die Ziffern in Klammern bezeichnen Seitenzahlen.

1 (26) = Unit 1, Seite 26

A

a [ə] ein, eine (10/11)
about [əˈbaʊt]: **about me/you/...** über mich/dich/... (14) **What about ... ?** Wie wäre es mit ... ? 5 (143) **What about you?** Und du? / Was ist mit dir? (10/11)
°**above** [əˈbʌv] oben; über, oberhalb (von)
°**act** [ækt] aufführen, spielen **act out** vorspielen, aufführen
action [ˈækʃn] die Aktion, die (spannende) Handlung 1 (32)
°**active** [ˈæktɪv] aktiv
activity [ækˈtɪvəti] die Aktivität, die Tätigkeit 3 (85)
add [æd] hinzufügen; addieren 5 (142)
address [əˈdres] die Adresse 2 (60)
after [ˈɑːftə]:
1. **after (school)** nach (der Schule) 1 (30)
2. **after (you read)** nachdem (du liest) 1 (30)
afternoon [ɑːftəˈnuːn] der Nachmittag 3 (81) **in the afternoon** nachmittags, am Nachmittag 3 (81)
again [əˈgen] wieder, noch einmal 2 (60)
°**agree on** [əˈgriː ɒn] sich einigen auf
all [ɔːl] alle(s) 1 (24) °**all your things** all deine Sachen °**(not) at all** überhaupt (nicht)
allergic (to) [əˈlɜːdʒɪk] allergisch (gegen) 5 (134/135)
alone [əˈləʊn] allein 2 (56)
alphabet [ˈælfəbet] das Alphabet 2 (60)
°**alphabetical** [ælfəˈbetɪkl] alphabetisch
already [ɔːlˈredi] schon 5 (140)
also [ˈɔːlsəʊ] auch 4 (115)
always [ˈɔːlweɪz] immer 1 (28)
am [æm] **I'm (= I am)** ich bin (10/11)
a.m. [eɪˈem]: **4 a.m.** 4 Uhr (früh)morgens 3 (78) **9 a.m.** 9 Uhr vormittags 3 (78)
amazing [əˈmeɪzɪŋ] erstaunlich; großartig 5 (147)
an [ən] ein/e *(vor Vokalen)* (14)
and [ænd], [ənd] und (10/11)

angry [ˈæŋgri] wütend 2 (56)
animal [ˈænɪml] das Tier (12)
°**another** [əˈnʌðə] ein/e andere/r/s; noch ein/e
answer [ˈɑːnsə]:
1. die Antwort 1 (23)
2. (be)antworten 1 (23)
any [ˈeni]: **Do you have any questions?** Habt ihr / Hast du (irgendwelche) Fragen? 4 (120) **there aren't any ...** es gibt keine ... 4 (120)
°**anything** [ˈeniθɪŋ]: **not (...) anything** nichts
app [æp] die App 1 (34)
apple [ˈæpl] der Apfel 1 (21)
April [ˈeɪprəl] der April 4 (116)
are [ɑː]: **they are** sie sind 1 (20) **they aren't** sie sind nicht 1 (20) **you are** du bist / ihr seid 1 (20)
area [ˈeəriə] der Bereich, die Gegend, die Fläche 2 (51)
art [ɑːt] die Kunst 1 (26)
°**as** [æz], [əz]: **the same as ...** der-/die/dasselbe, das gleiche wie ...
ask [ɑːsk]:
1. fragen 1 (23) **ask a question** eine Frage stellen 1 (23)
2. **ask sb. for sth.** jn. um etwas bitten 3 (86) **ask sb. to do sth.** jn. bitten, etwas zu tun 3 (86)
assembly [əˈsembli] die Schulversammlung 1 (26)
at [æt], [ət] an; in; bei; auf 1 (18/19) **at 8 o'clock** um 8 Uhr 3 (78) **at the cinema** im Kino 4 (104/105) **at the top (of)** oben, am oberen Ende (von); an der Spitze (von) (16) **at work** bei der Arbeit, am Arbeitsplatz 2 (56) **be good at sth. / at doing sth.** etwas gut können; gut in etwas sein 5 (147) **Open your books at page 10.** Schlagt eure Bücher auf Seite 10 auf. 1 (23) °**at least** wenigstens, zumindest
August [ˈɔːgəst] der August 5 (136)
aunt [ɑːnt] die Tante 2 (44/45)
away [əˈweɪ] weg, fort 1 (31)

B

°**back** [bæk] zurück **at the back** hinten **on the back of the card** auf der Rückseite der Karte
bad [bæd] schlecht; schlimm 1 (29)
bag [bæg] die Tasche 1 (28)
°**baking powder** [ˈbeɪkɪŋ paʊdə] das Backpulver
ball [bɔːl] der Ball 5 (148)
balloon [bəˈluːn] der Ballon 5 (139)
banana [bəˈnɑːnə] die Banane 5 (145)
band [bænd] die Band, die Musikgruppe 3 (82)
bark (at sb.) [bɑːk] (jn. an)bellen 4 (117)
basketball [ˈbɑːskɪtbɔːl] der Basketball 3 (82)
bathroom [ˈbɑːθruːm] das Bad(ezimmer) 2 (51)
be [biː] sein 1 (20)
beach [biːtʃ] der Strand 1 (30) **on the beach** am Strand 1 (30) **to the beach** zum Strand, an den Strand 1 (30)
because [bɪˈkɒz] weil 1 (29)
bed [bed] das Bett 2 (52) **go to bed** ins Bett gehen 2 (52)
bedroom [ˈbedruːm] das Schlafzimmer 2 (51)
before [bɪˈfɔː]:
1. **before (school / the lesson)** vor (der Schule / der Unterrichtsstunde) 3 (79)
2. **before (you read)** bevor (du liest) 3 (79)
behind [bɪˈhaɪnd] hinter 2 (53)
°**below** [bɪˈləʊ] unten; unter(halb von)
best [best] beste(r, s); am besten 1 (32)
big [bɪg] groß (15)
bike [baɪk] das Fahrrad (15)
°**biology** [baɪˈɒlədʒi] die Biologie
°**bird** [bɜːd] der Vogel
birthday [ˈbɜːθdeɪ] der Geburtstag 5 (134/135) **Happy birthday!** Herzlichen Glückwunsch zum Geburtstag! 5 (134/135) **My birthday is in April.** Ich habe im April Geburtstag. 5 (134/135) **on my birthday** an meinem Geburtstag 5 (134/135) **When's your birthday?** Wann hast du Geburtstag? 5 (134/135)

black [blæk] schwarz (10/11)
blue [bluː] blau (10/11)
board [bɔːd] die Tafel (17)
boat [bəʊt] das Boot; das Schiff 4 (104/105)
book [bʊk] das Buch (17)
°**boring** [ˈbɔːrɪŋ] langweilig
°**bowl** [bəʊl] die Schüssel, die Schale
bowling [ˈbəʊlɪŋ] das Bowling, das Kegeln 4 (104/105)
°**box** [bɒks] die Box, der Kasten
boy [bɔɪ] der Junge 1 (25)
bread [bred] das Brot 5 (134/135)
break [breɪk] die Pause 1 (24)
°**break sth.** [breɪk] etwas zerbrechen
breakfast [ˈbrekfəst] das Frühstück 3 (79)
bring [brɪŋ] bringen, mitbringen 4 (117)
Britain [ˈbrɪtn] Großbritannien 1 (20)
British [ˈbrɪtɪʃ] britisch 1 (20)
°**bro** [brəʊ] (infml für brother) der Bruder, der Kumpel
brother [ˈbrʌðə] der Bruder 2 (44/45)
brown [braʊn] braun (10/11)
brush [brʌʃ]:
1. bürsten 3 (81)
brush your teeth (sich) die Zähne putzen 3 (81)
2. die Bürste 3 (81)
building [ˈbɪldɪŋ] das Gebäude 1 (28)
bully [ˈbʊli]:
1. der Mobber, die Mobberin; der Tyrann, die Tyrannin 1 (30)
2. tyrannisieren, mobben 1 (30)
bus [bʌs] der Bus 3 (76/77) **by bus** mit dem Bus 3 (76/77) **on the bus** im Bus 3 (76/77)
busy [ˈbɪzi] (viel)beschäftigt 1 (20) **be busy** beschäftigt sein, (viel) zu tun haben 1 (20)
but [bʌt], [bət] aber 1 (24)
butter [ˈbʌtə] die Butter 5 (142)
buy [baɪ] kaufen 4 (108)
by [baɪ]: **by bus** mit dem Bus 3 (76/77) **by the sea** am Meer, an der See 3 (82)
Bye. [baɪ] Tschüs. 1 (30)

C

cafe [ˈkæfeɪ] das Café 3 (79)
cake [keɪk] der Kuchen, die Torte 5 (134/135)
°**calendar** [ˈkælɪndə] der Kalender
called [kɔːld] **be called** heißen 5 (145)
can [kæn], [kən] können (12) **I can't** (= cannot) ich kann nicht (12)
canteen [kænˈtiːn] die Kantine, die (Schul-)Mensa 1 (28)
cap [kæp] die (Schirm-)Mütze, die Kappe (15)
car [kɑː] das Auto 3 (76/77)
card [kɑːd] die Karte 3 (92) **playing card** die Spielkarte 3 (92)
careful [ˈkeəfl] vorsichtig (10/11)
carrot [ˈkærət] die Möhre, die Karotte 5 (141)

case [keɪs] das Etui, der Behälter, der Kasten 1 (21)
cat [kæt] die Katze (14)
°**Celsius** [ˈselsiəs]: **degree Celsius (°C)** der Grad Celsius
centre [ˈsentə] das Zentrum; die Mitte 4 (106)
chair [tʃeə] der Stuhl 2 (52)
°**change** [tʃeɪndʒ] (sich) (ver)ändern; wechseln
check [tʃek]:
1. (über)prüfen, kontrollieren 3 (79)
2. die (Über-)Prüfung, die Kontrolle 3 (79)
°**checkpoint** [ˈtʃekpɔɪnt] der Kontrollpunkt
cheese [tʃiːz] der Käse 5 (134/135)
chicken [ˈtʃɪkɪn] das Huhn; das (Brat-)Hähnchen 5 (145)
°**China** [ˈtʃaɪnə] China
chips (pl) [tʃɪps] die Pommes frites 4 (104/105) **fish and chips** der Fisch mit Pommes frites 4 (104/105)
chocolate [ˈtʃɒklət] die Schokolade 2 (52) **hot chocolate** der Kakao, die heiße (Trink-)Schokolade 4 (115)
°**choose** [tʃuːz] (aus)wählen
cinema [ˈsɪnəmə] das Kino 4 (104/105) **at the cinema** im Kino 4 (104/105)
circle [ˈsɜːkl] der Kreis 2 (44/45)
circus [ˈsɜːkəs] der Zirkus 5 (136)
city [ˈsɪti] die (Groß-)Stadt 4 (104/105)
°**clap** [klæp] klatschen
class [klɑːs] die Klasse; der Unterricht; der Kurs (10/11) **in class** im Unterricht 1 (23)
class teacher [ˈklɑːs tiːtʃə] der Klassenlehrer, die Klassenlehrerin 1 (22)
°**classmate** [ˈklɑːsmeɪt] der Mitschüler, die Mitschülerin
classroom [ˈklɑːsruːm] das Klassenzimmer 1 (23)
°**classroom phrase** [ˈklɑːsruːm freɪz] der Satz, den man im Klassenraum braucht
clean [kliːn]:
1. sauber 4 (106)
2. sauber machen, putzen 4 (106)
clean sth. up etwas aufräumen, sauber machen 4 (116)
clean-up [ˈkliːn ʌp] das Säubern, das Saubermachen 4 (116)
clean-up day [ˈkliːn ʌp deɪ] der Dreck-weg-Tag (Aktionstag zum Müllsammeln) 4 (116)
cleaner [ˈkliːnə] die Reinigungskraft 3 (90)
clearly [ˈklɪəli]: **speak clearly** deutlich sprechen 3 (93)
clever [ˈklevə] schlau, klug 1 (30)
clock [klɒk] die (Wand-, Stand-, Turm-)Uhr 3 (78)
close [kləʊz] schließen, zumachen 4 (115)
closed [kləʊzd] geschlossen (17)
clothes (pl) [kləʊðz] die Kleidung, die Kleidungsstücke 2 (52)

clothes swap [ˈkləʊðz swɒp] der Kleidertausch, die Kleidertauschparty 4 (115)
cloud [klaʊd] die Wolke 4 (114)
cloudy [ˈklaʊdi] wolkig, bewölkt 4 (114)
clown [klaʊn] der Clown 5 (142)
club [klʌb] der Klub, der Verein 3 (82) **school club** die AG (in der Schule) 3 (82) °**join a club** in einen Klub eintreten
cocoa [ˈkəʊkəʊ] der Kakao 5 (144)
code [kəʊd] programmieren (Computer); kodieren 1 (18/19)
coding [ˈkəʊdɪŋ] das Programmieren (Computer) 1 (18/19)
coffee [ˈkɒfi] der Kaffee 5 (145)
cola [ˈkəʊlə] die Cola 5 (141)
cold [kəʊld]:
1. kalt 4 (115)
be cold frieren 4 (115)
2. die Kälte 4 (115)
3. die Erkältung 4 (115)
have a cold erkältet sein 4 (115)
collect [kəˈlekt] (ein)sammeln 3 (92)
colour [ˈkʌlə] die Farbe (10/11) **What colour is …?** Welche Farbe hat …? (10/11)
come [kʌm] (mit)kommen 4 (111)
comic [ˈkɒmɪk] der Comic 3 (93)
°**comment on sth.** [ˈkɒment] etwas kommentieren
°**compare** [kəmˈpeə] vergleichen
competition [kɒmpəˈtɪʃn] der Wettbewerb 3 (79)
°**complete** [kəmˈpliːt] vervollständigen
computer [kəmˈpjuːtə] der Computer 1 (28)
computing [kəmˈpjuːtɪŋ] die Informatik 1 (26)
console [kənˈsəʊl] die Konsole 3 (90)
°**conversation** [kɒnvəˈseɪʃn] das Gespräch
cook [kʊk]:
1. der Koch, die Köchin 1 (18/19)
2. kochen 1 (18/19)
cooking [ˈkʊkɪŋ] das Kochen 1 (18/19)
cool [kuːl] cool (10/11)
°**copy** [ˈkɒpi] kopieren, abschreiben
°**correct** [kəˈrekt]:
1. korrekt
2. korrigieren
°**correctly** [kəˈrektli] korrekt (Adv.)
cost [kɒst]:
1. die Kosten; der Preis 4 (114)
2. kosten 4 (114)
°**count** [kaʊnt] zählen
country [ˈkʌntri] das Land, (auch:) die ländliche Gegend 3 (81)
course [kɔːs]:
1. **main course** das Hauptgericht 5 (145)
°2. der Kurs(us)
cousin [ˈkʌzn] der Cousin, die Cousine 2 (44/45)
crafts (pl) [krɑːfts] das Kunsthandwerk, das Basteln 4 (108)

Dictionary

English – German

cream [kriːm] die Sahne 5 (134/135)
cricket [ˈkrɪkɪt] das Kricket (Mannschaftssportart) 3 (82)
°**cross** [krɒs] mit einem Kreuz versehen
°**culture** [ˈkʌltʃə] die Kultur
cushion [ˈkʊʃn] das Kissen 2 (52)
cut [kʌt]:
 1. der Schnitt 5 (142)
 2. schneiden 5 (142)
 °**cut sth. out** etwas ausschneiden
cute [kjuːt] niedlich, süß 2 (48)
cycle [ˈsaɪkl] Rad fahren 3 (83)
cycling [ˈsaɪklɪŋ] das Radfahren 3 (83)

D

dad [dæd] der Papa, der Vati (12)
°**daily** [ˈdeɪli] täglich
dance [dɑːns]:
 1. tanzen (15)
 2. der Tanz (15)
dancer [ˈdɑːnsə] der Tänzer, die Tänzerin (15)
dancing [ˈdɑːnsɪŋ] das Tanzen (15)
date [deɪt] das Datum 5 (137) **birthday date** das Datum des Geburtstags 5 (137)
day [deɪ] der Tag 1 (25) **the days of the week** (pl) die Wochentage 1 (25) **work long days** lange arbeiten, lange Arbeitstage haben 3 (79)
dead [ded] tot 4 (117)
December [dɪˈsembə] der Dezember 5 (136)
°**decide** [dɪˈsaɪd] beschließen, sich entscheiden
°**degree Celsius (°C)** [dɪgriː ˈselsiəs] der Grad Celsius
°**delicious** [dɪˈlɪʃəs] köstlich, lecker
°**describe** [dɪˈskraɪb] beschreiben
°**description** [dɪˈskrɪpʃn] die Beschreibung
design [dɪˈzaɪn] die Gestaltung, das Design 1 (26)
design and technology [dɪzaɪn ən tekˈnɒlədʒi] das Werken, der Werkunterricht 1 (26)
desk [desk] der Schreibtisch 1 (21)
dessert [dɪˈzɜːt] die Nachspeise, das Dessert 5 (134/135) **for dessert** zum/ als Nachtisch 5 (134/135)
°**dialogue** [ˈdaɪəlɒg] Dialog
°**dice** [daɪs], pl **dice** der Würfel **throw the dice** würfeln
°**dictionary** [ˈdɪkʃənri] das Wörterbuch, das (alphabetische) Wörterverzeichnis
°**diff bank** [ˈdɪf bæŋk] die Aufgaben zur Differenzierung
difference [ˈdɪfrəns] der Unterschied 5 (139)
different (to) [ˈdɪfrənt] verschieden; anders (als) 2 (50)
dig [dɪg] graben 4 (117)
°**digital** [ˈdɪdʒɪtl] digital
dining area [ˈdaɪnɪŋ eəriə] der Essbereich, die Essecke 2 (51)

dining room [ˈdaɪnɪŋ ruːm] das Esszimmer 2 (51)
dinner [ˈdɪnə] das Abendessen 2 (57) **for dinner** zum Abendessen 2 (57)
dirty [ˈdɜːti] schmutzig 4 (106)
dish [dɪʃ]:
 1. die Schüssel, die Schale 5 (134/135)
 2. das Gericht (die Mahlzeit) 5 (134/135) **main dish** das Hauptgericht 5 (145)
do [duː] machen, tun 2 (48) **do your homework** Hausaufgaben machen 2 (48) °**my favourite thing to do** das, was ich am liebsten tue
dog [dɒg] der Hund (12)
done [dʌn]: **Well done.** Gut gemacht! 3 (89)
door [dɔː] die Tür 2 (53)
°**double** [ˈdʌbl] doppelt, Doppel-
°**down there** [daʊn ˈðeə] dort runter, dort hinunter; dort unten
°**drama club** [ˈdrɑːmə klʌb] die Theater-AG
draw [drɔː] zeichnen (15)
drawing [ˈdrɔːɪŋ]:
 1. die Zeichnung (15)
 2 das Zeichnen (15)
dream [driːm]:
 1. der Traum 2 (48)
 2. **dream (of/about sth.)** träumen (von etwas) 2 (48)
°**dress** [dres]:
 1. das Kleid
 2. **dress up (as)** sich schick anziehen; sich verkleiden (als)
dressed [drest]: **get dressed** sich anziehen 3 (81)
drink [drɪŋk]:
 1. das Getränk (12)
 2. trinken (12)
drone [drəʊn] die Drohne 5 (140)
°**duke** [djuːk] der Herzog

E

°**each** [iːtʃ] jede(r, s) (einzelne), jeweils
easy [ˈiːzi] einfach, leicht 5 (143)
eat [iːt] essen; fressen (12)
egg [eg] das Ei 5 (144)
eight [eɪt] acht (12)
eighteen [eɪˈtiːn] achtzehn 3 (78)
eighty [ˈeɪti] achtzig 3 (78)
°**electric** [ɪˈlektrɪk] elektrisch, Elektro-
elephant [ˈelɪfənt] der Elefant (14)
eleven [ɪˈlevən] elf (12)
end [end]:
 1. enden; beenden 3 (78)
 2. das Ende, der Schluss 3 (78) **at the end (of)** am Ende (von) 3 (78) **in the end** schließlich; zum Schluss 3 (78)
°**ending** [ˈendɪŋ] die Endung; das Ende (Text, Geschichte)
England [ˈɪŋglənd] England (17)
English [ˈɪŋglɪʃ] Englisch; englisch (17)
enjoy [ɪnˈdʒɔɪ] genießen 5 (134/135) **enjoy doing sth.** es genießen, etwas zu tun 5 (134/135)
enjoy [ɪnˈdʒɔɪ] genießen 5 (134/135) **enjoy doing sth.** es genießen, etwas

zu tun 5 (134/135) **Enjoy!** Viel Vergnügen! / Guten Appetit! 5 (134/135)
°**enough** [ɪˈnʌf] genug
°**erm** [ɜːm] äh (Verlegenheitslaut)
estate [ɪˈsteɪt] die Wohnsiedlung; das Gewerbegebiet 4 (106)
euro [ˈjʊərəʊ], pl **euros** Euro 3 (90)
°**ever** [ˈevə]: **the best party ever** die beste Party überhaupt / die beste Party, die man sich wünschen kann 5 (147)
°**every** [ˈevri] jede(r, s)
everybody [ˈevrɪbɒdi] jeder; alle 3 (81) **Hello everybody!** Hallo/ Servus allerseits! 3 (81)
everyone [ˈevriwʌn] jeder; alle (4) 117
°**everything** [ˈevriθɪŋ] alles
everywhere [ˈevriweə] überall 4 (111)
°**example** [ɪgˈzɑːmpl] das Beispiel **for example** zum Beispiel
Excuse me, ... [ɪksˈkjuːz miː] Entschuldigung, ... / Entschuldigen Sie, ... 4 (112)
exercise [ˈeksəsaɪz] die Übung, die Aufgabe 1 (21)
exercise book [ˈeksəsaɪz bʊk] das Schulheft, das Übungsheft 1 (21)
expensive [ɪkˈspensɪv] teuer 4 (115)
explain sth. to sb. [ɪkˈspleɪn] jm. etwas erklären 4 (108)
explanation [ekspləˈneɪʃn] die Erklärung 4 (108)
°**eye** [aɪ] das Auge

F

°**fact** [fækt] die Tatsache
°**false** [fɔːls] falsch, unrichtig
family [ˈfæməli] die Familie 2 (44/45)
fan [fæn] der Fan 2 (47)
°**far** [fɑː] weit (entfernt)
fast [fɑːst] schnell 2 (48)
favourite [ˈfeɪvərɪt]:
 1. der Liebling, der Favorit, die Favoritin (14)
 2. Lieblings- (14)
 °**my favourite thing to do** das, was ich am liebsten tue
February [ˈfebruəri] der Februar 5 (136)
°**feed** [fiːd] füttern **Don't feed the seagulls.** Füttert / Füttern Sie nicht die Möwen.
°**feedback** (no pl) [ˈfiːdbæk] das Feedback (die Rückmeldung)
feel [fiːl] fühlen; sich fühlen 2 (56) **feel sorry for sb.** Mitleid haben mit jm. 3 (88)
feeling [ˈfiːlɪŋ] das Gefühl 2 (56)
fifteen [fɪfˈtiːn] fünfzehn 3 (78)
fifty [ˈfɪfti] fünfzig 3 (78)
file [faɪl] die Datei; der Ordner, die Liste 1 (34)
°**fill in** [fɪl ˈɪn] einsetzen; ausfüllen
film [fɪlm] der Film 4 (104/105)
finally [ˈfaɪnəli] schließlich, endlich 4 (120)
find [faɪnd] finden 2 (48) **find out (about)** herausfinden; sich informieren (über) 4 (117)

°**fine** [faɪn]: I'm fine. / Leo is fine. Mir/Leo geht es gut.
first [fɜːst]:
 1. erste(r, s) 1 (22)
 2. zuerst, als Erstes 1 (22)
 at first zuerst, am Anfang 1 (22)
fish [fɪʃ], *pl* **fish** der Fisch (14)
fish and chips [fɪʃ ən ˈtʃɪps] Fisch mit Pommes frites 4 (104/105)
five [faɪv] fünf (12)
flat [flæt] die Wohnung 2 (50)
floor [flɔː]:
 1. der Fußboden 2 (50)
 2. die Etage, der Stock, das Stockwerk 2 (50)
 top floor die oberste Etage, der oberste Stock, das oberste Stockwerk 2 (50)
flour [ˈflaʊə] das Mehl 5 (144)
°**fly** [flaɪ] fliegen
food [fuːd] das Essen, das Lebensmittel, das Futter 1 (29)
football [ˈfʊtbɔːl] der Fußball (10/11)
for [fɔː] für (17) **What's for homework?** Was haben wir als Hausaufgabe(n) auf? 2 (48) °**for 30 seconds** für 30 Sekunden, 30 Sekunden lang
°**forget** [fəˈget] vergessen **Don't forget.** Vergiss (es) nicht.
°**form** [fɔːm] das Formular
°**formula** [ˈfɔːmjələ] die Formel
forty [ˈfɔːti] vierzig 3 (78)
four [fɔː] vier (12)
fourteen [fɔːˈtiːn] vierzehn (12)
°**France** [frɑːns] Frankreich
free [friː]:
 1. frei 1 (31)
 free time die Freizeit, die freie Zeit 1 (31) **Are you free after school?** Hast du nach der Schule Zeit? 1 (31)
 2. kostenlos 1 (31)
Friday [ˈfraɪdeɪ], [ˈfraɪdi] der Freitag 1 (25)
fried [fraɪd] frittiert, gebraten 5 (145)
friend [frend] der Freund, die Freundin 1 (25)
friendly [ˈfrendli] freundlich, nett 1 (30)
from [frɒm] von, aus 1 (30)
front: **a house with trees in front** ein Haus mit Bäumen davor 2 (53) **in front of** vor 2 (53) **in front of** vor 2 (53)
fruit [fruːt] das Obst 5 (134/135)
fry [fraɪ] braten; frittieren 5 (145)
frying pan [ˈfraɪɪŋ pæn] die Bratpfanne 5 (145)
fun [fʌn]: **be fun** Spaß machen; lustig sein 3 (82) **have fun** Spaß haben 3 (82) °**Have fun!** Viel Spaß!
funny [ˈfʌni] witzig, komisch 2 (56)

G

°**gallery** [ˈgæləri] die Galerie
game [geɪm] das Spiel 2 (57)
°**gap** [gæp] die Lücke
garden [ˈgɑːdn] der Garten 2 (50)
geography [dʒiˈɒgrəfi] die Geografie, die Erdkunde 1 (26)
German [ˈdʒɜːmən] deutsch; Deutsch; Deutsche/r 4 (112)
Germany [ˈdʒɜːməni] Deutschland 4 (112)
get [get]:
 1. bekommen 3 (90)
 get sth. sich etwas holen/besorgen 3 (90)
 2. werden 4 (112)
 get warm warm werden 4 (112)
 3. **get up** aufstehen 3 (79)
girl [gɜːl] das Mädchen 1 (25)
give [gɪv] geben 3 (90)
°**glasses** *(pl)* [ˈglɑːsɪz] die Brille
glue [gluː] der Kleber, der Klebstoff 1 (21)
glue stick [ˈgluː stɪk] der Klebestift 1 (21)
go [gəʊ]:
 1. gehen; fahren 1 (30)
 °**I must go.** Ich muss Schluss machen. *(am Telefon/Briefschluss)*
 2. werden 4 (118)
 go red erröten, rot werden 4 (118) **go green** grün/umweltfreundlich werden 4 (118)
gold [gəʊld]:
 1. das Gold 4 (117)
 2. goldfarben 4 (117)
good [gʊd] gut 1 (20) **be good at sth.** etwas gut können; gut in etwas sein 5 (147) **be good with ...** gut umgehen können mit ... 1 (31)
Goodbye. [gʊdˈbaɪ] Auf Wiedersehen! / Servus. (12)
°**gram (g)** [græm] das Gramm
grandma [ˈgrænmɑː] die Oma 1 (29)
grandpa [ˈgrænpɑː] der Opa 1 (29)
°**grass** [grɑːs] das Gras; der Rasen
great [greɪt] großartig, toll 1 (20)
Great Britain [greɪt ˈbrɪtn] Großbritannien 1 (20)
green [griːn]:
 1. grün (10/11)
 2. umweltbewusst 4 (118)
 go green grün/umweltfreundlich werden 4 (118)
grey [greɪ] grau (10/11)
ground [graʊnd] der (Erd-) Boden 2 (50)
ground floor [graʊnd ˈflɔː] das Erdgeschoss 2 (50)
group [gruːp] die Gruppe 3 (92)
guess [ges]:
 1. die Vermutung 5 (143)
 2. (er)raten 5 (143)
 guessing game das Ratespiel 5 (143)
 3. glauben, annehmen 5 (143)
 I guess ich glaube, ich nehme an 5 (143)
guide [gaɪd]:
 1. führen, leiten 4 (111)
 2. (= tour guide) der Reiseleiter, die Reiseleiterin / der Fremdenführer, die Fremdenführerin 4 (111)
guide dog [ˈgaɪd dɒg] der Blindenhund 4 (111)
guitar [gɪˈtɑː] die Gitarre 2 (56)

H

hall [hɔːl]:
 1. der Flur, die Diele 1 (28)
 2. die Halle, der Saal 1 (28)
 sports hall die Sporthalle 1 (28)
ham [hæm] der Schinken 5 (141)
hamster [ˈhæmstə] der Hamster 2 (46)
hand [hænd] die Hand (17) **put your hand up** sich melden, aufzeigen (17)
°**happen (to sb.)** [ˈhæpən] (jm.) geschehen, passieren
happy [ˈhæpi] glücklich, froh 1 (20) **Happy birthday!** Herzlichen Glückwunsch zum Geburtstag! 5 (134/135)
hard [hɑːd] schwer, schwierig; hart 2 (48)
has [hæz], [həz]: **he/she/it has** er/sie/es hat 2 (55)
hat [hæt] der Hut, die Mütze (16)
have [hæv] haben 1 (20)
he [hiː] er 1 (24) **he's (= he is)** er ist 1 (24)
head [hed] der Kopf 4 (111)
headphones *(pl)* [ˈhedfəʊnz] der Kopfhörer 2 (57)
hear [hɪə] hören 4 (106)
Hello. [həˈləʊ] Hallo. / Servus. (10/11) **Hello everybody!** Hallo/Servus allerseits! 3 (81) °**Say hello to ....** Begrüße .... / Begrüßt ....
help [help]:
 1. helfen 1 (23)
 2. die Hilfe 1 (23)
helpful [ˈhelpfl] hilfsbereit; hilfreich, nützlich 1 (30)
her [hɜː], [hə]:
 1. sie; ihr 3 (88)
 2. **her friends** ihre Freunde/Freundinnen 1 (31)
here [hɪə] hier; hierher (12) **Here you are.** Bitte schön. / Hier, bitte. 1 (23)
Hi. [haɪ] Hallo. (10/11)
°**high** [haɪ] hoch
highlight [ˈhaɪlaɪt]:
 1. der Höhepunkt, das Schlaglicht 3 (93)
 2. hervorheben, markieren, unterstreichen 3 (93)
him [hɪm] ihm, ihn 1 (30)
his room [hɪz] sein Zimmer *(zu „he")* 2 (49)
history [ˈhɪstri] die Geschichte *(vergangene Zeiten)* 1 (26)
hobby [ˈhɒbi] das Hobby (15)
hockey [ˈhɒki] das Hockey 3 (83)
°**hole** [həʊl] das Loch
holiday [ˈhɒlədeɪ] Urlaub (12) **holidays** Ferien (12) **on holiday** im/in den Urlaub (12)

Dictionary — English – German

home [həʊm]:
1. das Heim, das Zuhause 2 (44/45)
at home zu Hause 2 (44/45)
2. nach Hause 2 (44/45)
go home nach Hause gehen 2 (44/45)
homework [ˈhəʊmwɜːk] die Hausaufgabe(n) 2 (48) **do your homework** Hausaufgaben machen 2 (48) **What's for homework?** Was haben wir als Hausaufgabe(n) auf? 2 (48)
horrible [ˈhɒrəbl] schrecklich 1 (20)
horse [hɔːs] das Pferd (14)
hospital [ˈhɒspɪtl] das Krankenhaus 4 (110)
hot [hɒt] heiß, warm 4 (115)
hot chocolate [hɒt ˈtʃɒklət] der Kakao, die heiße (Trink-)Schokolade 4 (115)
hot meal [hɒt ˈmiːl] die warme Mahlzeit 4 (118)
°**hot seat** [hɒt ˈsiːt] der heiße Stuhl *(der Platz im Zentrum der Aufmerksamkeit)*
hour [ˈaʊə] die Stunde 3 (78)
house [haʊs] das Haus 2 (46)
how [haʊ] wie 1 (18/19) **how to do sth.** wie man etwas tut / tun kann / tun soll 5 (147) °**How are you?** Wie geht's? / Wie geht es dir/euch/Ihnen? 2 (44/45)
hundred [ˈhʌndrəd]: **a/one hundred** (ein)hundert 3 (78)
hungry [ˈhʌŋgri] hungrig (10/11) **I'm hungry.** Ich habe Hunger. (10/11)
husband [ˈhʌzbənd] der Ehemann 3 (79)

I

I [aɪ] ich (10/11) **I'm (= I am)** ich bin (10/11)
ice cream [aɪs ˈkriːm] das (Speise-)Eis 4 (107)
ice rink [ˈaɪs rɪŋk] die Schlittschuhbahn 4 (110)
icing [ˈaɪsɪŋ] die Glasur, der Zuckerguss 5 (144)
icing sugar [ˈaɪsɪŋ ʃʊɡə] der Puderzucker 5 (144)
idea [aɪˈdɪə] die Idee 2 (58)
if [ɪf]:
1. wenn, falls 5 (136)
What if? Was wäre, wenn? 5 (136)
2. ob 5 (136)
°**important (for/to sb.)** [ɪmˈpɔːtnt] wichtig (für jn.)
in [ɪn] in; auf (12) **in English** auf Englisch (17) **in the afternoon** nachmittags, am Nachmittag 3 (81) **in the country** auf dem Land 3 (81) **in the morning** morgens, am Morgen 3 (81) **in the photo** auf dem Foto (15) **in the picture** auf dem Bild (12) **in town** in der Stadt 4 (109) °**in the sky** am Himmel
°**India** [ˈɪndiə] Indien
°**Indian** [ˈɪndiən] indisch; der Inder, die Inderin

information [ɪnfəˈmeɪʃn] die Information(en) 4 (112) **visitor information centre** die Touristeninformation, das Fremdenverkehrsbüro 4 (112)
°**ingredient** [ɪnˈɡriːdiənt] die Zutat
inside [ɪnˈsaɪd] innerhalb (von) 4 (115) **inside the house** im Haus 4 (115)
interesting [ˈɪntrəstɪŋ] interessant 2 (48)
internet [ˈɪntənet] das Internet 2 (61)
°**interview** [ˈɪntəvjuː] befragen, interviewen
°**into** [ˈɪntu], [ˈɪntə]: **into the classroom** ins Klassenzimmer (hinein)
°**introduce myself** [ɪntrəˈdjuːs maɪˈself] mich vorstellen
invitation (to) [ɪnvɪˈteɪʃn] die Einladung (zu, nach) 5 (136)
invite (to) [ɪnˈvaɪt] einladen (zu, nach) 5 (136)
is [ɪz] *(er/sie/es)* ist (10/11) **he isn't (= is not)** er ist nicht 1 (24)
it [ɪt] es *(bei Sachen und Tieren auch:* er; sie*)* (10/11)
°**Italy** [ˈɪtəli] Italien
its [ɪts] sein/seine, ihr/ihre *(besitzanzeigend: Dinge und Tiere)* 2 (55)

J

January [ˈdʒænjuəri] der Januar 5 (136)
°**jewellery making** [ˈdʒuːəlri] Schmuck herstellen *(als Hobby)*
jigsaw (puzzle) [ˈdʒɪɡsɔː] das Puzzle 3 (92)
°**join a club** [dʒɔɪn] in einen Klub eintreten
journey [ˈdʒɜːni] die Reise, die Fahrt; der Weg 3 (76/77)
juggle [ˈdʒʌɡl] jonglieren 5 (138)
July [dʒʊˈlaɪ] der Juli 5 (136)
June [dʒuːn] der Juni 5 (136)
just [dʒʌst] nur, bloß; einfach 5 (147) **It's just us.** Es sind nur wir. 5 (147)

K

°**kangaroo** [kæŋɡəˈruː] das Känguru
°**key** [kiː] der Schlüssel; Schlüssel-
kid [kɪd] das Kind, der/die Jugendliche 3 (79)
kind [kaɪnd] nett, freundlich 3 (90)
kind (of) [kaɪnd] die Art (von), die Sorte (von) 5 (141)
kitchen [ˈkɪtʃɪn] die Küche 2 (51)
know [nəʊ] wissen; kennen 1 (20)

L

lamp [læmp] die Lampe 2 (52)
°**language** [ˈlæŋɡwɪdʒ] die Sprache
°**language file** [ˈlæŋɡwɪdʒ faɪl] der Grammatikanhang
late [leɪt] (zu) spät 1 (22) **I'm late.** Ich habe mich verspätet. 1 (22)

later [ˈleɪtə] später 2 (56) **Speak later.** Tschüs. / Bis später. 2 (56)
learn [lɜːn] lernen 1 (34)
°**least** [liːst]: **at least** wenigstens, zumindest
lemon [ˈlemən] die Zitrone 5 (141)
lemonade [leməˈneɪd] die Limonade 5 (141)
lesson [ˈlesn] die (Unterrichts-)Stunde 1 (24)
let's (= let us) [lets] lass(t) uns 1 (22)
°**letter** [ˈletə] der Buchstabe
library [ˈlaɪbrəri] die Bücherei, die Bibliothek 4 (110)
°**life** [laɪf], *pl* **lives** das Leben
°**life skills** *(pl)* [ˈlaɪf skɪlz] die Alltagskompetenzen, die lebenswichtigen Fertigkeiten
light [laɪt] das Licht; die Lampe 3 (93)
like [laɪk] mögen (10/11) **I like singing.** Ich singe gerne. (10/11) **I'd (= I would) like …** Ich hätte gern … / Ich möchte … 3 (86) **I'd (= I would) like to meet ….** Ich würde mich gerne mit … treffen. 3 (86)
like [laɪk]: **like this** so, auf diese Art 2 (60) **a story like this** so/solch eine Geschichte 2 (60) **What's … like?** Wie ist …? / Wie sieht … aus? 4 (114)
line [laɪn]:
1. die Reihe 4 (118)
2. die Zeile 4 (118)
lion [ˈlaɪən] der Löwe (14)
list [lɪst]:
1. die Liste 5 (141)
2. (auf)listen 5 (141)
listen (to) [ˈlɪsn] (sich etwas) anhören; zuhören (15) **listening to music** Musik (an)hören (15)
°**little** [ˈlɪtl] klein
live [lɪv] leben, wohnen 2 (46)
°**lives** [laɪvz] *Plural von* life
living room [ˈlɪvɪŋ ruːm] das Wohnzimmer 2 (51)
lizard [ˈlɪzəd] die Eidechse 2 (48)
long [lɒŋ] lang 2 (58) **work long days** lange arbeiten, lange Arbeitstage haben 3 (79)
look [lʊk]:
1. aussehen 4 (117)
2. sehen, schauen (17)
look at sth. sich etwas anschauen (17)
look sth. up etwas nachschlagen 3 (92) °**Look out!** Vorsicht! / Pass(t) auf!
°**lost** [lɒst]: **a lost visitor** ein Besucher / eine Besucherin, der/die sich verlaufen hat **I'm lost.** Ich habe mich verlaufen/verirrt.
lot [lɒt]: **a lot (of) / lots (of)** viel/e 2 (46) **a lot** sehr 2 (46)
loud [laʊd] laut 2 (46)
loudly [ˈlaʊdli]: **speak more loudly** lauter sprechen 4 (121)
love [lʌv]:
1. die Liebe (15)

2. lieben, sehr mögen (15)
I'd (= I would) love ... Ich hätte liebend gern ... / Ich möchte liebend gern... 3 (86) **I'd (= I would) love to meet ....** Ich würde mich liebend gerne mit ... treffen. 3 (86)
lucky [ˈlʌki]: **be lucky** Glück haben 1 (25)
lunch [lʌntʃ] das Mittagessen 1 (26) **What's for lunch?** Was gibt es zum Mittagessen? 1 (26)
°**lunchtime** [ˈlʌntʃtaɪm] die Mittagszeit **at lunchtime** zur Mittagszeit

M

°**magazine** [mægəˈziːn] die Zeitschrift
°**magic** [ˈmædʒɪk]:
 1. magisch, Zauber-
 2. die Zauberei
 do magic zaubern
°**magic set** [ˈmædʒɪk set] der Zauberkasten
°**magic trick** [ˈmædʒɪk trɪk] der Zaubertrick
main [meɪn] Haupt-, wichtigste(r, s) 5 (145)
main course [meɪn ˈkɔːs] das Hauptgericht 5 (145)
main dish [meɪn ˈdɪʃ] das Hauptgericht 5 (145)
make [meɪk] machen, herstellen 1 (25) °**make sb./sth. do sth.** jn./etwas dazu bringen, etwas zu tun
many [ˈmeni] viele 4 (109) **how many?** wie viele? 4 (109)
map [mæp] die Landkarte, der Stadtplan 1 (28)
March [mɑːtʃ] der März 5 (136)
marina [məˈriːnə] der Jachthafen 4 (104/105)
market [ˈmɑːkɪt] der Markt 4 (110)
married (to) [ˈmærid] verheiratet (mit) 4 (117)
°**match** [mætʃ]:
 1. das Gegenstück, das (zusammenpassende) Paar
 2. (passend) zusammenfügen
 match to zuordnen
match [mætʃ] das Spiel, der Wettkampf 4 (113)
°**material** [məˈtɪəriəl] das Material; der Stoff
maths [mæθs] die Mathe(matik) 1 (26)
°**mattar paneer** [mʌtr pʌˈnɪə] das Mattar Paneer *(nordindisches Gericht)*
May [meɪ] der Mai 5 (136)
maybe [ˈmeɪbi] vielleicht 4 (117)
me [miː]:
 1. mich (14)
 2. mir (14)
 3. *(in bestimmten Wendungen)* ich (14) **It's me.** Ich bin's. (14) **Not me!** Ich nicht! *(= Ich bin/war/habe/... es/das nicht!)* 2 (55)

meal [miːl] die Mahlzeit, das Essen 4 (118) **hot meal** die warme Mahlzeit 4 (118)
mean [miːn]:
 1. gemein, fies 1 (30)
 2. bedeuten 4 (118)
 3. meinen *(sagen wollen)* 4 (118)
meaning [ˈmiːnɪŋ] die Bedeutung 4 (118)
meat [miːt] das Fleisch 5 (134/135)
°**mediation** [miːdiˈeɪʃn] die Vermittlung, die Sprachmittlung
meet [miːt] kennenlernen; (sich) treffen (10/11) **Nice to meet you.** Freut mich, dich/euch/Sie kennenzulernen. (10/11)
melon [ˈmelən] die Melone 5 (141)
mess [mes] das Chaos, die Unordnung 2 (46)
message [ˈmesɪdʒ] die Nachricht, die Mitteilung 1 (25)
messy [ˈmesi] unordentlich 2 (46)
mice [maɪs] *Plural von* **mouse**
°**middle** [ˈmɪdl] die Mitte **in the middle (of)** in der Mitte (von)
milk [mɪlk] die Milch 5 (145)
°**millilitre (ml)** [ˈmɪliliːtə] der Milliliter
°**mime** [maɪm] vorspielen, pantomimisch darstellen
mind map [ˈmaɪnd mæp] Gedankenkarte, Wörternetz, Mindmap 1 (34)
mini [ˈmɪni] Mini- 5 (140)
mini-drone [mɪni ˈdrəʊn] die Minidrohne 5 (140)
minute [ˈmɪnɪt] die Minute 1 (24)
°**miss** [mɪs] verpassen, versäumen, auslassen
°**mistake** [mɪˈsteɪk] der Fehler
mix [mɪks] (ver)mischen 5 (144) °**mix sth. up** etwas (durcheinander) mischen
mixture [ˈmɪkstʃə] die Mischung 5 (144)
°**modern** [ˈmɒdn] modern
moment [ˈməʊmənt] der Moment 5 (138) **at the moment** im Moment, zurzeit 5 (138)
Monday [ˈmʌndeɪ], [ˈmʌndi] der Montag 1 (25)
money [ˈmʌni] das Geld 3 (89)
monkey [ˈmʌŋki] der Affe (14)
month [mʌnθ] der Monat 5 (136)
more [mɔː] mehr, weitere 5 (142) **speak more loudly** lauter sprechen 4 (121) **three more** noch drei, drei weitere 5 (142)
morning [ˈmɔːnɪŋ] der Morgen 3 (81) **in the morning** morgens, am Morgen 3 (81)
most schools [məʊst] die meisten Schulen 3 (82)
mouse [maʊs], pl **mice** die Maus 2 (49)
°**move** [muːv] (sich) bewegen
Mr Lee [ˈmɪstə] Herr Lee 1 (22)
Mrs Lee [ˈmɪsɪz] Frau Lee *(Anrede für verheiratete Frauen)* 1 (22)

Ms Lee [mɪz] Frau Lee *(allgemeine Anrede f. Frauen)* 1 (22)
much [mʌtʃ] viel; sehr 3 (90) **Thank you very much.** Vielen Dank. / Danke vielmals. 3 (90)
mum [mʌm] die Mama, die Mutti (12)
museum [mjuˈziːəm] das Museum 4 (110)
music [ˈmjuːzɪk] die Musik (15)
must [mʌst] müssen 5 (138) °**I must go.** Ich muss Schluss machen. *(am Telefon/Briefschluss)*
my [maɪ] mein/e (14)
°**myself** [maɪˈself]: **introduce myself** mich vorstellen

N

name [neɪm] der Name (10/11) **What's your name?** Wie heißt du? (10/11)
near [nɪə] nahe (bei), in der Nähe von 1 (28)
°**necessary** [ˈnesəsəri] notwendig, nötig, erforderlich
need [niːd] brauchen 5 (138) **need to do sth.** etwas tun müssen 5 (138)
neighbour [ˈneɪbə] der Nachbar, die Nachbarin 2 (44/45)
neighbourhood [ˈneɪbəhʊd] die Nachbarschaft, die Gegend, das Viertel 2 (44/45)
never [ˈnevə] nie, niemals 3 (83)
new [njuː] neu (17)
news [njuːz] die Nachrichten 3 (89)
newspaper [ˈnjuːspeɪpə] die (Tages-)Zeitung 3 (88)
next [nekst]:
 1. nächste(r, s) 4 (115) **the next day** am nächsten Tag 4 (115)
 2. **Next ...** Als Nächstes ... 4 (115)
next to [ˈnekst tə] neben 2 (53)
nice [naɪs] nett, schön (10/11)
°**Nigeria** [naɪˈdʒɪəriə] Nigeria
°**Nigerian** [naɪˈdʒɪəriən] nigerianisch; der Nigerianer, die Nigerianerin
°**night** [naɪt] die Nacht
nine [naɪn] neun (12)
nineteen [naɪnˈtiːn] neunzehn 3 (78)
ninety [ˈnaɪnti] neunzig 3 (78)
no [nəʊ]:
 1. nein 1 (22)
 2. kein/e; verboten 5 (134/135) **No dogs!** Hunde verboten! 5 (134/135)
noise [nɔɪz] das Geräusch; der Lärm 4 (116)
noisy [ˈnɔɪzi] laut, voller Lärm; lärmend 4 (116)
°**north** [nɔːθ] der Norden; nördlich; Nord-
not [nɒt] nicht 1 (20) **I'm not a boy.** Ich bin kein Junge. 1 (20)
note [nəʊt] die Notiz; der kurze Brief 4 (117) **make notes** (sich) Notizen machen *(zur Vorbereitung)* 4 (117)

Dictionary

English – German

November [nəʊˈvembə] der November 5 (136)
now [naʊ] nun, jetzt 1 (22)
number [ˈnʌmbə] die Zahl, die Ziffer, die Nummer (12)

O

o'clock [əˈklɒk]: **at 8 o'clock** um 8 Uhr 3 (78)
October [ɒkˈtəʊbə] der Oktober 5 (136)
°**odd word out** [ɒd wɜːd ˈaʊt] das Wort, das nicht zu den anderen passt
of [ɒv], [əv] von 1 (22) **bags of rubbish** Tüten/Säcke mit/voller Müll 4 (117) **the days of the week** (pl) die Wochentage 1 (25)
of course [əv ˈkɔːs] natürlich, selbstverständlich 2 (56)
office [ˈɒfɪs] das Büro 2 (51)
often [ˈɒfn], [ˈɒftən] oft 3 (80)
oh [əʊ] Null (im gesprochenen Englisch) 2 (60)
°**oil** [ɔɪl] das Öl
OK [əʊˈkeɪ] okay, in Ordnung 1 (20) **Are you OK?** Geht es dir gut? / Bist du okay? 2 (46) **I'm OK.** Es geht mir gut. 2 (46)
old [əʊld] alt 1 (18/19)
on [ɒn] auf 1 (25) **on holiday** im/in den Urlaub (12) **on Monday** am Montag 1 (25) **on Mondays** an jedem Montag, montags 1 (25) **on my birthday** an meinem Geburtstag 5 (134/135) **on the beach** am Strand 1 (30) **on the bus** im Bus 3 (76/77)
°**once** [wʌns] einmal
one [wʌn] eins (12)
online [ɒnˈlaɪn] online, Online- 3 (85)
only [ˈəʊnli]:
1. nur, bloß, erst 2 (47)
2. **the only thing(s)** die einzige Sache / die einzigen Dinge
open [ˈəʊpən]:
1. öffnen; aufschlagen (Buch) (17)
2. offen, geöffnet (17)
°**opinion** [əˈpɪnjən] die Meinung **in my opinion** meiner Meinung nach
opposite [ˈɒpəzɪt] das Gegenteil 1 (32)
or [ɔː] oder; sonst 1 (34)
orange [ˈɒrɪndʒ]:
1. orange(farben) (10/11)
2. die Orange, die Apfelsine (10/11)
°**order** [ˈɔːdə] Reihenfolge **put in the right order** in die richtige Reihenfolge bringen
°**organize** [ˈɔːɡənaɪz] organisieren
other [ˈʌðə] andere(r, s) 3 (81) **the others** die anderen 3 (81)
our [ˈaʊə] unser/e 1 (30)
outside [aʊtˈsaɪd] außerhalb (von) 4 (115) **outside the house** außerhalb des Hauses 4 (115)
oven [ˈʌvn] der Backofen 5 (144)
over [ˈəʊvə]: **over 50** über / mehr als 50 4 (117) **over here** hier herüber; hier drüben 4 (117) **over there** da drüben, dort drüben 4 (117) °**over the sea** über dem Meer

own [əʊn]: **my/your own room** mein/dein/ein eigenes Zimmer 2 (55)

P

packet [ˈpækɪt] die Packung, das Päckchen 5 (141)
page (= p.) [peɪdʒ] die (Buch-/Heft-)Seite 1 (23) **Open your books at page 10.** Schlagt eure Bücher auf Seite 10 auf. 1 (23)
°**pair** [peə] das Paar
°**palace** [ˈpæləs] der Palast, das Schloss
pan [pæn] die Pfanne 5 (145)
paper [ˈpeɪpə]:
1. die (Tages-)Zeitung 3 (88)
2. das Papier 3 (88)
°**piece of paper** das Stück Papier, der Zettel
°**paragraph** [ˈpærəɡrɑːf] der (Text-)Abschnitt
°**parallel** [ˈpærəlel] parallel, Parallel-
parents (pl) [ˈpeərənts] die Eltern 2 (56)
park [pɑːk] der Park 3 (80)
parkour [pɑːˈkʊə] der Parkour (akrobatischer Hindernislauf in der Stadt) 1 (18/19)
parrot [ˈpærət] der Papagei (14)
part (of) [pɑːt] der Teil (von) 3 (89)
partner [ˈpɑːtnə] der Partner, die Partnerin 1 (34)
party [ˈpɑːti] die Party 3 (90)
pasta [ˈpæstə] die Pasta (italienische Bezeichnung für Teigwaren) 5 (141)
pay (for sth.) [peɪ] zahlen; (etwas) bezahlen 3 (90)
PE (= physical education) [piː ˈiː] der (Schul-)Sport 1 (26)
pea [piː] die Erbse 5 (134/135)
pen [pen] der Kugelschreiber, der Stift; der Füller 1 (21)
pencil [ˈpensl] der Bleistift 1 (21)
pencil case [ˈpensl keɪs] das Federmäppchen 1 (21)
pencil sharpener [ˈpensl ʃɑːpnə] der Bleistift(an)spitzer 1 (21)
people (pl) [ˈpiːpl] die Leute, die Menschen 1 (32)
perfect [ˈpɜːfɪkt] perfekt 5 (140)
perfectly (still) [ˈpɜːfɪktli] ganz/völlig (still) 5 (140)
person [ˈpɜːsn] die Person 2 (54)
pet [pet] das (Haus-)Tier 2 (46)
phone [fəʊn]:
1. anrufen; telefonieren (15)
2. das Telefon (15)
on the phone am Telefon 2 (58)
phone number [ˈfəʊn nʌmbə] die Telefonnummer (15)
photo [ˈfəʊtəʊ] das Foto (15) **in the photo** auf dem Foto (15) **take photos** Fotos machen (15) **taking photos** das Fotografieren (Hobby) (15)
°**phrase** [freɪz] die Ausdruck, die (Rede-)Wendung

physical education (PE) [fɪzɪkl edʒuˈkeɪʃn] der (Schul-)Sport 1 (26)
°**pick** [pɪk] (aus)wählen, aussuchen
picnic [ˈpɪknɪk] das Picknick 4 (104/105) **have a picnic** ein Picknick machen 4 (104/105)
picture [ˈpɪktʃə] Bild (12)
°**piece** [piːs] das Stück, das Teil
°**piece of paper** [piːs əv ˈpeɪpə] das Stück Papier, der Zettel
pier [pɪə] der Pier, die Seebrücke 4 (104/105)
pig [pɪɡ] das Schwein 5 (147)
pink [pɪŋk] rosa (10/11)
place [pleɪs] der Ort, der Platz 1 (28)
°**placemat** [ˈpleɪsmæt] das Platzdeckchen
°**plan** [plæn]:
1. der Plan
2. planen
°**plantain** [ˈplæntɪn] die Kochbanane
play [pleɪ] spielen 2 (57)
player [ˈpleɪə] der Spieler, die Spielerin 2 (57)
playing card [ˈpleɪɪŋ kɑːd] die Spielkarte 3 (92)
playlist [ˈpleɪlɪst] die Playlist 5 (143)
please [pliːz] bitte (17)
p.m. [piːˈem]: **4 p.m.** 4 Uhr nachmittags, 16 Uhr 3 (78) **9 p.m.** 9 Uhr abends, 21 Uhr 3 (78)
point [pɔɪnt] der Punkt 5 (143)
°**point (at/to)** [pɔɪnt] zeigen, deuten (auf)
°**Poland** [ˈpəʊlənd] Polen
polite [pəˈlaɪt] höflich 2 (47)
pool [puːl] (kurz für swimming pool) das Schwimmbad 4 (107)
popular [ˈpɒpjələ] beliebt, populär 5 (143)
pork [pɔːk] das Schweinefleisch 5 (147)
post [pəʊst]:
1. der Post (Teil eines Blogs) 4 (109)
2. posten (im Internet veröffentlichen) 4 (109)
poster [ˈpəʊstə] das Poster 1 (35)
potato [pəˈteɪtəʊ], pl **potatoes** die Kartoffel 5 (150)
pound (£) [paʊnd] das Pfund (britische Währung) 3 (90)
powder [ˈpaʊdə] das Pulver 5 (144)
°**practice** [ˈpræktɪs] die Übung(en)
°**practise** [ˈpræktɪs] üben
present [ˈpreznt] das Geschenk 5 (140)
present sth. (to sb.) [prɪˈzent] (jm.) etwas präsentieren, vorstellen 2 (61)
presentation [preznˈteɪʃn] das Referat, die Präsentation 2 (61)
prize [praɪz] der Preis, der Gewinn 3 (89)
prize show [ˈpraɪz ʃəʊ] die Preisverleihung (Zeremonie) 3 (89)
problem [ˈprɒbləm] das Problem 2 (57)
project [ˈprɒdʒekt] das Projekt 3 (81)
purple [ˈpɜːpl] violett, lila (10/11)

put [pʊt] *(etwas wohin)* tun, legen, stellen, stecken 15 **put your hand up** sich melden, aufzeigen 17 °**put in the right order** in die richtige Reihenfolge bringen
puzzle [ˈpʌzl] das Rätsel 3 (92)

Q

question [ˈkwestʃən] die Frage 1 (23) **ask a question** eine Frage stellen 1 (23)
°**question mark** [ˈkwestʃən mɑːk] das Fragezeichen
°**questionnaire** [kwestʃəˈneə] der Fragebogen
°**quick** [kwɪk] schnell
°**quicker** [ˈkwɪkə] schneller
quiet [ˈkwaɪət] ruhig, still, leise 2 (46)
quiz [kwɪz], *pl* **quizzes** das Quiz, das Ratespiel; der Test 4 (115) **do a quiz** ein Quiz / ein Ratespiel / einen Test machen 4 (115)
quizzes [ˈkwɪzɪz] *Plural von* **quiz**

R

rabbit [ˈræbɪt] das Kaninchen 2 (46)
°**race** [reɪs] Rennen fahren; um die Wette laufen/reiten/...
rain [reɪn]:
1. der Regen 4 (107)
2. regnen 4 (107)
rainy [ˈreɪni] regnerisch 4 (107)
read [riːd] lesen 3 (88)
reader [ˈriːdə] der Leser, die Leserin 3 (88)
ready [ˈredi] fertig, bereit 17
really [ˈriːəli], [ˈrɪəli] wirklich 2 (57)
°**reason** [ˈriːzn] der Grund, die Begründung
recipe [ˈresəpi] das (Koch-)Rezept 5 (142)
recipe book [ˈresəpi bʊk] das Kochbuch 5 (142)
record [rɪˈkɔːd] aufnehmen, aufzeichnen 3 (93)
recording [rɪˈkɔːdɪŋ] die Aufnahme 3 (93)
red [red] rot 10/11 **go red** erröten, rot werden 4 (118)
°**registration** [redʒɪˈstreɪʃn] *die Anwesenheitskontrolle und Ankündigung aktueller Ereignisse vor dem Unterricht*
remember [rɪˈmembə]:
1. daran denken, nicht vergessen 12 **remember to do sth.** daran denken, etwas zu tun 12
2. sich erinnern an 12 **remember doing sth.** sich daran erinnern, etwas getan zu haben 12
°**repeat** [rɪˈpiːt] wiederholen
°**research** [rɪˈsɜːtʃ] erforschen, untersuchen, recherchieren
°**result** [rɪˈzʌlt] das Ergebnis
°**review** [rɪˈvjuː] der Bericht, die Rezension *(kritische Besprechung)*
°**rhythm** [ˈrɪðəm] der Rhythmus
rice [raɪs] der Reis 5 (134/135)

°**ride** [raɪd] die Fahrt; das Fahrgeschäft *(auf Volksfesten, in Vergnügungsparks)*
right [raɪt]:
1. richtig 10/11
be right Recht haben 1 (24)
°**2. right by the sea** direkt an der See, direkt am Meer
°**3. on the right** rechts, auf der rechten Seite
°**to the right** nach rechts
ring [rɪŋ] der Ring 4 (117)
road [rəʊd] die Straße *(in oder zwischen Orten)* 2 (60)
robot [ˈrəʊbɒt] der Roboter 2 (52)
°**rock** [rɒk] die Zuckerstange
°**role** [rəʊl] die Rolle *(Film, Theater)*
°**role-play** [ˈrəʊpleɪ] das Rollenspiel
room [ruːm] der Raum, das Zimmer 1 (24)
°**routine** [ruːˈtiːn] die Routine, der (Tages-/Übungs-)Ablauf
rubber [ˈrʌbə] das Radiergummi 1 (21)
rubbish [ˈrʌbɪʃ] der (Haus-)Müll, der Abfall 4 (106)
rucksack [ˈrʌksæk] der Rucksack (15)
°**rule** [ruːl] die Regel
ruler [ˈruːlə] das Lineal 1 (21)
run [rʌn] rennen, laufen 3 (82)
running [ˈrʌnɪŋ] das Laufen *(Sport)* 3 (82)
°**Russia** [ˈrʌʃə] Russland
°**Russian** [ˈrʌʃn] russisch, Russisch; der Russe, die Russin

S

sad [sæd] traurig 1 (30)
salad [ˈsæləd] der Salat *(als Gericht oder Beilage)* 5 (141)
°**salt** [sɔːlt] das Salz
same [seɪm]: **the same** gleich; derselbe/dieselbe/dasselbe; dieselben 4 (111)
sandwich [ˈsænwɪtʃ], [ˈsænwɪdʒ] das Sandwich 10/11
Saturday [ˈsætədeɪ], [ˈsætədi] der Samstag 1 (25)
sauce [sɔːs] die Soße 5 (134/135)
sausage [ˈsɒsɪdʒ] das (Brat-, Bock-)Würstchen, die Wurst 5 (141)
say [seɪ] sagen 2 (60)
scared [skeəd]: **be scared (of)** Angst haben (vor) 1 (29)
scene [siːn] die Szene 3 (93)
school [skuːl] die Schule 17 **at school** in der Schule 1 (18/19)
school club [ˈskuːl klʌb] die AG *(in der Schule)* 3 (82)
school uniform [skuːl ˈjuːnɪfɔːm] Schuluniform 1 (20)
science [ˈsaɪəns] die Naturwissenschaft 1 (26)
°**scooter** [ˈskuːtə] der (Tret-)Roller
sea [siː] das Meer, die See 3 (82) **by the sea** am Meer, an der See 3 (82)
seagull [ˈsiːgʌl] die Möwe 10/11
°**second** [ˈsekənd] die Sekunde **for 30 seconds** für 30 Sekunden, 30 Sekunden lang

second (2nd) [ˈsekənd] zweite(r, s) 5 (136)
°**secondary school** [ˈsekəndri skuːl] die weiterführende Schule
secret [ˈsiːkrət]:
1. geheim 3 (88)
2. das Geheimnis 3 (88)
see [siː] sehen 12 **See you soon.** Bis bald! 1 (25) **See you.** Bis dann. / Tschüs. 1 (25)
sell [sel] verkaufen 4 (113)
send [send] senden, schicken 3 (90)
°**sentence** [ˈsentəns] der Satz
September [sepˈtembə] der September 5 (136)
seven [ˈsevn] sieben 12
seventeen [sevnˈtiːn] siebzehn 3 (78)
seventy [ˈsevnti] siebzig 3 (78)
shame [ʃeɪm]: **a shame** schade; eine Schande 5 (147) **That's / It's a shame!** Das/Es ist schade! 5 (147) **What a shame!** Wie schade! 5 (147)
share [ʃeə] teilen 3 (90)
sharpener [ˈʃɑːpnə] Anspitzer 1 (21)
she [ʃiː] sie *(weibliche Person)* 1 (24) **she's (= she is)** sie ist 1 (24)
shelf [ʃelf], *pl* **shelves** das Regal 2 (52)
shelves [ʃelvz] *Plural von* **shelf**
shoe [ʃuː] der Schuh 2 (52)
shop [ʃɒp] das Geschäft, der Laden 4 (104/105) **be at the shops** Einkäufe erledigen 4 (104/105)
shopping [ˈʃɒpɪŋ] das Einkaufen; die Einkäufe 3 (80) **do the shopping** die Einkäufe erledigen, einkaufen gehen 3 (80) **go shopping** einkaufen gehen 3 (80)
shopping list [ˈʃɒpɪŋ lɪst] die Einkaufsliste 5 (141)
short [ʃɔːt] kurz; klein *(Person; Körpergröße)* 3 (76/77)
show [ʃəʊ]:
1. die Show, die Aufführung; die Ausstellung 3 (89)
prize show die Preisverleihung *(Zeremonie)* 3 (89)
°**2.** zeigen
shower [ˈʃaʊə] die Dusche 3 (79) **have a shower** (sich) duschen 3 (79)
°**sight** [saɪt] die Sehenswürdigkeit
simple [ˈsɪmpl] einfach 3 (93)
sing [sɪŋ] singen (16)
singer [ˈsɪŋə] der Sänger, die Sängerin (16)
singing [ˈsɪŋɪŋ] das Singen (16)
°**Sir** [sɜː] Anrede für einen Lehrer (GB)
sister [ˈsɪstə] die Schwester 2 (44/45)
sit [sɪt] sitzen; sich setzen 5 (139) **sit down** sich hinsetzen 17
six [sɪks] sechs 12
sixteen [sɪksˈtiːn] sechzehn 3 (78)
sixty [ˈsɪksti] sechzig 3 (78)
skateboard [ˈskeɪtbɔːd]:
1. das Skateboard 4 (104/105)
2. Skateboard fahren 4 (104/105)
skateboarding [ˈskeɪtbɔːdɪŋ] das Skateboardfahren 4 (104/105)

Dictionary English – German

skatepark [ˈskeɪt pɑːk] der Skatepark 3 (87)
°**skating** [ˈskeɪtɪŋ] das Skateboarden; das (Inline-)Skaten
ski [skiː]:
1. der Ski 4 (115)
2. Ski laufen, Ski fahren 4 (115)
go skiing (zum) Skilaufen gehen 4 (115)
°**skill** [skɪl]:
1. die Fähigkeit, die Fertigkeit
2. die Lern- und Arbeitstechnik
°**sky** [skaɪ] der Himmel **in the sky** am Himmel
sleep [sliːp]:
1. der Schlaf 5 (138)
2. schlafen 5 (138)
°**sleep in** ausschlafen
slide [slaɪd] das Dia; die Folie (Präsentationssoftware) 4 (120)
slow [sləʊ] langsam 1 (30)
small [smɔːl] klein 2 (48)
smart [smɑːt]:
1. schick 5 (140)
2. intelligent, clever 5 (140)
snake [sneɪk] die Schlange (14)
snow [snəʊ]:
1. der Schnee 4 (114)
2. schneien 4 (114)
snowy [ˈsnəʊi] schneebedeckt; verschneit 4 (114)
so [səʊ]:
1. so 1 (30)
so weird so seltsam, so komisch 1 (30)
2. also, daher 4 (115)
°3. **and so are we** und (das sind) wir auch
sofa [ˈsəʊfə] das Sofa 2 (52)
some [sʌm], [səm] einige, ein paar; etwas, ein wenig 3 (89)
somebody [ˈsʌmbədi] jemand 4 (117)
someone [ˈsʌmwʌn] jemand 4 (117)
something [ˈsʌmθɪŋ] etwas 4 (113)
sometimes [ˈsʌmtaɪmz] manchmal 3 (79)
son [sʌn] der Sohn 3 (79)
song [sɒŋ] das Lied (13)
°**soon** [suːn] bald
sorry [ˈsɒri]: Sorry. / I'm sorry. Tut mir leid. / Entschuldigung. 1 (22) **be / feel sorry for sb.** Mitleid haben mit jm. 3 (88) **I'm / I feel sorry for him.** Ich habe Mitleid mit ihm. / Er tut mir leid. 3 (88)
°**sound** [saʊnd]:
1. das Geräusch; der Klang, der Laut
2. klingen (sich ... anhören)
°**south** [saʊθ] der Süden; südlich; Süd-
speak (to) [spiːk] sprechen (mit) 2 (56) **Speak later.** Tschüs. / Bis später. 2 (56)
speaking [ˈspiːkɪŋ] das Sprechen 2 (56)
special [ˈspeʃl] besondere(r, s) 2 (48) **... is special** ... ist etwas Besonderes 2 (48) **What's special about this place?** Was ist das Besondere an diesem Ort? 2 (48)
°**speech** [spiːtʃ] die Rede, die Ansprache
°**speech bubble** [ˈspiːtʃ bʌbl] die Sprechblase
spell [spel] buchstabieren 2 (60)
spelling [ˈspelɪŋ] die Schreibweise, die Rechtschreibung 2 (60)
spice [spaɪs] das Gewürz 5 (134/135)
spicy [ˈspaɪsi] würzig 5 (134/135)
°**spoon** [spuːn] der Löffel
sport [spɔːt] der Sport; die Sportart (15)
sports hall [ˈspɔːts hɔːl] die Sporthalle 1 (28)
stadium [ˈsteɪdiəm] das Stadion 4 (110)
°**stand** [stænd] stehen; sich (hin)stellen
stand up [stænd ˈʌp] aufstehen (17)
start [stɑːt]:
1. der Anfang, der Start 1 (22)
2. beginnen, anfangen (mit) 1 (22)
station [ˈsteɪʃn] der Bahnhof 4 (110)
stay [steɪ]:
1. bleiben; übernachten 4 (115)
2. der Aufenthalt 4 (115)
step [step] die Stufe; der Schritt 1 (35)
still [stɪl]:
1. (immer) noch 1 (31)
2. trotzdem 1 (31)
stop [stɒp]:
1. (an)halten; stoppen; aufhören (mit) 1 (31)
2. der Halt, der Haltepunkt; die Unterbrechung 1 (31)
story [ˈstɔːri] die Geschichte (Erzählung) 1 (30)
strawberry [ˈstrɔːbəri] die Erdbeere 5 (134/135)
structure [ˈstrʌktʃə]:
1. strukturieren, aufbauen 4 (120)
2. die Struktur 4 (120)
student [ˈstjuːdnt] der Schüler, die Schülerin / der Student, die Studentin 1 (18/19)
°**study** [ˈstʌdi] lernen (auch z.B. für Prüfungen)
°**study skills** (pl) [ˈstʌdi skɪlz] die Lerntechniken
subject [ˈsʌbdʒɪkt] das (Schul-)Fach 1 (26)
sugar [ˈʃʊgə] der Zucker 5 (141)
summer [ˈsʌmə] der Sommer 4 (112)
sun [sʌn] die Sonne 4 (114)
Sunday [ˈsʌndeɪ], [ˈsʌndi] der Sonntag 1 (25)
sunglasses (pl) [ˈsʌnglɑːsɪz] die Sonnenbrille 5 (139)
sunny [ˈsʌni] sonnig 4 (114) **It's sunny.** Die Sonne scheint. 4 (114)
supermarket [ˈsuːpəmɑːkɪt] der Supermarkt 4 (110)
sure [ʃʊə], [ʃɔː] sicher 5 (140)
surfing [ˈsɜːfɪŋ] das Surfing 3 (83)
surprised [səˈpraɪzd] überrascht 3 (88)
swap [swɒp]:
1. tauschen 4 (115)
2. der Tausch 4 (115)
clothes swap der Kleidertausch, die Kleidertauschparty 4 (115)
sweatshirt [ˈswetʃɜːt] das Sweatshirt 5 (140)
sweet [swiːt]:
1. süß 2 (55)
2. das Bonbon 2 (55)
sweets (pl) [swiːts] die Süßigkeiten 2 (55)
swim [swɪm] schwimmen (15)
swimmer [ˈswɪmə] der Schwimmer, die Schwimmerin (15)
swimming [ˈswɪmɪŋ] das Schwimmen (15)
swimming pool [ˈswɪmɪŋ puːl] das Schwimmbad 4 (107)
°**symbol** [ˈsɪmbl] das Symbol

T

T-shirt [ˈtiː ʃɜːt] das T-Shirt 5 (139)
°**Ta-dah!** [tʌˈdɑː] Tada! / Siehe da!
table [ˈteɪbl]:
1. der Tisch 2 (52)
°2. die Tabelle
table tennis [ˈteɪbl tenɪs] das Tischtennis 3 (82)
take [teɪk]:
1. (mit)nehmen; bringen 1 (22)
take photos Fotos machen (15)
2. dauern, (Zeit) brauchen, in Anspruch nehmen 3 (79)
talk [tɔːk]:
1. **talk (to)** sprechen, reden (mit) 2 (56)
talk about sprechen, reden über 2 (56)
2. das Gespräch; die Rede, der Vortrag 2 (56)
°**task** [tɑːsk] die Aufgabe
tea [tiː] der Tee 5 (145)
°**teach** [tiːtʃ] lehren, unterrichten **teach sb. to do sth.** jm. beibringen, etwas zu tun
teacher [ˈtiːtʃə] der Lehrer, die Lehrerin 1 (22)
team [tiːm] das Team, die Mannschaft 1 (25)
°**teaspoon** [ˈtiːspuːn] der Teelöffel
tech [tek] (infml) siehe **technology**
technology [tekˈnɒlədʒi], infml auch: **tech** die Technik, der Technikunterricht; die Technologie 1 (26)
teeth [tiːθ] Plural von **tooth brush your teeth** (sich) die Zähne putzen 3 (81)
tell [tel] erzählen, sagen 2 (51)
ten [ten] zehn (12)
tennis [ˈtenɪs] Tennis 3 (82)
terrarium [teˈreəriəm] das Terrarium 2 (55)
test [test]:
1. der Test; die Klassenarbeit 1 (34)
2. testen 1 (34)

text [tekst]:
1. der Text 3 (79)
2. die SMS 5 (136)
3. **text sb.** jm. eine SMS schicken 5 (136)

thank you [ˈθæŋk juː] danke (schön) (10/11) **Thank you very much.** Vielen Dank. / Danke vielmals. 3 (90)

thanks [θæŋks] danke (schön) (10/11)

that [ðæt]:
1. das (dort) 1 (30)
that's (= that is) das (da) ist 1 (30)
2. der, die, das *(Relativpronomen)* 4 (118)
things that people can use Dinge, die Menschen gebrauchen/benutzen können 4 (118)

the [ðə] der, die, das (10/11)

their [ðeə] ihr/e *(Plural)* 3 (76/77)

them [ðem], [ðəm] sie, ihnen 1 (35)

then [ðen] dann, danach 1 (30)

there [ðeə] da, dort; dahin, dorthin 2 (50) **there are** es sind ... / es gibt ... 2 (50) **there's (= there is)** es ist ... / es gibt ... 2 (50)

these [ðiːz] diese (hier) 1 (31) **These are my friends.** Das hier sind meine Freunde/Freundinnen. 1 (31)

they [ðeɪ] sie *(Plural)* 1 (20) **they're (= they are)** sie sind 1 (20)

thing [θɪŋ] das Ding, die Sache (12)

think [θɪŋk] denken, meinen, glauben 1 (24) **I think ...** Ich denke/meine/glaube/finde, ... 1 (24) °**think about sth.** nachdenken über °**think of sth.** sich etwas überlegen, ausdenken

third (3rd) [θɜːd] dritte(r, s) 5 (136)

thirteen [θɜːˈtiːn] dreizehn (12)

thirty [ˈθɜːti] dreißig 3 (78)

this [ðɪs] dies; diese(r, s) (15)

°**those** [ðəʊz] die dort, jene (dort)

three [θriː] drei (12)

°**throw** [θrəʊ] werfen

Thursday [ˈθɜːzdeɪ], [ˈθɜːzdi] der Donnerstag 1 (25)

°**tick** [tɪk] ankreuzen, abhaken

ticket [ˈtɪkɪt] die Eintrittskarte, die Fahrkarte, das Ticket 4 (114)

tidy [ˈtaɪdi]:
1. ordentlich 2 (53)
2. aufräumen 2 (53)

tie [taɪ] die Krawatte 1 (20)

°**till** [tɪl] bis

time [taɪm] die Zeit; die Uhrzeit 1 (20) **What's the time?** Wie spät ist es? 3 (78)

timetable [ˈtaɪmteɪbl] der Stundenplan 1 (24)

tired [ˈtaɪəd] müde 1 (20)

title [ˈtaɪtl] der Titel, die Überschrift 4 (120)

to [tuː], [tə]:
1. zu, nach 1 (30)
to sb. an jn. *(z.B. schreiben an jn., eine E-Mail an jn.)* 1 (30) **the answer to the question** die Antwort auf die Frage 1 (23) °**Say hello to ....** Begrüße .... / Begrüßt ....
2. bis 5 (136)
(from) 2 o'clock to 5 o'clock (von) 2 Uhr / 14 Uhr bis 5 Uhr / 17 Uhr 5 (136)
3. (um) zu (12)
how to do sth. wie man etwas tut / tun kann / tun soll 5 (147) **things to eat** Dinge zum Essen (12) °**my favourite thing to do** das, was ich am liebsten tue

°**toad** [təʊd] die Kröte

today [təˈdeɪ] heute 2 (55)

together [təˈgeðə] zusammen 4 (117)

toilet [ˈtɔɪlət] die Toilette 1 (28)

tomato [təˈmɑːtəʊ], *pl* **tomatoes** die Tomate 5 (134/135)

tomato sauce [təˈmɑːtəʊ sɔːs] die Tomatensoße 5 (134/135)

too [tuː]:
1. auch (10/11)
from Berlin too auch aus Berlin (10/11)
2. **too slow** zu langsam 1 (30)

tooth [tuːθ], *pl* **teeth** Zahn 3 (81)

top [tɒp] die Spitze, das obere Ende (16) **top floor** die oberste Etage, der oberste Stock, das oberste Stockwerk 2 (50) **at the top (of)** oben, am oberen Ende (von); an der Spitze (von) (16) **the top five hobbies** die fünf besten/beliebtesten Hobbys (16)

°**topic** [ˈtɒpɪk] das Thema

tour (of) [tʊə] Tour, Reise, Rundgang/Rundfahrt 2 (50)

tour guide [ˈtʊə gaɪd] der Reiseleiter, die Reiseleiterin / der Fremdenführer, die Fremdenführerin 4 (111)

tourist [ˈtʊərɪst] der Tourist, die Touristin 4 (112)

°**tower** [ˈtaʊə] der Turm

town [taʊn] die Stadt 4 (109)

town centre [taʊn ˈsentə] das Stadtzentrum 4 (109)

toy [tɔɪ] das Spielzeug 4 (118)

train [treɪn] der Zug, die Eisenbahn 3 (76/77)

train station [ˈtreɪn steɪʃn] der Bahnhof 4 (110)

trainer [ˈtreɪnə] der Trainer, die Trainerin 3 (90)

trampoline [ˈtræmpəliːn] das Trampolin 3 (82)

trampolining [ˈtræmpəliːnɪŋ] das Trampolinspringen/-turnen 3 (82)

°**transport** *(no pl)* [ˈtrænspɔːt] das Fortbewegungsmittel; die Beförderung

travel [ˈtrævl]:
1. das Reisen 4 (115)
2. reisen, fahren 4 (115)

tree [triː] der Baum 2 (50)

trick [trɪk] der Trick, das Kunststück 5 (140)

trouble [ˈtrʌbl] der Ärger, Schwierigkeiten 1 (30) **be in trouble** Ärger haben, in Schwierigkeiten sein 1 (30)

°**true** [truː] wahr, richtig

Tuesday [ˈtjuːzdeɪ], [ˈtjuːzdi] der Dienstag 1 (25)

°**Turkey** [ˈtɜːki] die Türkei

turn [tɜːn] (sich) (um)drehen 4 (115) **Turn it upside down.** Dreh/Stell es auf den Kopf. 4 (115) **turn sth. (over)** etwas umdrehen 4 (115)

turn [tɜːn]: **it is sb.'s turn (to do sth.)** jd. ist dran / an der Reihe (etwas zu tun) 5 (147) **take turns (to do sth.)** sich abwechseln; sich dabei abwechseln, etwas zu tun 5 (147)

TV [tiːˈviː] der Fernseher; das Fernsehen 3 (79)

twelfth (12th) [twelfθ] zwölfte(r, s) 5 (136)

twelve [twelv] zwölf (12)

twenty [ˈtwenti] zwanzig 3 (78)

two [tuː] zwei (12)

U

°**Ugh!** [ɜː] Bah!

uncle [ˈʌŋkl] der Onkel 2 (44/45)

under [ˈʌndə] unter 2 (53)

°**understand** [ʌndəˈstænd] verstehen

unfriendly [ʌnˈfrendli] unfreundlich 4 (106)

uniform [ˈjuːnɪfɔːm] Uniform 1 (20) **(school) uniform** die (Schul-) Uniform 1 (20)

unit [ˈjuːnɪt] die Unit *(die Lerneinheit)* 1 (18/19)

upside down [ˌʌpsaɪd ˈdaʊn] verkehrt herum, auf dem Kopf 4 (115)

us [ʌs], [əs] uns 1 (22) **It's just us.** Es sind nur wir. 5 (147)

use [juːz] benutzen, verwenden 1 (23)

°**useful** [ˈjuːsfl] nützlich, hilfreich

user [ˈjuːzə] der (Be-)Nutzer, die (Be-)Nutzerin 1 (23)

V

vanilla [vəˈnɪlə] die Vanille 5 (144)

vegetables *(pl)* [ˈvedʒtəblz] das/die Gemüse 5 (134/135)

vegetarian [ˌvedʒəˈteəriən], *infml auch* **veggie**:
1. der/die Vegetarier/in 5 (134/135)
2. vegetarisch 5 (134/135)

veggie [ˈvedʒi] *siehe* **vegetarian**

°**verse** [vɜːs] der Vers, die Strophe *(Lied)*

very [ˈveri] sehr 1 (31)

vet [vet] der Tierarzt, die Tierärztin 2 (46)

video [ˈvɪdiəʊ] das Video; Video- 2 (57)

video game [ˈvɪdiəʊ geɪm] das Videospiel 2 (57)

°**viewing** [ˈvjuːɪŋ] das Fernsehen, das Betrachten *(von DVDs, Filmen usw.)*

village [ˈvɪlɪdʒ] das Dorf 4 (109)

Dictionary — English – German

visit [ˈvɪzɪt]:
1. der Besuch 4 (112)
2. besuchen 4 (112)

visitor [ˈvɪzɪtə] der Besucher, die Besucherin; der Gast 4 (112)

visitor information centre [vɪzɪtə ɪnfəˈmeɪʃn sentə] die Touristeninformation, das Fremdenverkehrsbüro 4 (112)

vocab [ˈvəʊkæb] *siehe* **vocabulary**

vocabulary [vəˈkæbjələri], *infml auch* **vocab** der Wortschatz, das Vokabular; das Vokabelverzeichnis 1 (34)

W

walk [wɔːk]:
1. der Spaziergang 1 (18/19)
2. (zu Fuß) gehen, wandern 1 (18/19)
°**walk around** umhergehen

walking [ˈwɔːkɪŋ] das Wandern 1 (18/19)

°**wall** [wɔːl] die Wand, die Mauer **on the wall** an die Wand; an der Wand

want [wɒnt] wollen 3 (85) **want to do sth.** etwas tun wollen 3 (85)

wardrobe [ˈwɔːdrəʊb] der Kleiderschrank 2 (52)

warm [wɔːm] warm 4 (112)

watch (sth.) [wɒtʃ] (sich etwas) anschauen; (etwas) beobachten 3 (79)

water [ˈwɔːtə] das Wasser 4 (113)

wave (to sb.) [weɪv] (jm. zu)winken 5 (146)

°**way** [weɪ] die Art (und Weise) **in different ways** unterschiedlich *(Adv.)*

we [wiː] wir 1 (24) **we're (= we are)** wir sind 1 (24)

wear [weə] tragen, anhaben *(Kleidung)* 5 (139)

weather [ˈweðə] das Wetter, die Witterung 4 (114)

Wednesday [ˈwenzdeɪ], [ˈwenzdi] der Mittwoch 1 (25)

week [wiːk] die Woche 1 (25) **the days of the week** *(pl)* die Wochentage 1 (25)

weekday [ˈwiːkdeɪ] der Werktag, der Wochentag 3 (78)

weekend [wiːkˈend] das Wochenende 2 (46) **at the weekend** am Wochenende 2 (46) **at weekends** an den Wochenenden *(= an vielen/allen Wochenenden)* 2 (46)

weird [wɪəd] seltsam, komisch 1 (30)

welcome [ˈwelkəm]: **Welcome (to ...)!** Willkommen (in/an ...)! 1 (23) **You're welcome.** Bitte, gern geschehen. / Nichts zu danken. 1 (23)

well [wel]:
1. gut *(Adv.)* 3 (89)
Well done. Gut gemacht! 3 (89)
°2. **Well, ...** Nun, .../ Also, .../ Na ja, ...

what [wɒt]:
1. was (10/11)
2. welche(r, s) 1 (23)
What about a ... ? Wie wäre es mit einer/einem ... ? 5 (143) **What about you?** Und du? / Was ist mit dir? (10/11) **What's your name?** Wie heißt du? (10/11)

wheelchair [ˈwiːltʃeə] der Rollstuhl 3 (79)

when [wen]:
1. wann 2 (46)
2. wenn *(zeitlich)* 1 (32)

where [weə] wo; wohin 1 (28)

which [wɪtʃ] welche(r, s) 3 (89) **Which part(s) ...?** Welcher Teil ...? / Welche Teile ...? 3 (89)

white [waɪt] weiß (10/11)

who [huː] wer 1 (30)

why [waɪ] warum 2 (46)

win [wɪn] gewinnen 3 (79)

wind [wɪnd] der Wind 4 (114)

window [ˈwɪndəʊ] das Fenster 1 (22)

windsurfing [wɪndsɜːfɪŋ] das Windsurfing 3 (82)

windy [ˈwɪndi] windig 4 (114)

winner [ˈwɪnə] der Gewinner, die Gewinnerin / der Sieger, die Siegerin 3 (79)

winter [ˈwɪntə] der Winter 4 (112)

with [wɪð] mit; bei (15)

°**woman** [ˈwʊmən], *pl* **women** die Frau

°**women** [ˈwɪmɪn] *Plural von* **woman**

word [wɜːd] das Wort 1 (23)

°**wordbank** [ˈwɜːdbæŋk] die Wortbank *(die Sammlung von Wörtern zu einem Thema)*

work [wɜːk]:
1. arbeiten; funktionieren 2 (56)
work long days lange arbeiten, lange Arbeitstage haben 3 (79)
2. die Arbeit 2 (56)
at work bei der Arbeit, am Arbeitsplatz 2 (56)

°**workbook** [ˈwɜːkbʊk] das Arbeitsheft

would [wʊd]: **I'd (= I would) like/love ...** Ich hätte (liebend) gern ... / Ich möchte (liebend gern)... 3 (86) **I'd love/like to meet ....** Ich würde mich (liebend) gerne mit ... treffen. 3 (86)

°**Wow!** [waʊ] Wow! / Mensch!

write [raɪt] schreiben 2 (60)

wrong [rɒŋ] falsch (10/11) **be wrong** Unrecht haben 1 (24) °**What's wrong with ...?** Was stimmt nicht mit ...? / Was ist an ... falsch?

Y

°**yeah** [jeə] *(infml)* ja

year [jɪə] das Jahr; der Jahrgang 1 (18/19)

yellow [ˈjeləʊ] gelb (10/11)

yes [jes] ja 1 (22)

yoga [ˈjəʊgə] das Yoga 1 (18/19)

you [juː] du; dich; dir; ihr; euch; Sie; Ihnen (10/11)

your [jɔː], [jə] dein/e; euer/eure; Ihr/e (10/11)

°**yourself** [jəˈself] du/dir/dich (selbst)

youth [juːθ] die Jugend; der Jugendliche 4 (106)

youth centre [ˈjuːθ sentə] das Jugendzentrum 4 (106)

°**Yuck!** [jʌk] Igitt!

°**yum** [jʌm] *(infml)* lecker

Z

°**zoo** [zuː] der Zoo

German – English Dictionary

Das *German-English Dictionary* enthält den **Lernwortschatz** deines Schulbuchs. Es kann dir eine erste Hilfe sein, wenn du vergessen hast, wie etwas auf Englisch heißt.
Wenn du wissen möchtest, wo das englische Wort zum ersten Mal in deinem Schulbuch vorkommt, dann kannst du im *English-German Dictionary* (Seiten 236–246) nachschlagen.

Es werden folgende **Abkürzungen und Symbole** verwendet:

infml = informal (umgangssprachlich)   pl = plural (Mehrzahl)
sb. = somebody (jemand)   sth. = something (etwas)
jd. = jemand   jm. = jemandem   jn. = jemanden

A

Abend evening [ˈiːvnɪŋ] **am Abend** in the evening
Abendessen dinner [ˈdɪnə] **zum Abendessen** for dinner
abends in the evening [ˈiːvnɪŋ] **9 Uhr abends** (21 Uhr) 9 p.m. [piːˈem]
aber but [bʌt], [bət]
A bis Z: (von) A bis Z (from) A to Z [eɪ tu zed]
Abfall rubbish [ˈrʌbɪʃ]
abwechseln: sich abwechseln take turns [tɜːn] **sich dabei abwechseln, etwas zu tun** take it in turns (to do sth.)
acht eight [eɪt]
achtzehn eighteen [eɪˈtiːn]
achtzig eighty [ˈeɪti]
addieren add [æd]
Adresse address [əˈdres]
Affe monkey [ˈmʌŋki]
AG *(in der Schule)* school club [skuːl klʌb]
aktiv active [ˈæktɪv]
Aktivität activity [ækˈtɪvəti]
albern stupid [ˈstjuːpɪd]
alle(s) all [ɔːl] **alle 30 Minuten** every 30 minutes [ˈevri]
allein alone [əˈləʊn]
allergisch (gegen) allergic (to) [əˈlɜːdʒɪk]
Alphabet alphabet [ˈælfəbet]
also so [səʊ] **Also, ...** Well, ... [wel]
alt old [əʊld] **Wie alt bist du?** How old are you?
am: am Anfang at first [æt], [ət] **am Arbeitsplatz** at work **am besten** best [best] **am Ende (von)** at the end (of) **am größten** biggest [ˈbɪɡɪst] **am Meer** by the sea [baɪ] **am Montag** on Monday [ɒn] **am Morgen** in the morning [ɪn] **am Nachmittag** in the afternoon **am nächsten Tag** the next day **am oberen Ende (von)** at the top (of) **am Strand** on the beach **am Telefon** on the phone **am Wochenende** at the weekend
an at [æt], [ət]
anbraten: *(Gemüse- oder Fleischstücke)* **unter Rühren scharf anbraten** stir-fry [ˈstɜː fraɪ]
andere(r, s) other [ˈʌðə] **die anderen** the other **ein/e andere(r, s)** another [əˈnʌðə]
anders different [ˈdɪfrənt]
Anfang start [stɑːt] **am Anfang** at first [æt], [ət]
anfangen (mit) start [stɑːt]
Angst: Angst haben be scared (of) [skeəd]
anhaben *(Kleidung)* wear [weə]
anhalten stop [stɒp]
anhören: sich etwas anhören listen to sth. [ˈlɪsn]
anlächeln: jn. anlächeln smile at sb. [smaɪl]
Anruf (phone) call [ˈfəʊn kɔːl]
anrufen call [kɔːl]; phone [fəʊn]
anschauen: etwas/jn. anschauen look at sth./sb. [lʊk] **sich etwas anschauen** watch sth. [wɒtʃ]
Anspitzer sharpener [ˈʃɑːpnə]
Anteil share [ʃeə]
Antwort answer [ˈɑːnsə] **Antwort auf die Frage** the answer to the question
antworten answer [ˈɑːnsə]
Anweisung instruction [ɪnˈstrʌkʃn]
anziehen: sich anziehen get dressed [drest]
App app [æp]
Appetit: Guten Appetit! Enjoy! [ɪnˈdʒɔɪ]
April April [ˈeɪprəl]
Arbeit work [wɜːk] **bei der Arbeit, am Arbeitsplatz** at work
arbeiten work [wɜːk] **lange arbeiten** work long days [lɒŋ]
Ärger trouble [ˈtrʌbl] **Ärger kriegen** be in trouble
Art way [weɪ] **auf diese Art** (in) this way, like this [laɪk] **auf unterschiedliche Art** in different ways **eine Art (von) ...** a kind (of) ... [kaɪnd], sort (of) [sɔːt]
Artikel article [ˈɑːtɪkl]
auch also [ˈɔːlsəʊ]; too [tuː] **auch aus Berlin** from Berlin too
auf at [æt], [ət]; in [ɪn]; on [ɒn] **auf dem Bild, auf dem Foto** in the picture **auf dem Kopf** upside down [ʌpsaɪd ˈdaʊn] **auf dem Land** in the country **auf der Weide** in the field **auf Englisch** in English **Auf Wiedersehen!** Goodbye. [ɡʊdˈbaɪ]
Aufführung show [ʃəʊ]
Aufgabe exercise [ˈeksəsaɪz]
aufhören (mit) stop [stɒp]
auflisten list [lɪst]
aufpassen auf look after [lʊk]
aufräumen tidy [ˈtaɪdi] **etwas aufräumen** clean sth. up [kliːn]
aufschlagen *(Buch)* open [ˈəʊpən] **Schlagt eure Bücher auf Seite 10 auf.** Open your books at page 10.
aufstehen *(aus dem Bett)* get up [ɡet ˈʌp]; *(sich hinstellen)* stand up [stænd ˈʌp]
August August [ɔːˈɡʌst]
aus from [frɒm]
Ausdruck phrase [freɪz]
ausruhen: sich ausruhen relax [rɪˈlæks]
aussehen look [lʊk]
außerhalb (von) outside [ˌaʊtˈsaɪd]
Ausstellung show [ʃəʊ]
auswählen choose [tʃuːz]
Auto car [kɑː]
Autoscheinwerfer car light [ˈkɑː laɪt]

B

backen bake [beɪk]
Backofen oven [ˈʌvn]
Backpulver baking powder [ˈbeɪkɪŋ paʊdə]
Bad(ezimmer) bathroom [ˈbɑːθruːm]
Badminton badminton [ˈbædmɪntən]
Bahnhof (train) station [ˈtreɪn steɪʃn]
bald soon [suːn]
Balkon balcony [ˈbælkəni]
Ball ball [bɔːl]
Ballon balloon [bəˈluːn]
Banane banana [bəˈnɑːnə]
Band band [bænd]
Basketball basketball [ˈbɑːskɪtbɔːl]
Basteln crafts (pl) [krɑːfts]
Baum tree [triː]
beantworten answer [ˈɑːnsə]
bedeuten mean [miːn]
Bedeutung meaning [ˈmiːnɪŋ]
beenden end [end]
beginnen start [stɑːt]
Behälter case [keɪs]
bei at [æt], [ət]; with [wɪð] **bei der Arbeit** at work **bei ihrer Mutter (zu Hause/daheim)** at her mum's (house)
beibringen: jm. beibringen, etwas zu tun teach sb. to do sth. [tiːtʃ]
Beispiel example [ɪɡˈzɑːmpl] **zum Beispiel** for example **wie zum Beispiel** like [laɪk]
bekommen get [ɡet]
belebt busy [ˈbɪzi]
bellen: (jn. an)bellen bark (at sb.) [bɑːk]

Dictionary

German – English

benutzen use [juːz]
Benutzer/in user [ˈjuːzə]
beobachten: (etwas) beobachten watch (sth.) [wɒtʃ]
bereit ready [ˈredi]
beschäftigt: (viel) beschäftigt busy [ˈbɪzi] **du bist beschäftigt** you're busy
beschreiben describe [dɪˈskraɪb]
Beschreibung description [dɪˈskrɪpʃn]
besondere(r, s) special [ˈspeʃl]
besorgen: (sich etwas) besorgen get sth. [get]
beste(r, s) best [best] **der beste Sohn überhaupt / der beste Sohn, den man sich wünschen kann** the best son ever [ˈevə]
Besuch visit [ˈvɪzɪt]
besuchen visit [ˈvɪzɪt]
Besucher/in visitor [ˈvɪzɪtə]
Bett bed [bed] **ins Bett gehen** go to bed
bevor before [bɪˈfɔː] **bevor du liest** before you read
bewegen: sich bewegen move [muːv]
bewölkt cloudy [ˈklaʊdi]
Bibliothek library [ˈlaɪbrəri]
Bild picture [ˈpɪktʃə] **auf dem Bild** in the picture [ɪn]
Bildschirmpräsentation slide show [ˈslaɪd ʃəʊ]
Biologie biology [baɪˈɒlədʒi]
bis to [tu], [tə] **Bis bald!** See you soon. [ˈsiː juː], [ˈsiː jə] **Bis dann.** See you. **Bis später.** Speak later. [ˈleɪtə]
bisschen: ein bisschen a little [ˈlɪtl]
bitte please [pliːz] **Bitte schön. / Hier, bitte.** Here you are. [hɪə ju ˈɑː] **Bitte, gern geschehen.** You're welcome. [ˈwelkəm]
bitten: jn. bitten, etwas zu tun ask sb. to do sth. [ɑːsk] **jn. um etwas bitten** ask sb. for sth.
blau blue [bluː]
Blazer (das Jackett, oft Teil der Schuluniform) blazer [ˈbleɪzə]
Bleistift pencil [ˈpensl]
Bleistift(an)spitzer pencil sharpener [ˈpensl ˈʃɑːpnə]
Blindenhund guide dog [ˈgaɪd dɒg]
blöd stupid [ˈstjuːpɪd]
bloß just [dʒʌst]; only [ˈəʊnli]
Bockwurst sausage [ˈsɒsɪdʒ]
Boden ground [graʊnd]
Bonbon sweet [swiːt]
Bowling bowling [ˈbəʊlɪŋ]
Boxen boxing [ˈbɒksɪŋ]
boxen box [bɒks]
braten fry [fraɪ] **gebraten** fried [fraɪd]
Brathähnchen chicken [ˈtʃɪkɪn]
Bratwurst sausage [ˈsɒsɪdʒ]
brauchen need [niːd]; (Zeit) take [teɪk]
braun brown [braʊn]
brav good [gʊd]
Brief letter [ˈletə] **der kurze Brief** note [nəʊt]

bringen bring [brɪŋ]; take [teɪk]
britisch British [ˈbrɪtɪʃ]
Brot bread [bred]
Browser (Computerprogramm zum Finden und Lesen von Websites) browser [ˈbraʊzə]
Bruder brother [ˈbrʌðə]
Buch book [bʊk]
Buchseite page (p.) [peɪdʒ]
Bücherei library [ˈlaɪbrəri]
Buchstabe letter [ˈletə]
buchstabieren spell [spel]
Bürste brush [brʌʃ]
bürsten brush [brʌʃ]
Bus bus [bʌs] **im Bus** on the bus **mit dem Bus** by bus
Bushaltestelle bus stop [ˈbʌs stɒp]
Butter butter [ˈbʌtə]

C

Café cafe [ˈkæfeɪ]
Cent cent [sent]
Chaos mess [mes]
clever smart [smɑːt]
Code code [kəʊd]
codieren code [kəʊd]
Cola cola [ˈkəʊlə]
Comic comic [ˈkɒmɪk]
Computer computer [kəmˈpjuːtə]
cool cool [kuːl]
Cousin/e cousin [ˈkʌzn]
Cricket (Mannschaftssportart) cricket [ˈkrɪkɪt]
Curry (Gewürz und auch Gericht) curry [ˈkʌri]
Custard (Vanillesoße) custard [ˈkʌstəd]

D

da there [ðeə] **da drüben** over there
Dachgeschoss top floor [tɒp ˈflɔː]
daher so [səʊ]
dahin there [ðeə]
damit so that [səʊ ðæt]
danach then [ðen]
Dank: Vielen Dank. Thank you very much. [ˈθæŋk juː]
Danke(schön). Thank you. [ˈθæŋk juː]; thanks [θæŋks] **Danke vielmals.** Thank you very much. [mʌtʃ]
danken: Nichts zu danken. You're welcome. [ˈwelkʌm]
dann then [ðen]
das
  1. (Artikel) the [ðə]
  2. (Relativpronomen) that [ðæt]
das (dort) that [ðæt] **das (da)** that's (= that is)
dasselbe the same [seɪm]
Datei file [faɪl]
Datum date [deɪt] **Datum des Geburtstags** birthday date [ˈbɜːθdeɪ]
dauern take [teɪk]
dein/e your [jɔː], [jə]
dekorieren decorate [ˈdekəreɪt]

denken think [θɪŋk] **daran denken (etwas zu tun)** remember (to do sth.) [rɪˈmembə] **Ich denke, …** I think …
der
  1. (Artikel) the [ðə]
  2. (Relativpronomen) that [ðæt]
derselbe the same [seɪm]
Design design [dɪˈzaɪn]
Dessert dessert [dɪˈzɜːt]
deutlich clear [klɪə] **deutlich sprechen** speak clearly [spiːk ˈklɪəli]
Deutsch; deutsch German [ˈdʒɜːmən]
Deutsche German [ˈdʒɜːmən]
Deutschland Germany [ˈdʒɜːməni]
Dezember December [dɪˈsembə]
die
  1. (Artikel) the [ðə]
  2. (Relativpronomen) that [ðæt]
die dort those [ðəʊz]
Diele hall [hɔːl]
Dienstag Tuesday [ˈtjuːzdeɪ]
diese (hier) these [ðiːz]
diese(r, s) this [ðɪs]
dieselbe(n) the same [seɪm]
Ding: Dinge, die Menschen gebrauchen/benutzen können things that people can use [θɪŋ] **Dinge zum Essen** things to eat
Donnerstag Thursday [ˈθɜːzdeɪ]
Dorf village [ˈvɪlɪdʒ]
dort there [ðeə] **dort drüben** over there [ˈəʊvə]
dorthin there [ðeə]
dran: jd. ist dran it is sb.'s turn [tɜːn] **Wann bin ich dran (etwas zu tun)?** When is (it) my turn (to do sth.)?
draußen; nach draußen outside [aʊtˈsaɪd]
Dreck-weg-Tag (Aktionstag zum Müllsammeln) clean-up day [ˈkliːn ʌp deɪ]
drehen turn [tɜːn] **Dreh etwas auf den Kopf.** Turn it upside down. [ˈʌpsaɪd ˈdaʊn] **etwas umdrehen** turn sth. (over)
drei three [θriː]
dreißig thirty [ˈθɜːti]
dreizehn thirteen [θɜːˈtiːn]
drinnen; nach drinnen inside [ɪnˈsaɪd]
dritte(r, s) third (3rd) [θɜːd]
Drohne drone [drəʊn]
du you [juː] **du bist** you're (= you are) [jɔː] **du bist beschäftigt** you're busy [ˈbɪzi]
dumm stupid [ˈstjuːpɪd]
Dusche shower [ˈʃaʊə]
duschen: (sich) duschen have a shower [ˈʃaʊə]

E

Ehemann husband [ˈhʌzbənd]
Ei egg [eg]
Eidechse lizard [ˈlɪzəd]
eigene(r, s): mein/ein eigenes Zimmer my own room [əʊn]

Eimer *(Mülleimer)* bin [bɪn]
ein(e) *(Artikel)* a [ə]; *(vor Vokalen)* an [ən] **ein paar** some [sʌm], [səm] **ein wenig** some; a little [ˈlɪtl] **noch ein(e)** another [əˈnʌðə]
einfach just [dʒʌst]
Einführung introduction [ɪntrəˈdʌkʃn]
einige some [sʌm], [səm]
Einkäufe shopping [ˈʃɒpɪŋ] **Einkäufe erledigen** do the shopping, be at the shops [ʃɒp]
Einkaufen shopping [ˈʃɒpɪŋ]
einkaufen gehen do the shopping [ˈʃɒpɪŋ]; go shopping
Einkaufsliste shopping list [ˈʃɒpɪŋ lɪst]
Einkaufszentrum shopping centre [ˈʃɒpɪŋ sentə]
Einladung (zu, nach) invitation (to) [ˌɪnvɪˈteɪʃn]
Einleitung introduction [ɪntrəˈdʌkʃn]
einmal: noch einmal again [əˈgen]
eins one [wʌn]
einsammeln collect [kəˈlekt]
Eintrittskarte ticket [ˈtɪkɪt]
Eisenbahn train [treɪn]
Elefant elephant [ˈelɪfənt]
elektrisch, Elektro- electric [ɪˈlektrɪk]
elf eleven [ɪˈlevn]
Eltern parents *(pl)* [ˈpeərənts]
Ende end [end] **das obere Ende** top [tɒp] **am oberen Ende** at the top (of)
enden end [end]
England England [ˈɪŋglənd]
Englisch; englisch English [ˈɪŋglɪʃ] **auf Englisch** in English [ɪn]
Enkel grandson [ˈgrænsʌn]
Enkelin granddaughter [ˈgrændɔːtə]
Entschuldigung. Sorry / I'm sorry. [ˈsɒri] **Entschuldigung, ... / Entschuldigen Sie, ...** Excuse me, ... [ɪkˈskjuːz miː]
entspannen: sich entspannen relax [rɪˈlæks]
er he [hiː] **er ist** he's (= he is) **er ist nicht** he isn't (= is not)
Erbse pea [piː]
Erdbeere strawberry [ˈstrɔːbəri]
Erdboden ground [graʊnd]
Erdgeschoss ground floor [graʊnd ˈflɔː]
Erdkunde geography [dʒiˈɒgrəfi]
erforschen research [rɪˈsɜːtʃ]
Erholung rest [rest]
erinnern: sich erinnern an remember [rɪˈmembə] **sich daran erinnern, etwas getan zu haben** remember doing sth.
erklären: jm. etwas erklären explain sth. to sb. [ɪkˈspleɪn]
erst only [ˈəʊnli]
erstaunlich amazing [əˈmeɪzɪŋ]
erste(r, s) first [fɜːst] **als Erstes** first
erzählen tell [tel]
es it [ɪt] **es ist** *(bei Sachen und Tieren auch: er ist; sie ist)* it's (= it is) **es ist ... / es gibt ...** there's [ðeəz] **es sind ... / es gibt ...** there are [ˈðeər ɑː]

Essen cooking [ˈkʊkɪŋ]; food [fuːd]; meal [miːl]
essen eat [iːt] **Dinge zum Essen** things to eat
Esslöffel tablespoon [ˈteɪblspuːn]
Esszimmer dining room [ˈdaɪnɪŋ ruːm]
Etage floor [flɔː] **die oberste Etage** top floor [tɒp ˈflɔː]
Etui case [keɪs]
etwas some [sʌm], [səm]; something [ˈsʌmθɪŋ]
euer/eure your [jɔː], [jə]
Euro euro, *pl* euros [ˈjʊərəʊ]

F

Fach subject [ˈsʌbdʒɪkt]
Fähigkeit skill [skɪl]
fahren go [gəʊ]; travel [ˈtrævl] **mit dem Fahrrad fahren** ride a bike [raɪd] **Rad fahren** cycle [ˈsaɪkl] **Skateboard fahren** skateboard [ˈskeɪtbɔːd]
Fahrkarte ticket [ˈtɪkɪt]
Fahrrad bike [baɪk]
Fahrt journey [ˈdʒɜːni]
Fakt fact [fækt]
falls if [ɪf]
falsch wrong [rɒŋ]
Familie family [ˈfæməli]
Familienname family name [ˈfæməli neɪm]
Fan fan [fæn]
Farbe colour [ˈkʌlə] **Welche Farbe hat ...?** What colour is ...?
Favorit/in favourite [ˈfeɪvərɪt]
Februar February [ˈfebruəri]
Federball badminton [ˈbædmɪntən]
Federmäppchen pencil case [ˈpensl keɪs]
Feedback *(Rückmeldung)* feedback *(no pl)* [ˈfiːdbæk]
Feier ceremony [ˈserəməni]
Feld field [fiːld]
Fenster window [ˈwɪndəʊ]
Ferien holidays *(pl)* [ˈhɒlədeɪz]
Fernsehen, Fernseher TV [ˌtiːˈviː]
fertig ready [ˈredi]
Fertigkeit skill [skɪl]
fies mean [miːn]
Film film [fɪlm] **die sechs besten Filme** the top six films [tɒp]
Filmstar star [stɑː]
finden find [faɪnd] **Ich finde, ...** I think ... [θɪŋk]
Finger finger [ˈfɪŋgə]
Fisch fish, *pl* fish [fɪʃ] **Fisch mit Pommes frites** fish and chips [fɪʃ ən ˈtʃɪps] **Imbissstube, die Fisch mit Pommes frites verkauft** fish and chip shop [ʃɒp]
Fleisch meat [miːt]
fliegen fly [flaɪ]
Flur hall [hɔːl]
Forschungen research [rɪˈsɜːtʃ]
fort away [əˈweɪ]
fortfahren continue [kənˈtɪnjuː] **etwas fortfahren** continue to do sth. [duː]

fortsetzen: (sich) fortsetzen continue [kənˈtɪnjuː]
Foto photo [ˈfəʊtəʊ] **auf dem Foto** in the photo **ein Foto machen** take a photo
Fotograf/in photographer [fəˈtɒgrəfə]
Frage question [kwestʃən] **Antwort auf die Frage** the answer to the question [ˈɑːnsə] **eine Frage stellen** ask a question **Habt ihr / Hast du (irgendwelche) Fragen?** Do you have any questions?
fragen ask [ɑːsk]
Frau woman, *pl* women [ˈwʊmən], [ˈwɪmɪn] **Frau Lee** *(Anrede für verheiratete Frauen)* Mrs Lee [ˈmɪsɪz] *(allgemeine Anrede für Frauen)* Ms Lee [mɪz]
frech rude [ruːd]
frei free [friː] **freie Zeit** free time [taɪm]
Freitag Friday [ˈfraɪdeɪ], [ˈfraɪdi]
Freizeit free time [ˈfriː taɪm]
Fremdenverkehrsbüro tourist information centre [tʊərɪst ɪnfəˈmeɪʃn sentə]
fressen eat [iːt]
freuen: Freut mich, dich/euch/ Sie kennenzulernen. Nice to meet you. [naɪs]
Freund/in friend [frend] **Das hier sind meine Freunde/Freundinnen.** These are my friends. [ðiːz] **ihre Freunde/Freundinnen** her friends [hɜː], [hə] **seine Freunde/Freundinnen** his friends [hɪz]
freundlich friendly [ˈfrendli]; kind [kaɪnd]
frieren be cold [kəʊld]
frittieren fry [fraɪ] **frittiert** fried [fraɪd]
froh happy [ˈhæpi]
Frühling spring [sprɪŋ]
Frühstück breakfast [ˈbrekfəst]
fühlen: sich fühlen feel [fiːl]
Füller pen [pen]
für for [fɔː] **für 30 Sekunden** for 30 seconds
fünf five [faɪv]
fünfzehn fifteen [fɪfˈtiːn]
fünfzig fifty [ˈfɪfti]
Fußball football [ˈfʊtbɔːl]
Fußboden floor [flɔː]
Futter food [fuːd]

G

ganz quite [kwaɪt] **ganz (still)** perfectly (still) [ˈpɜːfɪktli]
Garage garage [ˈgærɑːʒ]
Garten garden [ˈgɑːdn]
Gast visitor [ˈvɪzɪtə]
Gebäude building [ˈbɪldɪŋ]
geben give [gɪv] **es gibt ...** there's (= there is) ... [ðeəz]; there are ... [ˈðeər ɑː] **es gibt keine ...** there aren't any ... [ˈeni] **Was gibt es zum Mittagessen?** What's for lunch? [lʌntʃ]

Dictionary

German – English

Geburtstag birthday [ˈbɜːθdeɪ] **an meinem Geburtstag** on my birthday **Datum des Geburtstags** birthday date [deɪt] **Herzlichen Glückwunsch zum Geburtstag!** Happy birthday! [ˈhæpi] **Ich habe im April Geburtstag.** My birthday is in April. **Wann hast du Geburtstag?** When's your birthday?
Gedankenkarte mind map [ˈmaɪnd mæp]
Gegend: ländliche Gegend country [ˈkʌntri]
geheim secret [ˈsiːkrət]
Geheimnis secret [ˈsiːkrət]
gehen go [gəʊ] **ins Bett gehen** go to bed [bed] **nach Hause gehen** go home [həʊm] **Wie geht's? / Wie geht es dir / euch / Ihnen?** How are you? [haʊ] **(zu Fuß) gehen** walk [wɔːk]
gelb yellow [ˈjeləʊ]
Geld money [ˈmʌni]
Gelee jelly [ˈdʒeli]
gemein mean [miːn]
Gemüse vegetables (pl) [ˈvedʒtəblz]
genießen enjoy [ɪnˈdʒɔɪ] **es genießen, etwas zu tun** enjoy doing sth.
Geografie geography [dʒiˈɒgrəfi]
Geräusch noise [nɔɪz]
Gericht (Mahlzeit) dish [dɪʃ] das Gericht aus unter Rühren kurz angebratenen Zutaten, z. B. kleine Stücke Fleisch, Fisch und/oder Gemüse stir-fry [ˈstɜː fraɪ]
gern: ich hätte gern ... I'd (= I would) like ... [laɪk] **Ich hätte liebend gern ... / Ich möchte liebend gern...** I'd (= I would) love ... [lʌv] **Ich würde mich (liebend) gerne mit ... treffen.** I'd (= I would) like/love to meet ...
Geruch smell [smel]
Geschäft shop [ʃɒp]
geschehen: (jm.) geschehen happen (to sb.) [ˈhæpən] **Bitte, gern geschehen.** You're welcome. [ˈwelkʌm]
Geschenk present [ˈpreznt]
Geschichte (Erzählung) story [ˈstɔːri]; (vergangene Zeiten) history [ˈhɪstri] **so/solch eine Geschichte** a story like this [laɪk]
Gespräch talk [tɔːk]
Gestaltung design [dɪˈzaɪn]
Gestank smell [smel]
gesund healthy [ˈhelθi]
Gesundheit health [helθ]
Getränk drink [drɪŋk]
Gewerbegebiet estate [ɪˈsteɪt]
Gewinn prize [praɪz]
gewinnen win [wɪn]
Gewinner/in winner [ˈwɪnə] **als Gewinner/in** as the winner
Gewürz spice [spaɪs]
Gitarre guitar [gɪˈtɑː]
Glasur icing [ˈaɪsɪŋ]
glauben think [θɪŋk] **Ich glaube, ...** I think ...

gleich the same [seɪm]
Glück: Glücks-, lucky [ˈlʌki] **Glück haben** be lucky
glücklich happy [ˈhæpi]; lucky [ˈlʌki]
Glückszahl lucky number [lʌki ˈnʌmbə]
Gold gold [gəʊld]
goldfarben gold [gəʊld]
graben dig [dɪg]
Gramm gram (g) [græm]
Grad degree [dɪˈgriː]
grau grey [greɪ]
Grillen barbecue [ˈbɑːbɪkjuː]
Grillfest barbecue [ˈbɑːbɪkjuː]
groß big [bɪg] **der/die/das größte, am größten** biggest
großartig amazing [əˈmeɪzɪŋ]; great [greɪt]
Großbritannien (Great) Britain [ˈbrɪtn]
Großeltern grandparents (pl) [ˈgrænpeərənts]
Großstadt city [ˈsɪti]
grün green [griːn] **grün/umweltfreundlich werden** go green [gəʊ]
Gruppe group [gruːp]
gut good [gʊd]; (Adv.) well [wel] **Es geht mir gut.** I'm OK. [əʊˈkeɪ] **etwas gut können; gut in etwas sein** be good at sth. / at doing sth. **Guten Appetit!** Enjoy! [ɪnˈdʒɔɪ] **Gut gemacht!** Well done. [dʌn] **gut umgehen können mit ...** be good with ... **Mir geht es gut.** I'm fine. [faɪn] **so gut** so good [səʊ]

H

haben have [hæv] **er/sie/es hat** he/she/it has [hæz], [həz]
Hähnchen chicken [ˈtʃɪkɪn]
Halle hall [hɔːl]
Hallo. Hello. [həˈləʊ]; Hi. [haɪ] **Hallo allerseits!** Hello everybody! [ˈevribɒdi]
halten stop [stɒp]
Hamburger (Frikadelle) burger [ˈbɜːgə]
Hamster hamster [ˈhæmstə]
Hand hand [hænd] **Hand / Hände hochstrecken** put your hand / hands up [pʊt]
Handy phone [fəʊn]
hart hard [hɑːd]
Hass hate [heɪt]
hassen hate [heɪt]
Haupt- main [meɪn]
Hauptgericht main course [ˈkɔːs]; main dish [dɪʃ]
Haus house [haʊs] **nach Hause gehen** go home [həʊm] **im Haus** inside the house [ɪnˈsaɪd] **wieder zu Hause** back at home [bæk] **zu Hause** at home
Hausaufgabe(n) homework [ˈhəʊmwɜːk] **Hausaufgaben machen** do your homework **Was haben wir als Hausaufgabe(n) auf?** What's for homework? [wɒts fɔː]

Hausmüll rubbish [ˈrʌbɪʃ]
Haustier pet [pet]
heben lift [lɪft]
Heftseite page (p.) [peɪdʒ]
Heim home [həʊm]
heiß hot [hɒt] **heiße (Trink-) Schokolode** hot chocolate [ˈtʃɒklət]
heißen: Wie heißt du? What's your name? [wɒts jɔː ˈneɪm]
hektisch busy [ˈbɪzi]
helfen help [help]
herausfinden find out (about) [ˌfaɪnd ˈaʊt]
Herbst autumn [ˈɔːtəm]
Herr Lee Mr Lee [ˈmɪstə]
herstellen make [meɪk]
herunter down [daʊn]
hervorheben highlight [ˈhaɪlaɪt]
Herzog duke [djuːk]
heute today [təˈdeɪ]
hier here [hɪə] **Hier, bitte.** Here you are. **hier herüber; hier drüben** over here [ˈəʊvə]
hierher here [hɪə]
Highlight (Höhepunkt) highlight [ˈhaɪlaɪt]
Hilfe help [help]
hilfreich helpful [ˈhelpfl]; useful [ˈjuːsfl]
hilfsbereit helpful [ˈhelpfl]
hinauf up [ʌp]
hinsetzen: sich hinsetzen sit down [sɪt ˈdaʊn]
hinter behind [bɪˈhaɪnd]
hinunter down [daʊn]
hinzufügen add [æd]
Hobby hobby [ˈhɒbi]
hoch up [ʌp]
Hockey hockey [ˈhɒki]
höflich polite [pəˈlaɪt]
holen: (sich etwas) holen get sth. [get]
Honig honey [ˈhʌni]
hören hear [hɪə]
Hotdog (heißes Würstchen in einem Brötchen) hot dog [ˈhɒt dɒg]
Huhn chicken [ˈtʃɪkɪn]
Hund dog [dɒg]
Hunger: Ich habe Hunger. I'm hungry. [ˈhʌŋgri]
hungrig hungry [ˈhʌŋgri]
Hut hat [hæt]

I

ich I [aɪ] **Ich bin** I'm (= I am) [æm] **Ich bin's.** It's me. **Ich nicht!** (= Ich bin/war/habe/... es/das nicht!) Not me! [nɒt]
Idee idea [aɪˈdɪə]
ihm, ihn him [hɪm]
Ihnen (höfliche Anrede) you [juː]
ihnen them [ðem], [ðəm]
ihr (Plural von „du") you [juː] **ihr seid** you're (= you are) [ɑː]
Ihr/e ... (besitzanzeigend zur höflichen Anrede „Sie") your [jɔː], [jə]

ihr/e ... (vor Nomen; besitzanzeigend)
  1. (zu „she") her ... [hɜː, hə]
  2. (zu „it") its ... [ɪts]
  3. (zu „they") their ... [ðeə]
immer always [ˈɔːlweɪz]
immer noch still [stɪl]
in at [æt], [ət]; in [ɪn] **in den Urlaub** on holiday [ˈhɒlədeɪ] **in der Nähe von** near [nɪə] **in der Schule** at school [skuːl] **in der Stadt** in town [taʊn]
Indien India [ˈɪndiə]
Informatik computing [kəmˈpjuːtɪŋ]
Information information [ɪnfəˈmeɪʃn]
informieren: sich informieren (über) find out (about) [ˌfaɪnd ˈaʊt]
innen; nach innen inside [ɪnˈsaɪd]
innerhalb (von) inside [ˌɪnˈsaɪd]
intelligent smart [smɑːt]
interessant interesting [ˈɪntrəstɪŋ]
Internet internet [ˈɪntənet]

J

Ja. Yes. [jes] **Na ja, ...** Well, ... [wel]
Jachthafen marina [məˈriːnə]
Jahr year [jɪə] **Ich bin elf Jahre alt.** I'm eleven years old. [jɪəz]
Jahreszeit season [ˈsiːzn]
Jahrgang year [jɪə]
Januar January [ˈdʒænjuəri]
jede(r, s) every [ˈevri] **jede(r, s) einzelne** each [iːtʃ]
jeder everybody [ˈevribɒdi]
jemand somebody [ˈsʌmbədi]; someone [ˈsʌmwʌn]
jene (dort) those [ðəʊz]
jetzt now [naʊ]
jeweils each [iːtʃ]
jonglieren juggle [ˈdʒʌgl]
Jugend youth [juːθ]
Jugendliche kid [kɪd]; youth [juːθ]
Jugendzentrum youth centre [ˈjuːθ sentə]
Juli July [dʒuˈlaɪ]
Junge boy [bɔɪ] **Ich bin kein Junge.** I'm not a boy. [nɒt]
Juni June [dʒuːn]

K

Kaffee coffee [ˈkɒfi]
Kakao cocoa [ˈkəʊkəʊ]; hot chocolate [hɒt ˈtʃɒklət]
kalt cold [kəʊld] **kalt werden** get cold [get]
Kälte cold [kəʊld]
Kaninchen rabbit [ˈræbɪt]
Kantine canteen [kænˈtiːn]
Kappe cap [kæp]
Karaoke karaoke [kæriˈəʊki]
Karotte carrot [ˈkærət]
Karte card [kɑːd]
Kartoffel potato, pl potatoes [pəˈteɪtəʊ]
Käse cheese [tʃiːz]
Kasten case [keɪs]
Katze cat [kæt]
kaufen buy [baɪ]

Kebab kebab [kɪˈbæb]
Kegeln bowling [ˈbəʊlɪŋ]
kein/e no [nəʊ] **es gibt keine ...** there aren't any [ˈeni]
kennen know [nəʊ]
kennenlernen meet [miːt] **Freut mich, dich/euch/Sie kennenzulernen.** Nice to meet you. [naɪs]
Kette chain [tʃeɪn]
Kilometer kilometre (km) [ˈkɪləmiːtə]
Kind kid [kɪd]
Kino cinema [ˈsɪnəmə] **im Kino** at the cinema
Kiosk kiosk [ˈkiːɒsk]
Kissen cushion [ˈkʊʃn]
klar clear [klɪə]
Klasse class [klɑːs]
Klassenarbeit test [test]
Klassenlehrer/in class teacher [ˈklɑːs tiːtʃə]
Klassenzimmer classroom [ˈklɑːsruːm]
Kleber glue [gluː]
Klebestift glue stick [ˈgluː stɪk]
Klebstoff glue [gluː]
Kleiderschrank wardrobe [ˈwɔːdrəʊb]
Kleidertausch(party) clothes swap [ˈkləʊðz swɒp]
Kleidung clothes (pl) [kləʊðz]
Kleidungsstücke clothes (pl) [kləʊðz]
klein little [ˈlɪtl]; short [ʃɔːt]; small [smɔːl] **kleine Mahlzeit** snack [snæk]
Klub club [klʌb]
klug clever [ˈklevə]
Koch, Köchin cook [kʊk]
Kochbuch recipe book [ˈresəpi]
kochen cook [kʊk]; (in Wasser) boil [bɔɪl]
Kochen cooking [ˈkʊkɪŋ]
Kochrezept recipe [ˈresəpi]
komisch weird [wɪəd]
Komma (Dezimalzeichen) point [pɔɪnt] **1,6 (eins Komma sechs)** 1.6 (one point six)
kommen come [kʌm] **Wo kommst du her?** Where are you from?
können can [kæn], [kən] **etwas gut können** be good at sth. / at doing sth. [æt], [ət] **gut umgehen können mit ...** be good at ... [gʊd] **Ich kann ... sehen.** I can see ... **Ich kann ... nicht sehen.** I can't (= cannot) see ... [kɑːnt]
Konsole console [kənˈsəʊl]
Kontrolle check [tʃek]
kontrollieren check [tʃek]
Kopf head [hed] **Dreh/Stell es auf den Kopf.** Turn it upside down. [ʌpsaɪd ˈdaʊn]
Kopfhörer headphones (pl) [ˈhedfəʊnz]
Korridor corridor [ˈkɒrɪdɔː]
Kosten cost [kɒst]
kosten cost [kɒst]
kostenlos free [friː]
köstlich delicious [dɪˈlɪʃəs]
krank ill [ɪl]
Krankenhaus hospital [ˈhɒspɪtl]

Krankheit illness [ˈɪlnəs]
Krawatte tie [taɪ]
Kreis circle [ˈsɜːkl]
Küche kitchen [ˈkɪtʃɪn]
Kuchen cake [keɪk]
Kugelschreiber pen [pen]
Kultur culture [ˈkʌltʃə]
kümmern: sich kümmern um look after [lʊk]
Kunst art [ɑːt] **darstellende Kunst** drama [ˈdrɑːmə]
Kunsthandwerk crafts (pl) [krɑːfts]
Kunststück trick [trɪk]
Kurs class [klɑːs]
kurz short [ʃɔːt]

L

Lächeln smile [smaɪl]
lächeln smile [smaɪl]
Laden shop [ʃɒp]
Lampe lamp [læmp]; light [laɪt]
Land country [ˈkʌntri] **auf dem Land** in the country
Landkarte map [mæp]
lang(e) long [lɒŋ] **30 Sekunden lang** for 30 seconds [fɔː] **(für) eine lange Zeit** (for) a long time [taɪm] **lange arbeiten, lange Arbeitstage haben** work long days [wɜːk]
langsam slow [sləʊ] **zu langsam** too slow [tuː]
langweilig boring [ˈbɔːrɪŋ]
Lärm noise [nɔɪz]
lassen: lass(t) uns let's (= let us) [lets]
Laufen (Sport) running [ˈrʌnɪŋ]
laut loud [laʊd] **lauter sprechen** speak more loudly [mɔː]
leben live [lɪv]
Lebensmittel food [fuːd]
lecker delicious [dɪˈlɪʃəs]
legen: (etwas wohin) legen put [pʊt]
lehren teach [tiːtʃ]
Lehrer/in teacher [ˈtiːtʃə]
leidtun: Er tut mir leid. I'm / I feel sorry for him. [ˈsɒri]
leise quiet [ˈkwaɪət]
lernen learn [lɜːn]
lesen read [riːd]
Leser/in reader [ˈriːdə]
Leute people (pl) [ˈpiːpl]; (Anrede) guys (pl) [gaɪz]
Licht light [laɪt]
Liebe love [lʌv]
Liebe/r ... Dear ... [dɪə]
lieben love [lʌv] **Ich hätte liebend gern ... / Ich möchte liebend gern ...** I'd (= I would) love ... **Ich würde mich liebend gerne mit ... treffen.** I'd (= I would) love to meet ... [miːt]
Liebling favourite [ˈfeɪvərɪt]; love [lʌv]
Lieblings- favourite [ˈfeɪvərɪt]
Lied song [sɒŋ]
liegen lie [laɪ]
lila purple [ˈpɜːpl]
Limonade lemonade [leməˈneɪd]
Lineal ruler [ˈruːlə]
Liste file [faɪl]; list [lɪst]

Dictionary — German – English

listen list [lɪst]
Löffel spoon [spuːn]
Löwe lion [ˈlaɪən]
lustig (be) funny [ˈfʌni] **Was ist lustig an ...?** What's funny about ...?

M

machen do [duː]; make [meɪk]
Mädchen girl [ɡɜːl]
magisch magical [ˈmædʒɪkl]
Mahlzeit meal [miːl] **kleine Mahlzeit** snack [snæk] **warme Mahlzeit** hot meal [hɒt]
Mai May [meɪ]
Mama mum [mʌm]
manchmal sometimes [ˈsʌmtaɪmz]
markieren highlight [ˈhaɪlaɪt]
Markt market [ˈmɑːkɪt]
März March [mɑːtʃ]
Mathe(matik) maths [mæθs]
Mauer wall [wɔːl]
Maus mouse, pl mice [maʊs], [maɪs]
Meer sea [siː] **am Meer** by the sea
Mehl flour [ˈflaʊə]
mehr more [mɔː] **mehr als 50** over 50 [ˈəʊvə]
Meile (ca. 1,6 km) mile [maɪl] **mit 30 Meilen pro Stunde** at 30 miles per hour [pər ˈaʊə] **Meilen pro Stunde** miles per hour (mph)
mein/e my [maɪ]
meinen (sagen wollen) mean [miːn]; (denken, glauben) think [θɪŋk] **Ich meine, ...** I think ...
meiste(r, s): die meisten Schulen most schools [məʊst]
meistens usually [ˈjuːʒuəli]
Melone melon [ˈmelən]
Mensa canteen [kænˈtiːn]
Menschen people (pl) [ˈpiːpl]
Messer knife, pl knives [naɪf], [naɪvz]
Meinung opinion [əˈpɪnjən] **meiner Meinung nach** in my opinion
Meter metre [ˈmiːtə]
mich me [miː]
Milch milk [mɪlk]
Millimeter millilitre (ml) [ˈmɪliliːtə]
Mindmap mind map [ˈmaɪnd mæp]
Mini- mini [ˈmɪni]
Minidrohne mini-drone [mɪni ˈdrəʊn]
Minute minute [ˈmɪnɪt]
mir me [miː]
mischen mix [mɪks]
Mischung mixture [ˈmɪkstʃə]
mit with [wɪð]
mitbringen bring [brɪŋ]
mitkommen come [kʌm]
Mitleid: Mitleid haben mit jm. be/feel sorry for sb. [ˈsɒri]
mitnehmen take [teɪk]
Mittagessen lunch [lʌntʃ] **Was gibt es zum Mittagessen?** What's for lunch?
Mittagszeit lunchtime [ˈlʌntʃtaɪm] **zur Mittagszeit** at lunchtime
Mitte centre [ˈsentə]
Mitteilung message [ˈmesɪdʒ]
Mittwoch Wednesday [ˈwenzdeɪ], [ˈwenzdi]
mobben bully [ˈbʊli]
Mobber/in bully [ˈbʊli]
möchten: Ich möchte ... I'd (= I would) like ... [laɪk]
modern modern [ˈmɒdn]
mögen like [laɪk] **sehr mögen** love [lʌv]
Möhre carrot [ˈkærət]
Moment moment [ˈməʊmənt] **in diesem Moment** at the moment
Monat month [mʌnθ]
Montag Monday [ˈmʌndeɪ], [ˈmʌndi] **an jedem Montag** on Mondays
montags on Mondays [ˈmʌndeɪ], [ˈmʌndi]
Morgen morning [ˈmɔːnɪŋ] **am Morgen** in the morning
morgens in the morning [ˈmɔːnɪŋ] **4 Uhr (früh) morgens** 4 a.m. [eɪˈem]
Möwe seagull [ˈsiːɡʌl]
müde tired [ˈtaɪəd]
Museum museum [mjuːˈziːəm]
Musik music [ˈmjuːzɪk]
Musikgruppe band [bænd]
müssen must [mʌst] **etwas tun müssen** need to do sth. [niːd] **Ich muss Schluss machen.** (am Telefon/ Briefschluss) I must go.
Müll rubbish [ˈrʌbɪʃ] **Tüten/Säcke voller Müll** bags of rubbish [bæɡz]
Mülleimer bin [bɪn]
mutig brave [breɪv]
Mutti mum [mʌm]
Mütze cap [kæp]; hat [hæt]

N

na: Na ja, ... Well, ... [wel]
nach
1. (örtlich) to [tu], [tə] **nach draußen** outside [ˌaʊtˈsaɪd] **nach (dr)innen** inside [ˌɪnˈsaɪd]
2. (zeitlich) after [ˈɑːftə] **nach der Schule** after school
Nachbar/in neighbour [ˈneɪbə]
nachdem: nachdem du liest after you read [ˈɑːftə]
Nachmittag afternoon [ˌɑːftəˈnuːn] **am Nachmittag** in the afternoon
nachmittags in the afternoon [ɑːftəˈnuːn] **4 Uhr nachmittags** (16 Uhr) 4 p.m. [piːˈem]
Nachname family name [ˈfæməli neɪm]
Nachricht message [ˈmesɪdʒ]
Nachrichten news [njuːz]
nachschauen look sth. up [lʊk ˈʌp]
nachschlagen: etwas nachschlagen look sth. up [lʊk ˈʌp]
nächste(r, s) next [nekst] **Als nächstes ...** Next ...
Nachtisch dessert [dɪˈzɜːt] **zum/als Nachtisch** for dessert
nahe (bei) near [nɪə]
Nähe: in der Nähe von near [nɪə]
Name name [neɪm]
natürlich of course [əv ˈkɔːs]
Naturwissenschaft science [ˈsaɪəns]
neben next to [ˈnekst tə]
nehmen, in Anspruch nehmen take [teɪk]
nein no [nəʊ]
nennen call [kɔːl]
nett friendly [ˈfrendli]; kind [kaɪnd]; nice [naɪs]
neu new [njuː]
neun nine [naɪn]
neunzehn nineteen [naɪnˈtiːn]
neunzig ninety [ˈnaɪnti]
nicht not [nɒt]
nie never [ˈnevə]
niedlich cute [kjuːt]
niemals never [ˈnevə]
noch: (immer) noch still [stɪl] **noch drei** three more [mɔː] **noch ein/e** another [əˈnʌðə] **noch einmal** again [əˈɡen]
Norden north [nɔːθ]
nördlich; Nord- north [nɔːθ]
Nordosten; nordöstlich north-east [nɔːθˈiːst]
Nordwesten; nordwestlich northwest [nɔːθˈwest]
normalerweise usually [ˈjuːʒuəli]
Notiz note [nəʊt]
Notizen: (sich) Notizen machen (zur Vorbereitung) make notes
November November [nəʊˈvembə]
Nudeln noodles (pl) [nuːdlz]
Null (im gesprochenen Englisch) oh [əʊ]
Nummer number [ˈnʌmbə]
nun now [naʊ] **Nun, ...** Well, ... [wel]
nur just [dʒʌst]; only [ˈəʊnli] **Es sind nur wir.** It's just us.
Nutzer/in user [ˈjuːzə]
nützlich helpful [ˈhelpfl]; useful [ˈjuːsfl]

O

ob if [ɪf]
oben at the top (of) [tɒp]
Obergeschoss top floor [tɒp ˈflɔː]
Obst fruit [fruːt]
oder or [ɔː]
öffnen open [ˈəʊpən]
oft often [ˈɒfn], [ˈɒftən]
Oktober October [ɒkˈtəʊbə]
Öl oil [ɔɪl]
Oma grandma [ˈɡrænmɑː]
Onkel uncle [ˈʌŋkl]
online; Online- online [ˌɒnˈlaɪn]
Opa grandpa [ˈɡrænpɑː]
orange orange [ˈɒrɪndʒ]
Orange orange [ˈɒrɪndʒ]
ordentlich tidy [ˈtaɪdi]
Ordner file [faɪl]
Ort place [pleɪs]

P

paar: ein paar some [sʌm], [səm]
Päckchen packet [ˈpækɪt]
Packung packet [ˈpækɪt]
Palast palace [ˈpæləs]

Papa dad [dæd]
Papagei parrot [ˈpærət]
Papier paper [ˈpeɪpə] **Stück Papier** piece of paper [piːs]
Paprika pepper [ˈpepə]
Park park [pɑːk]
Parkour (akrobatischer Hindernislauf in der Stadt) parkour [pɑːˈkʊə]
Partner/in partner [ˈpɑːtnə]
Party party [ˈpɑːti]
passieren happen (to sb.) [ˈhæpən]
passiv passive [ˈpæsɪv]
Pasta (italienische Bezeichnung für Teigwaren) pasta [ˈpæstə]
Pause break [breɪk]; rest [rest] **Pause machen** take a rest [teɪk]
Penny (kleinste britische Münze) penny (p), pl pence [ˈpeni], [pens]
Peperoni pepper [ˈpepə]
perfekt perfect [ˈpɜːfɪkt]
Person person [ˈpɜːsn]
Pfeffer pepper [ˈpepə]
Pferd horse [hɔːs]
Pfund (britische Währung) pound (£) [paʊnd]
Picknick picnic [ˈpɪknɪk] **ein Picknich machen** have a picnic [hæv]
Pier pier [pɪə]
Plan plan [plæn]
planen plan [plæn] **planen, etwas zu tun** plan to do sth. [duː]
Platz place [pleɪs]
Playlist playlist [ˈpleɪlɪst]
Pommes frites chips (pl) [tʃɪps] **Fisch mit Pommes frites** fish and chips [fɪʃ ən ˈtʃɪps] **Imbissstube, die Fisch mit Pommes frites verkauft** fish and chip shop [ʃɒp]
Pool(billiard) pool [puːl]
Popcorn popcorn [ˈpɒpkɔːn]
Popstar star [stɑː]
Post (Teil eines Blogs) post [pəʊst]
posten (im Internet veröffentlichen) post [pəʊst]
Poster poster [ˈpəʊstə]
Präsentation presentation [preznˈteɪʃn]
präsentieren: (jm.) etwas präsentieren present sth. (to sb.) [prɪˈzent]
Preis (Kosten) cost [kɒst]; (Gewinn) prize [praɪz]
Preisverleihung prize ceremony [ˈpraɪz serəməni]
pro per [pɜː], [pə] **Meilen pro Stunde** miles per hour (mph) [maɪlz] **pro Stunde** per hour [ˈaʊə]
Problem problem [ˈprɒbləm]
Programmieren coding [ˈkəʊdɪŋ]
programmieren (Computer) code [kəʊd]
Projekt project [ˈprɒdʒekt]
prüfen check [tʃek]
Prüfung check [tʃek]
Puderzucker icing sugar [ˈaɪsɪŋ ʃʊgə]
Pulver powder [ˈpaʊdə]
putzen clean [kliːn] **(sich) die/deine Zähne putzen** brush your teeth [brʌʃ]
Puzzle jigsaw (puzzle) [ˈdʒɪgsɔː]

Q

Quiz quiz, pl quizzes [kwɪz], [ˈkwɪzɪz] **ein Quiz machen** do a quiz [duː]

R

Rad: Rad fahren cycle [ˈsaɪkl]
Radfahren cycling [ˈsaɪklɪŋ]
Radiergummi rubber [ˈrʌbə]
Ratespiel quiz, pl quizzes [kwɪz], [ˈkwɪzɪz] **Ratespiel machen** do a quiz [duː]
Rätsel puzzle [ˈpʌzl]
Raum room [ruːm]
Recherche(n) research [rɪˈsɜːtʃ]
recherchieren (do) research [rɪˈsɜːtʃ]
Recht: Recht haben be right [raɪt]
Rechtschreibung spelling [ˈspelɪŋ]
Rede talk [tɔːk]
reden (mit) talk (to) [tɔːk] **reden über** talk about [əˈbaʊt]
Redewendung phrase [freɪz]
Referat presentation [preznˈteɪʃn] **ein Referat halten** give a presentation [gɪv]
Regal shelf, pl shelves [ʃelf], [ʃelvz]
Regen rain [reɪn]
regen rain [reɪn]
regnerisch rainy [ˈreɪni]
Reihe line [laɪn]; turn [tɜːn] **Wann bin ich an der Reihe (etwas zu tun)?** When is (it) my turn (to do sth.)?
Reinigungskraft cleaner [ˈkliːnə]
Reis rice [raɪs]
Reise journey [ˈdʒɜːni]; tour [tʊə]
Reisen travel [ˈtrævl]
reisen travel [ˈtrævl]
Restaurant restaurant [ˈrestrɒnt]
Rezept recipe [ˈresəpi]
richtig right [raɪt]; true [truː]
riechen; schlecht riechen smell [smel]
Ring ring [rɪŋ]
Roboter robot [ˈrəʊbɒt]
Roller scooter [ˈskuːtə]
Rollstuhl wheelchair [ˈwiːltʃeə]
rosa pink [pɪŋk]
Rucksack rucksack [ˈrʌksæk]
Ruf call [kɔːl]
Ruhe rest [rest]
ruhen rest [rest]
ruhig quiet [ˈkwaɪət]
rühren stir [stɜː]
Rundfahrt (durch) tour (of) [tʊə]
Rundgang (durch) tour (of) [tʊə]

S

Saal hall [hɔːl]
Sack: Säcke voller Müll bags of rubbish [bægz]
sagen say [seɪ]; tell [tel]
Saison season [ˈsiːzn]
Salat (als Gericht oder Beilage) salad [ˈsæləd]
Salz salt [sɔːlt]
sammeln collect [kəˈlekt]
Samstag Saturday [ˈsætədeɪ], [ˈsætədi]
Sandwich sandwich [ˈsænwɪtʃ], [ˈsænwɪdʒ]
Sänger/in singer [ˈsɪŋə]
Satz sentence [ˈsentəns]
sauber clean [kliːn]
sauber machen clean (sth. up) [kliːn]
Saubermachen clean-up [ˈkliːn ʌp]
Säubern clean-up [ˈkliːn ʌp]
schade a shame [ʃeɪm]
Schande a shame [ʃeɪm]
schauen look [lʊk]
Schauspiel drama [ˈdrɑːmə]
schick smart [smɑːt]
schicken send [send]
Schinken ham [hæm]
Schirmmütze cap [kæp]
Schlaf sleep [sliːp]
schlafen be asleep [əˈsliːp]; sleep [sliːp]
Schlafzimmer bedroom [ˈbedruːm]
Schlange snake [sneɪk]
schlau clever [ˈklevə]
schlecht bad [bæd]
schließen close [kləʊz]
schließlich in the end [end]
schlimm bad [bæd]
Schlittschuhbahn ice rink [ˈaɪs rɪŋk]
Schloss palace [ˈpæləs]
Schluss end [end] **Ich muss Schluss machen.** (am Telefon/ Briefschluss) I must go. [mʌst gəʊ] **zum Schluss** in the end
schmücken decorate [ˈdekəreɪt]
schmutzig dirty [ˈdɜːti]
Schnee snow [snəʊ]
schneebedeckt snowy [ˈsnəʊi]
schneien snow [snəʊ]
Schokolade chocolate [ˈtʃɒklət] **heiße (Trink-)Schokolade** hot chocolate [hɒt]
schon already [ɔːlˈredi]
schön nice [naɪs]
schrecklich horrible [ˈhɒrəbl]
schreiben write [raɪt]
Schreibtisch desk [desk]
Schreibweise spelling [ˈspelɪŋ]
Schritt step [step]
Schuh shoe [ʃuː]
Schule school [skuːl] **Hast du nach der Schule Zeit?** Are you free after school? **in der Schule** at school **nach der Schule** after school **weiterführende Schule** secondary school [ˈsekəndri]
Schüler/in student [ˈstjuːdnt]
Schulfach subject [ˈsʌbdʒɪkt]
Schulheft exercise book [ˈeksəsaɪz bʊk]
Schulmensa canteen [kænˈtiːn]
Schulsport PE (= physical education) [piːˈiː], [fɪzɪkl edʒuˈkeɪʃn]
Schuluniform school uniform [skuːl ˈjuːnɪfɔːm]
Schulversammlung assembly [əˈsembli]
schwarz black [blæk]
schwer difficult [ˈdɪfɪkəlt]; hard [hɑːd]
Schwester sister [ˈsɪstə]

Dictionary

German – English

schwierig difficult [ˈdɪfɪkəlt]; hard [hɑːd]
Schwierigkeiten trouble [ˈtrʌbl] **in Schwierigkeiten sein** be in trouble
Schwimmen swimming [ˈswɪmɪŋ]
schwimmen swim [swɪm]
Schwimmer/in swimmer [ˈswɪmə]
sechs six [sɪks]
sechzehn sixteen [sɪksˈtiːn]
sechzig sixty [ˈsɪksti]
See *(Meer)* sea [siː] **an der See** by the sea [baɪ]
Seebrücke pier [pɪə]
sehen look [lʊk]; see [siː]
sehr lot [lɒt]; much [mʌtʃ]; very [ˈveri]
sein be [biː] **bist, sind, seid** are [ɑː] *(er/sie/es)* **ist** is [ɪz]
sein/e its [ɪts]
Seite page (p.) [peɪdʒ]
Sekunde second [ˈsekənd] **für 30 Sekunden** for 30 seconds [fɔː]
selbstverständlich of course [əv ˈkɔːs]
selten *(Adj.)* rare [reə]; *(Adv.)* rarely [ˈreəli]
seltsam funny [ˈfʌni]; weird [wɪəd]
senden send [send]
September September [sepˈtembə]
Servus. Goodbye. [gʊdˈbaɪ]; Hello. [həˈləʊ] **Servus allerseits.** Hello everybody. [ˈevribɒdi]
Show show [ʃəʊ]
sicher sure [ʃʊə], [ʃɔː]
Sie *(höfliche Anrede)* you [juː] **Sie sind** you're (= you are)
sie
1. *(weibliche Person)* her [hɜː], [hə]; she [ʃiː] **sie ist** she's (= she is)
2. *(bei Dingen und Tieren)* it [ɪt]
3. *(Plural)* them [ðem], [ðəm]; they [ðeɪ] **sie sind** they're (= they are) **sie sind nicht** they aren't
sieben seven [ˈsevn]
siebzehn seventeen [sevnˈtiːn]
siebzig seventy [ˈsevnti]
sieden boil [bɔɪl]
Sieger/in winner [ˈwɪnə]
Silber silver [ˈsɪlvə]
silberfarben silver [ˈsɪlvə]
Singen singing [ˈsɪŋɪŋ]
singen sing [sɪŋ]
sitzen sit [sɪt]
Skateboard (fahren) skateboard [ˈskeɪtbɔːd]
Skateboardfahren skateboarding [ˈskeɪtbɔːdɪŋ]
Skatepark skatepark [ˈskeɪtpɑːk]
Slideshow slide show [ˈslaɪd ʃəʊ]
SMS text [tekst] **jm. eine SMS schicken** text sb.
Snack snack [snæk]
so like this [laɪk]; so [səʊ]
sodass so that [səʊ ðæt]
Sofa sofa [ˈsəʊfə]
Software software [ˈsɒftweə]
Sohn son [sʌn]
Sommer summer [ˈsʌmə]

Sonne sun [sʌn] **Die Sonne scheint.** It's sunny. [ˈsʌni]
sonnig sunny [ˈsʌni]
Sonntag Sunday [ˈsʌndeɪ], [ˈsʌndi]
sonst or [ɔː]
Sorte (von) kind (of) [kaɪnd]
Soße sauce [sɔːs]
Spaghetti spaghetti [spəˈgeti]
Spaß fun [fʌn] **Spaß haben** have fun [hæv] **Spaß machen** be fun [bi]
spät: (zu) spät late [leɪt]
später later [ˈleɪtə]
Spaziergang walk [wɔːk]
Speisekarte menu [ˈmenjuː]
Spiegel mirror [ˈmɪrə]
Spiel game [geɪm]; match [mætʃ]
spielen play [pleɪ]
Spieler/in player [ˈpleɪə]
Spielkarte playing card [ˈpleɪɪŋ kɑːd]
Spielzeug toy [tɔɪ]
Spitze top [tɒp] **an der Spitze (von)** at the top (of) [æt], [ət]
Sport sport [spɔːt]; *(Schulsport)* PE (= physical education) [piː ˈiː], [fɪzɪkl edʒuˈkeɪʃn]
Sportart sport [spɔːt]
Sporthalle sports hall [ˈspɔːts hɔːl]
Sprechen speaking [ˈspiːkɪŋ]
sprechen (mit) speak (to) [spiːk] **deutlich sprechen** speak clearly [ˈklɪəli] **lauter sprechen** speak more loudly [mɔː] **sprechen über** speak about [əˈbaʊt]
Stadion stadium [ˈsteɪdiəm]
Stadt city [ˈsɪti]; town [taʊn]
Stadtplan map [mæp]
Stadtzentrum town centre [taʊn ˈsentə]
Standuhr clock [klɒk]
Star star [stɑː]
Start start [stɑːt]
stecken: (etwas wohin) stecken put [pʊt]
stehen stand [stænd]
stellen: (etwas wohin) stellen put [pʊt]; **sich (hin)stellen** stand [stænd]
Stiefbruder stepbrother [ˈstepbrʌðə]
Stiefmutter stepmother [ˈstepmʌðə]; stepmum [ˈstepmʌm]
Stiefschwester stepsister [ˈstepsɪstə]
Stiefsohn stepson [ˈstepsʌn]
Stieftochter stepdaughter [ˈstepdɔːtə]
Stiefvater stepdad [ˈstepdæd]; stepfather [ˈstepfɑːðə]
Stift pen [pen]
still quiet [ˈkwaɪət]
Stock(werk) floor [flɔː] **das oberste Stockwerk** top floor [tɒp ˈflɔː]
Strand beach [biːtʃ] **an den/zum Strand** to the beach [tu], [tə]
Straße *(in Ortschaften)* street [striːt]
Straßenmusik street music [ˈstriːt mjuːzɪk]
Streetdance *(Tanzstil)* street dance [ˈstriːt dɑːns]
Stück piece [piːs] **Stück Papier** piece of paper [ˈpeɪpə]

Student/in student [ˈstjuːdnt]
Stufe step [step]
Stuhl chair [tʃeə]
Stunde hour [ˈaʊə]; *(Unterrichtsstunde)* lesson [ˈlesn] **pro Stunde** per hour [pɜː], [pə]
Stundenplan timetable [ˈtaɪmteɪbl]
Superheld/in superhero, *pl* superheroes [ˈsuːpəhɪərəʊ]
Supermarkt supermarket [ˈsuːpəmɑːkɪt]
Surfing surfing [ˈsɜːfɪŋ]
süß cute [kjuːt]; sweet [swiːt]
Süßigkeiten sweets *(pl)* [swiːts]
Sweatshirt sweatshirt [ˈswetʃɜːt]

T

Tag day [deɪ]
Tageszeitung newspaper [ˈnjuːspeɪpə]; paper [ˈpeɪpə]
Tante aunt [ɑːnt]
Tanz dance [dɑːns]
Tanzen dancing [ˈdɑːnsɪŋ]
tanzen dance [dɑːns]
Tänzer/in dancer [ˈdɑːnsə]
Tasche bag [bæg]
Tätigkeit activity [ækˈtɪvɪti]
Tausch swap [swɒp]
tauschen swap [swɒp]
Technik technology [tekˈnɒlədʒi], *infml auch* tech
Technikunterricht technology [tekˈnɒlədʒi], *infml auch* tech
Technologie technology [tekˈnɒlədʒi], *infml auch* tech
Tee tea [tiː]
Teelöffel teaspoon [ˈtiːspuːn]
Teil part (of) [pɑːt]; piece [piːs]; share [ʃeə]
teilen share [ʃeə]
Telefon phone [fəʊn] **am Telefon** on the phone [ɒn]
Telefonanruf (phone) call [ˈfəʊn kɔːl]
telefonieren phone [fəʊn]
Telefonnummer phone number [ˈfəʊn nʌmbə]
Tennis tennis [ˈtenɪs]
Terrarium terrarium [teˈreəriəm]
Test test [test]; quiz, *pl* quizzes [kwɪz], [ˈkwɪzɪz] **Test machen** do a quiz [duː]
testen test [test]
teuer expensive [ɪkˈspensɪv]
Text text [tekst]
Thema topic [ˈtɒpɪk]
Ticket ticket [ˈtɪkɪt]
Tier animal [ˈænɪml]; pet [pet]
Tierarzt/Tierärztin vet [vet]
Tipp tip [tɪp]
Tisch table [ˈteɪbl]
Tischtennis table tennis [ˈteɪbl tenɪs]
Titel title [ˈtaɪtl]
Tochter daughter [ˈdɔːtə]
Toilette toilet [ˈtɔɪlət]
toll great [greɪt]
Tomate tomato, *pl* tomatoes [təˈmɑːtəʊ]

Tomatensauce tomato sauce [təˈmɑːtəʊ sɔːs]
Torte cake [keɪk]
tot dead [ded]
Tour tour [tʊə]
Tourist/in tourist [ˈtʊərɪst]
Touristeninformation tourist information centre [tʊərɪst ɪnfəˈmeɪʃn sentə]
Tradition tradition [trəˈdɪʃn]
traditionell traditional [trəˈdɪʃənl]
tragen wear [weə]
Trainer/in trainer [ˈtreɪnə]
Training training [ˈtreɪnɪŋ]
Trampolin trampoline [ˈtræmpəlɪn]
Trampolinspringen/-turnen trampolining [ˈtræmpəlɪnɪŋ]
Traum dream [driːm]
träumen (von etwas) dream (of/about sth.) [driːm]
traurig sad [sæd]
treffen: (sich) treffen meet [miːt]
Tretroller scooter [ˈskuːtə]
Trick trick [trɪk]
Trifle *(englischer Nachtisch)* trifle [ˈtraɪfl]
trinken drink [drɪŋk]
trotzdem still [stɪl]
Tschüs. Bye. [baɪ]; See you. [siː]; Speak later. [spiːk ˈleɪtə]
T-Shirt T-shirt [ˈtiː ʃɜːt]
tun do [duː]; **(etwas wohin) tun** put [pʊt] **du hast (viel) zu tun** you're busy [ˈbɪzi] **es genießen, etwas zu tun** enjoy doing sth. [ɪnˈdʒɔɪ] **etwas weiterhin tun** continue to do sth. [kənˈtɪnjuː] **wie man etwas tut / tun kann / tun soll** how to do sth. [haʊ]
Tür door [dɔː]
Turmuhr clock [klɒk]
Tüte: Tüten voller Müll bags of rubbish [bægz]
Tyrann/in bully [ˈbʊli]
tyrannisieren bully [ˈbʊli]

U

üben practice [ˈpræktɪs]
über
1. *(räumlich)* over [ˈəʊvə]
2. *(mehr als)* **über 50** over 50
3. about [əˈbaʊt] **über mich/dich/...** about me/you/...
überall everywhere [ˈevriweə]
überprüfen check [tʃek]
Überprüfung check [tʃek]
überrascht surprised [səˈpraɪzd]
Überschrift heading [ˈhedɪŋ]; title [ˈtaɪtl]
Übung(en) exercise [ˈeksəsaɪz]; practice [ˈpræktɪs]
Übungsheft exercise book [ˈeksəsaɪz bʊk]
Uhr clock [klɒk]
Uhrzeit time [taɪm]
um: um 8 Uhr at 8 o'clock [æt], [ət]
umdrehen turn [tɜːn]
umrühren stir [stɜː]
umweltbewusst green [griːn]
umweltfreundlich werden go green [gəʊ griːn]
und and [ænd], [ənd] **Und du?** What about you? [əˈbaʊt]
unfreundlich unfriendly [ʌnˈfrendli]
unhöflich rude [ruːd]
Uniform uniform [ˈjuːnɪfɔːm]
unordentlich messy [ˈmesi]
Unordnung mess [mes]
Unrecht: Unrecht haben be wrong [rɒŋ]
uns us [ʌs], [əs]
unser/e our [ˈaʊə]
unter under [ˈʌndə]
Unterricht class [klɑːs] **im Unterricht** in class
unterrichten teach [tiːtʃ]
Unterrichtsstunde lesson [ˈlesn]
Unterschied difference [ˈdɪfrəns]
unterstreichen highlight [ˈhaɪlaɪt]
untersuchen research [rɪˈsɜːtʃ]
Urlaub holiday [ˈhɒlədeɪ] **im/in den Urlaub** on holiday

V

Vanille vanilla [vəˈnɪlə]
Vati dad [dæd]
vegan vegan [ˈviːgən]
Veganer/in vegan [ˈviːgən]
Vegetarier/in vegetarian [vedʒəˈteəriən], *infml auch* veggie [ˈvedʒi]
vegetarisch vegetarian [vedʒəˈteəriən], *infml auch* veggie [ˈvedʒi]
verboten no [nəʊ]
Verein club [klʌb]
Vereinigtes Königreich the United Kingdom (the UK) [juːnaɪtɪd ˈkɪŋdəm], [juːˈkeɪ]
vergessen: nicht vergessen remember [rɪˈmembə]
verirren: Hast du dich verirrt? Are you lost? [lɒst]
Verkaufsbude kiosk [ˈkiːɒsk]
Verkaufsstand kiosk [ˈkiːɒsk]
verkehrt herum upside down [ʌpsaɪd ˈdaʊn]
verlaufen: Hast du dich verlaufen? Are you lost? [lɒst]
vermischen mix [mɪks]
vermisst missing [ˈmɪsɪŋ]
verschieden different [ˈdɪfrənt]
verschneit snowy [ˈsnəʊi]
verspäten: Ich habe mich verspätet. I'm late. [leɪt] **Verspäte dich nicht.** Don't be late.
verstehen understand [ʌndəˈstænd]
verwenden use [juːz]
Video; Video- video [ˈvɪdiəʊ]
viel/e a lot of [ə ˈlɒt əv], lots of [ˈlɒts əv]; many [ˈmeni]; much [mʌtʃ] **wie viele?** how many? [haʊ]
vielleicht maybe [ˈmeɪbi]
vier four [fɔː]
vierzehn fourteen [fɔːˈtiːn]
vierzig forty [ˈfɔːti]
violett purple [ˈpɜːpl]
Vokabelverzeichnis vocabulary [vəˈkæbjələri], *infml auch* vocab [ˈvəʊkæb]
Vokabular vocabulary [vəˈkæbjələri], *infml auch* vocab [ˈvəʊkæb]
völlig (still) perfectly (still) [ˈpɜːfɪktli]
von from [frɒm]; of [ɒv], [əv]
vor
1. *(zeitlich)* before [bɪˈfɔː] **vor der Schule / der Unterrichtsstunde** before school / the lesson [skuːl], [ˈlesn]
2. *(räumlich)* in front of [ɪn ˈfrʌnt əv]
vormittags: 9 Uhr vormittags 9 a.m. [eɪˈem]
Vorname first name [ˈfɜːst neɪm]
vorsichtig careful [ˈkeəfl]
vorstellen: (jm.) etwas vorstellen present sth. (to sb.) [prɪˈzent]
Vortrag talk [tɔːk]
Vorwahl(nummer) code [kəʊd]

W

Wackelpudding jelly [ˈdʒeli]
wählen choose [tʃuːz]
wahr true [truː]
Wand wall [wɔːl] **an der/die Wand** on the wall [ɒn]
Wandern hiking [ˈhaɪkɪŋ]; walking [ˈwɔːkɪŋ]
wandern hike [haɪk]; walk [wɔːk]
Wanduhr clock [klɒk]
wann when [wen]
warm hot [hɒt]; warm [wɔːm] **warm werden** get warm [get]
warum why [waɪ]
was what [wɒt] **Was ist mit dir?** What about you? [əˈbaʊt]
Wasser water [ˈwɔːtə]
Wassermelone water melon [ˈmelən]
Website website [ˈwebsaɪt]
Weg journey [ˈdʒɜːni]; way [weɪ]
weg away [əˈweɪ]
Weide field [fiːld] **auf der Weide** in the field
Weihnachten Christmas [ˈkrɪsməs]
Weihnachtstag Christmas Day [krɪsməs ˈdeɪ]
weil because [bɪˈkɒz]
Weise: Art und Weise way [weɪ] **auf diese Weise** (in) this way **auf unterschiedliche Weise** in different ways [ˈdɪfrənt]
weiß white [waɪt]
weitere more [mɔː] **drei weitere** three more [θriː]
weitermachen continue [kənˈtɪnjuː] **(mit) etwas weitermachen** continue to do sth. [duː]
welche(r, s) which? [wɪtʃ]; what [wɒt] **Welche AGs ...?** Which clubs ...? [klʌb]
Wendung phrase [freɪz]
wenn
1. *(falls)* if [ɪf] **Was wäre, wenn?** What if? [wɒt]
2. *(zeitlich)* when [wen]

Dictionary

German – English

wer who [huː]
werden get [gɛt]
Werken design and technology [dɪzaɪn ən tekˈnɒlədʒi]
Werktag weekday [ˈwiːkdeɪ]
Werkunterricht design and technology [dɪzaɪn ən tekˈnɒlədʒi]
Wetter weather [ˈweðə]
Wettkampf competition [kɒmpəˈtɪʃn]; match [mætʃ]
wichtig important [ɪmˈpɔːtnt]
wichtigste(r, s) main [meɪn]
wie *(ähnlich/so wie)* like [laɪk]
wie how [haʊ] **Wie alt bist du?** How old are you? **Wie geht es dir/euch/Ihnen?** How are you? **Wie heißt du?** What's your name? [wɒts] **Wie ist ...? / Wie sieht ... aus?** What's ... like? **wie viele?** how many? **Wie wäre es mit einer/einem ... ?** What about a ... ?
Willkommen in/an ... Welcome to ... [ˈwelkəm]
Wind wind [wɪnd]
windig windy [ˈwɪndi]
Windsurfen windsurfing [wɪndsɜːfɪŋ]
winken: (jm. zu-)winken wave (to sb.) [weɪv]
Winter winter [ˈwɪntə]
wir we [wiː] **Es sind nur wir.** It's just us. [ʌs], [əs] **wir sind** we're (= we are) **wir sind nicht** we aren't
wirklich really [ˈriːəli], [ˈrɪəli]
wissen know [nəʊ]
Witterung weather [ˈweðə]
witzig funny [ˈfʌni]
wo where [weə] **Wo kommst du her?** Where are you from?

Woche week [wiːk]
Wochenende weekend [wiːkˈend] **am Wochenende** at the weekend
Wochentag weekday [ˈwiːkdeɪ]
wohnen live [lɪv]
Wohnsiedlung estate [ɪˈsteɪt]
Wohnung flat [flæt]
Wohnzimmer living room [ˈlɪvɪŋ ruːm]
Wok *(chinesischer Kochtopf)* wok [wɒk]
Wolke cloud [klaʊd]
wolkig cloudy [ˈklaʊdi]
wollen want [wɒnt] **etwas tun wollen** want to do sth. [duː]
Wort word [wɜːd]
Wörternetz mind map [ˈmaɪnd mæp]
Wortschatz vocabulary [vəˈkæbjələri], *infml auch* vocab [ˈvəʊkæb]
Wurst, Würstchen sausage [ˈsɒsɪdʒ]
würzig spicy [ˈspaɪsi]
wütend angry [ˈæŋgri]

Y

Yoga yoga [ˈjəʊgə]

Z

Zahl number [ˈnʌmbə]
zahlen: (etwas be-)zahlen pay (for sth.) [peɪ]
Zahn tooth, *pl* teeth [tuːθ], [tiːθ]
Zauberei magic [ˈmædʒɪk]
Zauberkasten magic set [ˈmædʒɪk set]
zaubern do magic [duː ˈmædʒɪk]
Zaubertrick magic trick [ˈmædʒɪk trɪk]
zehn ten [ten]
zeichnen draw [drɔː]

Zeichnen drawing [ˈdrɔːɪŋ]
zeigen show [ʃəʊ]
Zeile line [laɪn]
Zeit time [taɪm] **(für) eine lange Zeit** (for) a long time [lɒŋ]
Zeitung newspaper [ˈnjuːspeɪpə]; paper [ˈpeɪpə]
Zentrum centre [ˈsentə]
zerbrechen: etwas zerbrechen break sth. [breɪk]
Zeremonie ceremony [ˈserəməni]
Zettel piece of paper [piːs ɒv ˈpeɪpə]
ziemlich quite [kwaɪt]
Ziffer number [ˈnʌmbə]
Zimmer room [ruːm]
Zirkus circus [ˈsɜːkəs]
Zitrone lemon [ˈlemən]
Zoo zoo [zuː]
zu; um zu to [tu], [tə]
Zucker sugar [ˈʃʊgə]
Zuckerguss icing [ˈaɪsɪŋ]
zuerst (at) first [fɜːst]
Zug train [treɪn]
Zuhause home [həʊm]
zuhören listen [ˈlɪsn]
zumachen close [kləʊz]
zurück back [bæk]
zurzeit at the moment [ˈməʊmənt]
zusammen together [təˈgeðə]
zwanzig twenty [ˈtwenti]
zwei two [tuː]
zweite(r, s) second (2nd) [ˈsekənd]
Zwiebel onion [ˈʌnjən]
zwölf twelve [twelv]
zwölfte(r, s) twelfth (12th) [twelfθ]

ALPHABET, SOUNDS

🔊 The English alphabet

a [eɪ]	h [eɪtʃ]	o [əʊ]	v [viː]
b [biː]	i [aɪ]	p [piː]	w [ˈdʌbljuː]
c [siː]	j [dʒeɪ]	q [kjuː]	x [eks]
d [diː]	k [keɪ]	r [ɑː]	y [waɪ]
e [iː]	l [el]	s [es]	z [zed]
f [ef]	m [em]	t [tiː]	
g [dʒiː]	n [en]	u [juː]	

🔊 English sounds

[iː] green, he, sea
[ɑː] ask, class, car, park
❗ [ɔː] or, ball, door, four, morning
[uː] ruler, blue, too, two, you
[ɜː] her, girl, work, T-shirt
[ɪ] in, big, expensive
[e] yes, bed, again, breakfast
[æ] animal, apple, black, cat
[ʌ] mum, bus, colour
[ɒ] song, on, dog, what
[ʊ] book, good, put, bully
[ə] again, today, a sister
[i] happy, monkey
[u] museum, you, to

[eɪ] name, eight, play, great
[aɪ] I, time, right, my
[ɔɪ] boy, toilet, noise
[əʊ] old, no, road, yellow
[aʊ] now, house
[eə] where, pair, share, their
[ɪə] here, material, really, year
[ʊə] tour

[b] bike, table, verb
[p] pen, paper, shop
[d] day, window, good
[t] ten, letter, at
[g] go, again, bag
[k] kitchen, car, back
[m] man, remember, mum
[n] no, one, ten
❗ [ŋ] wrong, young, uncle, thanks
[l] like, old, small
[r] ruler, friend, sorry
❗ [w] we, where, one
[j] yes, you, uniform
[f] family, after
❗ [v] very, seven, have
[s] six, poster, yes
❗ [z] zoo, quiz, his, music, please
[ʃ] she, station, English
[tʃ] teacher, watch
[dʒ] job, German, project, orange
❗ [θ] thing, three, bathroom, north
❗ [ð] the, weather, with
❗ [h] house, who, behind

💡 Die Lautschrift zeigt dir die Aussprache von Wörtern und Lauten *(sounds)*.

❗ Übe mit Hilfe der App besonders die Aussprache dieser Laute, denn sie kommen im Deutschen nicht vor oder werden anders geschrieben.

English numbers

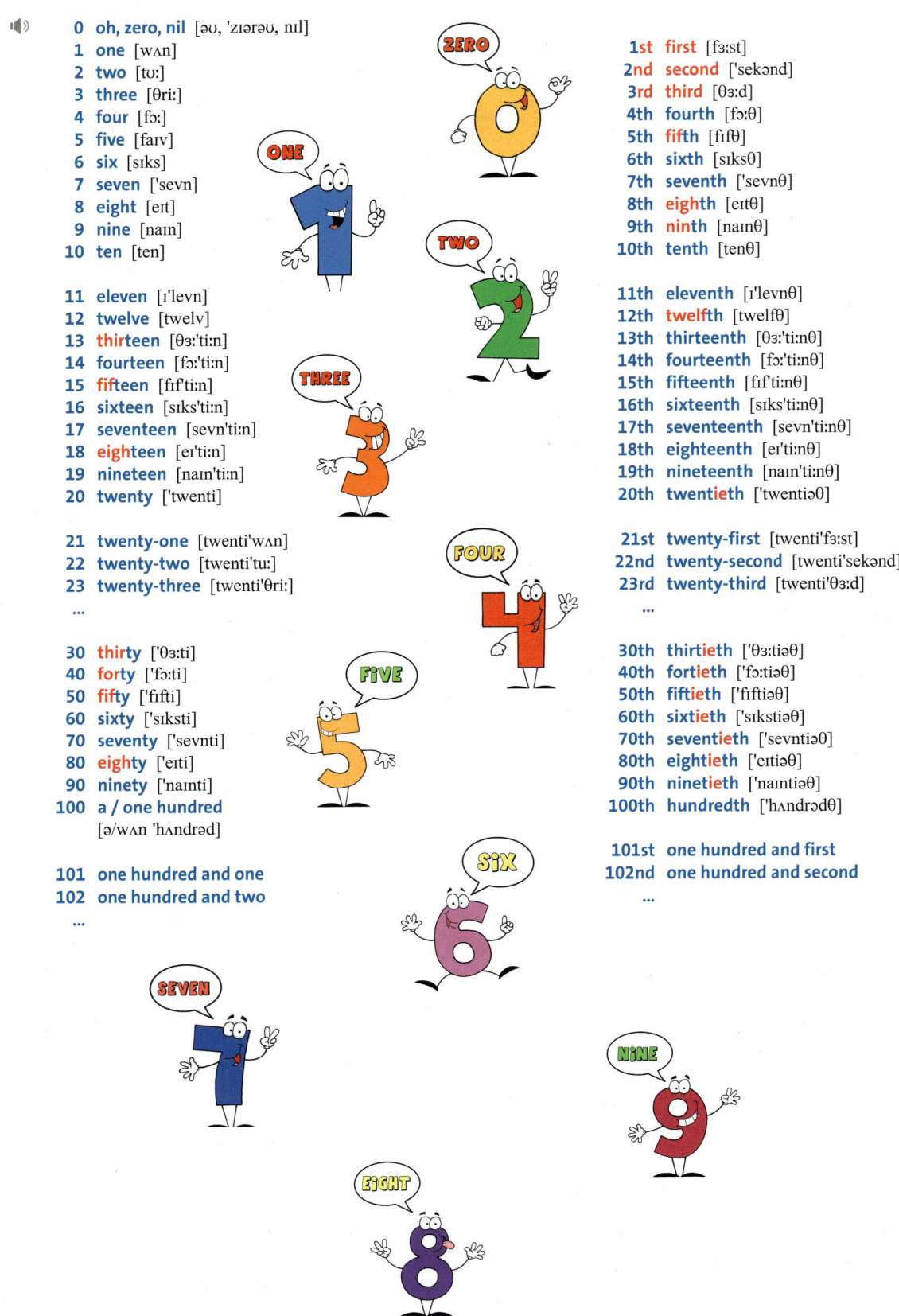

0	oh, zero, nil	[əʊ, 'zɪərəʊ, nɪl]
1	one	[wʌn]
2	two	[tuː]
3	three	[θriː]
4	four	[fɔː]
5	five	[faɪv]
6	six	[sɪks]
7	seven	['sevn]
8	eight	[eɪt]
9	nine	[naɪn]
10	ten	[ten]
11	eleven	[ɪ'levn]
12	twelve	[twelv]
13	thirteen	[θɜː'tiːn]
14	fourteen	[fɔː'tiːn]
15	fifteen	[fɪf'tiːn]
16	sixteen	[sɪks'tiːn]
17	seventeen	[sevn'tiːn]
18	eighteen	[eɪ'tiːn]
19	nineteen	[naɪn'tiːn]
20	twenty	['twenti]
21	twenty-one	[twenti'wʌn]
22	twenty-two	[twenti'tuː]
23	twenty-three	[twenti'θriː]
...		
30	thirty	['θɜːti]
40	forty	['fɔːti]
50	fifty	['fɪfti]
60	sixty	['sɪksti]
70	seventy	['sevnti]
80	eighty	['eɪti]
90	ninety	['naɪnti]
100	a / one hundred	[ə/wʌn 'hʌndrəd]
101	one hundred and one	
102	one hundred and two	
...		

1st	first	[fɜːst]
2nd	second	['sekənd]
3rd	third	[θɜːd]
4th	fourth	[fɔːθ]
5th	fifth	[fɪfθ]
6th	sixth	[sɪksθ]
7th	seventh	['sevnθ]
8th	eighth	[eɪtθ]
9th	ninth	[naɪnθ]
10th	tenth	[tenθ]
11th	eleventh	[ɪ'levnθ]
12th	twelfth	[twelfθ]
13th	thirteenth	[θɜː'tiːnθ]
14th	fourteenth	[fɔː'tiːnθ]
15th	fifteenth	[fɪf'tiːnθ]
16th	sixteenth	[sɪks'tiːnθ]
17th	seventeenth	[sevn'tiːnθ]
18th	eighteenth	[eɪ'tiːnθ]
19th	nineteenth	[naɪn'tiːnθ]
20th	twentieth	['twentiəθ]
21st	twenty-first	[twenti'fɜːst]
22nd	twenty-second	[twenti'sekənd]
23rd	twenty-third	[twenti'θɜːd]
...		
30th	thirtieth	['θɜːtiəθ]
40th	fortieth	['fɔːtiəθ]
50th	fiftieth	['fɪftiəθ]
60th	sixtieth	['sɪkstiəθ]
70th	seventieth	['sevntiəθ]
80th	eightieth	['eɪtiəθ]
90th	ninetieth	['naɪntiəθ]
100th	hundredth	['hʌndrədθ]
101st	one hundred and first	
102nd	one hundred and second	
...		

Quellenverzeichnis

Titelbild
Cornelsen/Personen: Anja Poehlmann, Brighton Pier: mauritius images/Steve Vidler

Illustrationen
Cornelsen/**Harald Ardeias:** (S. 4 un.re.; S. 17 1 A–F.; S. 21; S. 26; S. 27 9b; S. 29 alle außer Möwen; S. 30–31; S. 33 2A, 2B, 2C; S. 36–38; S. 40; S. 41 ob.; S. 43; S. 46 ob.; S. 49 1–8; S. 52–53; S. 54 Mi.re.; S. 55 7b; S. 56 1–3; S.57; S. 62 o.m., 63–65 un.re.; S. 70; S. 72–73; S. 78; S. 80 un.re.; S. 87 un.re.; S. 88–89; S. 95; S. 99 1–5; S. 100–101;S.110–111; S.112mi.; S.114; S.116; S.117; S.123 mi. a–f; S.124; S.128 ob.re.; S.137 mi.re.; S.138 ob.re.; S.139 mi.re.; S.140; S. 141 ob.re.; S. 145 ob.li.; S. 146 – 148; S. 152 un.re.; S. 153 ob.re., S. 154 un.li.+un.re.; S. 155; S. 156 ob.re.; S. 159 un. 1–6; S. 176 ob.li.; S. 189; S. 190). Cornelsen/Inhouse/**Josephine Bienert-Köhler:** (S. 67 1 bis 6; S. 97 1 bis 6; S. 165; S. 168 li.; S. 170 zweite v. un.re; S. 171 Mi.re. (M) siehe unten; S. 172 alle). Cornelsen/**Karen Donnelly** (S. 127 un.mi. +un.re.). Cornelsen/**Klara Luise Frankenberg:** (S. 164; S. 165 Mi + un.; S. 166; S. 167; S. 171 ob.re). Cornelsen/**Irina Zinner:** (Möwenbilder S. 1.; S. 4 ob.li.; S. 5–14; S. 15 1 bis 6; S. 16; S. 17 3 A–G; S. 23; S. 27 (Möwen); S. 29 (Möwen); S. 32; S. 34–35; S. 41–42(Möwenbilder); S. 46 un.re.; S. 47; S. 49 re.Mi.; S. 51; S. 54 1–6; S. 55 (Möwe); S. 60–61; S. 80; S. 81; S. 83; S. 85 mi.re. ; S. 86 un.li. ; S. 87 ob.re. ; S. 90; S. 92–93; S. 102 1–6; S. 103 ob.re., un.re.; S. 104 ob.re.; S.107, S.108 un.re, S.109, S.112 ob.re, un.li.; S.113 mi.re.; S.118; S.121; S.133; S.137 ob.re.; S.138 mi.re.; S.139 ob. re.+un.re.; S. 143 un.re.; S. 145 mi.re.; S.150–151, S.159 ob.re.; S. 162; S. 168 re.; S.169; S. 173–174; S. 175 ob.li.; S. 176 un.re. S. 177–182; S. 195–201; S.202 ob.re.; S. 236; S.264**;** Möwe auf Umschlagseite hinten (U3)).

Abbildungen
Umschlagseite vorne (U2): s. S.18, 20 und 30; **S. 1** s. S. 34, 35, 36; **S. 4–8:** Cornelsen/Anja Poehlmann; **S.12:** un.re. Shutterstock.com/New Africa; un.li. Shutterstock.com/Pete Pahham, un.Mi. Shutterstock.com/Djomas; **S. 14:** 1 stock.adobe.com/Arija, 2 Panther Media GmbH/Gertrud Böttcher, 3 Shutterstock.com/Dmitrijs Mihejevs, 4 Shutterstock.com/Iakov Filimonov, 5 Shutterstock.com/Eric Isselee, 6 Shutterstock.com/Alex Staroseltsev, 7Shutterstock.com/bluedog studio, 8 Shutterstock.com/Susan Schmitz; **S.15:** phone Shutterstock.com/Denis Semenchenko, Emoticons Shutterstock.com/Yefym Turkin, football Shutterstock.com/R-O-M-A, rucksack Shutterstock.com/AmaPhoto, bike Shutterstock.com/Gilang Prihardono, cap Shutterstock.com/Pixfiction; **S.16:** Shutterstock.com/Eric Isselee; **S. 18–19:** alle Cornelsen/Anja Poehlmann; **S. 20:** ob. Cornelsen/Anja Poehlmann, un.li. Shutterstock.com/AnnaStills, un.re. Shutterstock.com/Golden Pixels LLC; **S. 21:** Shutterstock. com/Monkey Business Images; **S. 22:** ob.Mi. Shutterstock.com/Pavlo S. ob.re. Shutterstock.com/Photo Melon, 7aCornelsen/Anja Poehlmann; **S. 23:** Shutterstock.com/AnnaStills; **S. 24:** alle außer Bild 2**:** Cornelsen/Anja Poehlmann, 2 Shutterstock.com/Vova_31; **S. 25:** ob.re. + 4 ob. Cornelsen/Anja Poehlmann; 4 un. Shutterstock. com/antoniodiaz; **S. 26** Tintenflecke: mauritius images/alamy stock photo/Daniil Chaban; **S. 28:** A+C+E Cornelsen/Anja Poehlmann, B mauritius images/alamy stock photo/Greg Balfour Evans, D mauritius images/alamy stock photo/James Winspear-VIEW; **S. 32:** Cornelsen/Anja Poehlmann; **S. 33:** Filmstills ob.re. + 3: Cornelsen/ Grasshopper Films; **S. 35:** un.re. Shutterstock.com/Monkey Business Images; **S. 36:** A Shutterstock.com/file404, B Shutterstock.com/Quinn Martin, C Shutterstock.com/Monkey Business Images, D Shutterstock.com/guig120; **S. 39:** alle Cornelsen/Anja Poehlmann; **S. 42:** li. 1.v.ob. Cornelsen/Anja Poehlmann, li. 2.v.ob. Shutterstock.com/ antoniodiaz; **S. 44:** Bild oben li. Montage: Cornelsen/li. (Sunita): Cornelsen/Anja Poehlmann, Mitte: Shutterstock. com/insta_photos, re.: Shutterstock.com/V.S.Anandhakrishna, C: Shutterstock.com/Txema Gerardo, D: Shutterstock.com/JacquiMoore, unten li.: Cornelsen/Anja Poehlmann, unten re. (family): Shutterstock.com/StockImageFactory.com; **S. 45:** Cornelsen/Anja Poehlmann; **S. 47:** Shutterstock.com/all_about_people; **S. 48:** A Shutterstock. com/Volodymyr Plysiuk, B mauritius images/alamy stock photo/Maximilian Weinzierl, C Shutterstock.com/cbpix, Rex: Shutterstock.com/Ga_photo, Axel: Shutterstock.com/FlavoredPixels, Maude: Shutterstock.com/D.Bond, un. li. Cornelsen/Anja Poehlmann; **S. 49:** un.re. Shutterstock.com/Monkey Business Images; **S. 50:** A mauritius images/alamy stock photo/Natalie Jezzard„ B mauritius images/Novarc Images, C mauritius images/alamy stock photo/Edward Simons, D mauritius images/alamy stock photo/Paul Thompson Images; **S. 51:** Filmstills A–F: Cornelsen/Grasshopper Films, un.Mi. Cornelsen/Anja Poehlmann; **S. 52:** 2 Shutterstock.com/Tokarchuk Andrii; **S. 53:** Cornelsen/Anja Poehlmann; **S. 55:** un. Mi. Shutterstock.com/Aluna1; **S. 56+57:** Emoticons Shutterstock. com/Yefym Turkin; **S. 58:** A Shutterstock.com/Reservoir Dots, B Shutterstock.com/Mircea Pavel, C Shutterstock. com/Aleksandra Duda, D Shutterstock.com/maximmmmum, E Shutterstock.com/ES. Professional, F Shutterstock. com/blackzheep, LOOK-foto/Rainer Martini; **S. 59:** Filmstills ob.re. + 1–6: Cornelsen/Grasshopper Films, hug Shutterstock.com/fizkes, postbox Shutterstock.com/nimon, letter Shutterstock.com/Bborriss.67, tree stock. adobe.com/Cienpies Design; **S. 60:** Shutterstock.com/Syda Productions; **S. 62:** un.re. Cornelsen/Anja Poehlmann, un.Mi. Shutterstock.com/Nenad Aksic; **S. 65:** 1 Shutterstock.com/Johannes Menge, 2 Shutterstock.com/ HRP_Photography; **S. 66:** Emoticon Shutterstock.com/Yefym Turkin, Mi.li. stock.adobe.com/Fly_dragonfly, Mi.re. Shutterstock.com/Robles Designery, un.re. Shutterstock.com/Moravian; **S. 67:** Mi.re. stock.adobe.com/Renat, Türen Shutterstock.com/Bibadash; **S. 68:** ob.re. stock.adobe.com/Pixel-Shot, cookies Shutterstock.com/Vladimir Kruglove, turkey stock.adobe.com/Brent Hofacker, socks stock.adobe.com/gertrudda, Mi.li. Shutterstock.com/ hvatkosha; **S. 69:** ob.li. ClipDealer GmbH/szefei, Mi.re. Shutterstock.com/Pichaya Pureesrisak, un.li. stock.adobe.

Quellenverzeichnis

com/themorningglory; **S. 75:** Shutterstock.com/T-Vision; **S. 76:** A+B Cornelsen/Anja Poehlmann, Emoticon: Shutterstock.com/Yefym Turkin, Herz Shutterstock.com/pink.mousy; **S. 77:** C–E (M) Cornelsen/Anja Poehlmann, E Hintergrund mauritius images/alamy stock photo/PDMPhotos; **S. 78:** Sonne/Mond Shutterstock.com/BesticonPark; **S. 79** (M): Junge Cornelsen/Anja Poehlmann, Mädchen und Hintergrund Shutterstock.com/Michael-puche; **S. 81:** A Shutterstock.com/Jovanovic Dejan, B Shutterstock.com/S. Travel Photo and Video, C Shutterstock.com/DUSAN ZIDAR, D Shutterstock.com/Ju PhotoStocker, E Shutterstock.com/Africa Studio, F Shutterstock.com/Leah-Anne Thompson, Mi. (Zane): Cornelsen/Anja Poehlmann; **S. 82:** 1 Shutterstock.com/CHARAN RATTANA-SUPPHASIRI, 2 Shutterstock.com/wavebreakmedia, 3 Shutterstock.com/BearFotos, 4 Shutterstock.com/SpeedKingz, 5 Shutterstock.com/Manny DaCunha, 6 Shutterstock.com/YanLev, 7 Shutterstock.com/mariakray, 8 Shutterstock.com/sakkmesterke; **S. 83:** 3b Shutterstock.com/valeryvoronessa; **S. 84:** 1.v.ob. Shutterstock.com/Ten03, 2.v.ob. Shutterstock.com/Brian McEntire, 3.v.ob. Shutterstock.com/TunedIn by Westend61; **S. 85:** ob.re. Shutterstock.com/Pressmaster, un.li. Shutterstock.com/Daisy Daisy,; **S. 86:** un.re. Cornelsen/Anja Poehlmann; **S. 91:** A Shutterstock.com/Krakenimages.com, B Shutterstock.com/matimix, C Shutterstock.com/Image Source Collection, D Shutterstock.com/Dentan, E Shutterstock.com/altan can, F Shutterstock.com/Purple Clouds, ob.re. + 1–6 Cornelsen/Grasshopper Films; **S. 93:** Shutterstock.com/SpeedKingz; **S. 94:** Daumen(rot+grün) Shutterstock.com/Azizunnahar Sadeq, un.re. (außer Daumen) Shutterstock.com/Panuwach, Daumen(gelb) Shutterstock.com/Cosmic_Design, un.li. Shutterstock.com/Asier Romero, Emoticons Shutterstock.com/Yefym Turkin; **S. 96:** alle Shutterstock.com/Chaim Devine; **S. 97:** ob.re. Shutterstock.com/Monkey Business Images; **S. 99:** un.re. Shutterstock.com/LightField Studios; **S. 101:** Würfel Shutterstock.com/art-sonik; **S. 102:** ob.re. Shutterstock.com/valeryvoronessa; **S. 103:** mi.li. Shutterstock.com/Elena Yakusheva; **S. 104:** 1 Shutterstock.com/Gill Copeland, 2 mauritius images/alamy stock photo/Simon Dack News, 3 mauritius images/alamy stock photo/Chris Harris; **S. 105:** 4 Cornelsen/Grasshopper Films, 5 mauritius images/alamy stock photo/Peter Moulton, 6 mauritius images/alamy stock photo/Life's Like That, 7 Shutterstock.com/Marius_Comanescu; **S. 106** ob.li. Cornelsen/Mädchen: Anja Poehlmann, Fensterrahmen: Shutterstock.com/Dawid Galecki, Ausblick: mauritius images/alamy stock photo/Nigel Bowles, Auge + Ohr: stock.adobe.com/nikolae; **S. 108** ob.re. Shutterstock.com/Nirat.pix; **S. 113** Seebrücke mauritius images/alamy stock photo/Steve Vidler, Achterbahn mauritius images/alamy stock photo/Amongstthemiddlin, rote Stange Shutterstock.com/CKP1001, Schaukel mauritius images/alamy stock photo/K I Photography; **S. 115** mauritius images/alamy stock photo/Eye Ubiquitous; **S. 119** ob.re. + A–F Cornelsen/Grasshopper Films, un.re. stock.adobe.com/gibustudio; **S. 120** Shutterstock.com/Nataliya Dorokhina; **S. 122** Shutterstock.com/cktravels.com; **S. 123** un.li. A mauritius images/alamy stock photo/Simon Dack, B mauritius images/alamy stock photo/Nick Hawkes; **S. 125** 1 mauritius images/alamy stock photo/Simon Dack, 2 Shutterstock.com/Gill Copeland, 3 Seil: Shutterstock.com/DenisNata, Ball Shutterstock.com/VikiVector, Schirm Shutterstock.com/Romolo Tavani, Tischtennis Shutterstock.com/Rawpixel.com, Jugendliche Shutterstock.com/Rawpixel.com, Kinosaal Shutterstock.com/Mr.Music, Fragezeichen Shutterstock.com/4zevar; **S. 126** Cornelsen/Anja Poehlmann; **S 127** ob.re. mauritius images/alamy stock photo/Simon Dack, Briefmarke Shutterstock.com/andromina, unten li.: mauritius images/alamy stock photo/Scott Ramsey, unten re.: mauritius images/alamy stock photo/Andrew Hasson; **S. 128** mi.re. mauritius images/alamy stock photo/Eye Ubiquitous; **S. 131** Cornelsen/Anja Poehlmann; **S. 132** Shutterstock.com/Laenz; **S. 134** Torte: Shutterstock.com/AS Food studio, Noah: Cornelsen/Anja Poehlmann; **S. 135** Essen: Shutterstock.com/vm2002, Sunita: Cornelsen/Anja Poehlmann; **S. 136** Poster: Shutterstock.com/aurielaki, Junge: Cornelsen/Anja Poehlmann; **S. 141** mi.re. Junge: Cornelsen/Anja Poehlmann, Mann: Shutterstock.com/stockfour; **S. 142** ob.mi. Shutterstock.com/Nastya22, ob.re. Shutterstock.com/kuvona, A–F; **S. 143** mi.re. Shutterstock.com/Cienpies Design; **S. 144** Digital Learning Associates Ltd; **S. 145** Emoticons: Shutterstock.com/Yefym Turkin, mi.re. stock.adobe.com/uckyo, Fish & Chips: Shutterstock.com/MaraZe, Kafee: Shutterstock.com/nw10photography; **S. 149** Cornelsen/Grasshopper Films; **S. 152** 1 Shutterstock.com/Nattika, 2 Shutterstock.com/Maks Narodenko, 3 Shutterstock.com/PixaHub, 4 Shutterstock.com/V.S.Anandhakrishna, 5 Shutterstock.com/DenisMArt, 6 Shutterstock.com/baibaz, 7 Shutterstock.com/studiovin, 8 Shutterstock.com/Shnycel; **S. 153** Stadion: Shutterstock.com/ktsdesign, Torte: Shutterstock.com/Natalia Ruedisueli; **S. 154** mi.li. Shutterstock.com/nelea33; **S. 156** mi.li. Shutterstock.com/Syda Productions, mi.re. +un.re. Shutterstock.com/Monkey Business Images, un.li. Shutterstock.com/LightField Studios; **S. 163:** Shutterstock.com/MicroOne; **S. 171:** Mi.re. (M): Cornelsen/Josephine Bienert-Köhler/Möwe: mauritius images/Nature in Stock, Bildschirm: Shutterstock.com/Passatic; **S. 173:** Schirm Shutterstock.com/chuyuss; **S. 175:** Pferde Shutterstock.com/YIK2007, Personen Shutterstock.com/hisa_nishiya, Bücher Shutterstock.com/robuart, Hose Shutterstock.com/DenisProduction.com; **S. 176:** Fahrrad Shutterstock.com/stockphoto-graf, Stift Shutterstock.com/OrangeVector, Tasche Shutterstock.com/dashadima; **S. 183:** Shutterstock.com/owatta; **S. 184:** Zahlen Shutterstock.com/HitToon, un. Shutterstock.com/Africa Studio; **S. 185:** 1.R. li. stock.adobe.com/perpis, 1.R. Mi. ClipDealer GmbH/yuliang11, 1.R. re. stock.adobe.com/katrin sauerwein/EyeEm, 2.R. li. stock.adobe.com/slowmotiongli, 2.R. Mi. Shutterstock.com/Luka Hercigonja, 2.R. re. stock.adobe.com/Daniel Prudek, 3.R. li. Shutterstock.com/Mrinal Pal, 3.R. re. stock.adobe.com/martinkubik, 4.R. li. stock.adobe.com/leungchopan, 4.R. Mi. stock.adobe.com/www.dgwildlife.com/giedriius, 4.R. re. Shutterstock.com/Stu Porter, 5.R. li. ClipDealer GmbH/Vitolef, 5.R. Mi.

stock.adobe.com/bertie10, 5.R. re. stock.adobe.com/© Seal Photographs/Craig Lambert Photo; **S.186:** 1.R.li. stock.adobe.com/DragonImages, 1.R. Mi. stock.adobe.com/Viacheslav Lakobchuk, 1.R. re. Shutterstock.com/LightField Studios, 2.R. li. stock.adobe.com/zhukovvvlad, 2.R. Mi. stock.adobe.com/DragonImages, 2.R. re. Shutterstock.com/Jacek Chabraszewski, 3.R. li. Shutterstock.com/Lapina, 3.R. re. mauritius images/Masterfile RM, 4.R. li. Shutterstock.com/Aleksey Mnogosmyslov, 4.R. Mi. stock.adobe.com/Jacob Lund, 4.R. re. Shutterstock.com/Kaderov Andrii, 5.R. li. Shutterstock.com/CroMary, 5.R. Mi. Shutterstock.com/Fotokostic, 5.R. re. Shutterstock.com/LightField Studios; **S.187:** 1.R. li. Shutterstock.com/buabunya, 1.R. Mi. Shutterstock.com/Draftfolio, 1.R. re. Shutterstock.com/Lorelyn Medina, 2.R. li. Shutterstock.com/SpicyTruffel, 2.R. Mi. Shutterstock.com/mentalmind, 2.R. re. Shutterstock.com/ekler, 3.R. li. Shutterstock.com/Tasha Vector, 3.R. Mi. Shutterstock.com/Peter Hermes Furian, 3.R. re. Shutterstock.com/Olga Krichevtseva, 4.R. li. Shutterstock.com/Merfin, 4.R. Mi. Shutterstock.com/Glinskaja Olga, 4.R. re. Shutterstock.com/ProStockStudio; **S.188:** 1.R. li. stock.adobe.com/Mr. Music/Mr., 1.R. Mi. Shutterstock.com/vipman, 1.R. re. stock.adobe.com/Daisy Daisy, 2.R. li. stock.adobe.com/Ivan, 2.R. Mi. Shutterstock.com/wavebreakmedia, 2.R. re. stock.adobe.com/Monkey Business, 3.R. li. Shutterstock.com/goodluz, 3.R. Mi. stock.adobe.com/S ROBIN/OceanProd, 3.R. re. Shutterstock.com/Rawpixel.com, 4.R. li. Shutterstock.com/Rawpixel.com, 4.R. Mi. Shutterstock.com/DGLimages, 4.R. re. Panther Media GmbH/Benis Arapovic; **S.190:** budgie stock.adobe.com/dieter76, chicken Shutterstock.com/Moonborne, ferret Shutterstock.com/Couperfield, guniea pig Shutterstock.com/Tettania, kitten Shutterstock.com/Nils Jacobi, lizard Shutterstock.com/Michaelpuche, mouse Shutterstock.com/Ziga Camernik, puppy stock.adobe.com/arezin.com/Aleksey, rabbit Shutterstock.com/Victoria Paladiy, rat Shutterstock.com/George Dolgikh; **S.191:** Uhren Shutterstock.com/Skocko, Himmel Shutterstock.com/Apple_Mac; **S.192:** bakery Shutterstock.com/milanzeremski, supermarket Shutterstock.com/Lizardflms, ice rink Shutterstock.com/begalphoto, theme park Shutterstock.com/SIHASAKPRACHUM, bus stop stock.adobe.com/Kay Ransom, mosque Shutterstock.com/Victor Moussa, synagogue mauritius images/alamy stock photo/Peter Llewellyn, church Shutterstock.com/Jono Photography, scooters Shutterstock.com/Bohdan Malitskiy, car park stock.adobe.com/© Sai Chan/Zoe, temple mauritius images/alamy stock photo/Edward Herdwick; **S.193:** lettuce Shutterstock.com/PotaeRin, cucumber Shutterstock.com/Maks Narodenko, banana Shutterstock.com/bergamont, butter Shutterstock.com/bigacis, cupcakes Shutterstock.com/Wealthylady, tomato Shutterstock.com/Tim UR, ice cream Shutterstock.com/stockcreations, potato Shutterstock.com/Anna Kucherova, peas Shutterstock.com/WIPHARAT CHAINUPAPHA, cream Shutterstock.com/grey_and, apple Shutterstock.com/Roman Samokhin, cabbage Shutterstock.com/JIANG HONGYAN, eggs Shutterstock.com/Nattika, sausages Shutterstock.com/Einsteinstudio, melon Shutterstock.com/Boonchuay1970, cheese Shutterstock.com/Tanya Sid, orange Shutterstock.com/Valentyn Volkov, popcorn Shutterstock.com/Jiri Hera, beef Shutterstock.com/MaraZe, carrot Shutterstock.com/Valentina Razumova, onion Shutterstock.com/Yeti studio, pepper Shutterstock.com/DronG, lemon Shutterstock.com/Maks Narodenko, strawberry Shutterstock.com/Tim UR, mango Shutterstock.com/Valentyn Volkov, chicken Shutterstock.com/JIANG HONGYAN, jelly Shutterstock.com/cigdem, donuts Shutterstock.com/Sergey Skleznev, muffins Shutterstock.com/Binh Thanh Bui, broccoli Shutterstock.com/smspsy, pork Shutterstock.com/CSDesign, lamb Shutterstock.com/TheBusinessMan, milk Shutterstock.com/New Africa; **S.194:** add Shutterstock.com/Nitr, bake Shutterstock.com/IC Production, boil Shutterstock.com/Gorlov-KV, cut Shutterstock.com/husjur02, fry Shutterstock.com/fotopai, mix stock.adobe.com/Africa Studio, pour Shutterstock.com/Deer worawut, roll out Shutterstock.com/Igor Zvencom, stir Shutterstock.com/Nebojsa Markovic, saucepan Shutterstock.com/Lipskiy, frying pan Shutterstock.com/grey_and, oven Shutterstock.com/taist2, plate Shutterstock.com/Suradech Prapairat, bowl Shutterstock.com/Khumthong, fork/knife/spoon/tablespoon Shutterstock.com/grey_and; **S.202:** small seagulls Mi.re. Shutterstock.com/s_oleg; **S.203:** Shutterstock.com/wee dezign; **S.204:** Junge Shutterstock.com/karelnoppe, Frau Shutterstock.com/Andresr, Fische Shutterstock.com/Tatyana Vyc, Elefant Shutterstock.com/Teguh Mujiono, Schlange Shutterstock.com/Teguh Mujiono; **S.205:** ob.re. Shutterstock.com/Le_Mon, Mi.re. Shutterstock.com/OneLineStock.com, un.re. Shutterstock.com/MicroOne; **S.206:** ob.re. Shutterstock.com/Adam Gregor, un.re. Shutterstock.com/Lapina; **S.207:** alle außer ob.re.+un.re. Shutterstock.com/jcttaonni, ob.re. Shutterstock.com/miniwide, un.re. Shutterstock.com/jakkapan; **S.208:** Shutterstock.com/EugeneEdge, **S.209:** Shutterstock.com/bsd; **S.210:** maths Shutterstock.com/Lyudmyla Ishchenko, science Shutterstock.com/Monkey Business Images; **S.211:** grandma Shutterstock.com/Oguz Aral, dogs Shutterstock.com/Pixel-Shot, bags Shutterstock.com/Anna Tyukhmeneva; **S.212:** Shutterstock.com/Outsider321; **S.213:** ob.re. Shutterstock.com/Rawpixel.com, un.re. Shutterstock.com/4 PM production; S.214 Kreis Shutterstock.com/ChristianChan, Kanninchen Shutterstock.com/Pavel L Photo and Video, Tierarzt Shutterstock.com/Noi1990, Haus Shutterstock.com/Studio Harmony; **S.215** Eidechse Shutterstock.com/krolya25, Maus Shutterstock.com/Utekhina Anna, Socken Shutterstock.com/Paleka; **S.216** Garten Shutterstock.com/brgfx, Wohnblock Shutterstock.com/dedi57, Kleiderschrank Shutterstock.com/Pavel Adashkevich, Roboter Shutterstock.com/Lecter, **S.217** Tisch Shutterstock.com/Lecter, Schreibtisch Shutterstock.com/donatas1205, Schuhe Shutterstock.com/pikepicture, Stühle Shutterstock.com/photka; **S.218** Shutterstock.com/dantess; **S.220** Uhr Shutterstock.com/Gemenacom, Rollstuhl Shutterstock.com/Nerthuz; **S.221** Shutterstock.com/Sashkin; **S.222** Shutterstock.com/Ljupco Smokovski; **S.224** ob.re. Shutterstock.com/pjcross, mi.li.

Quellenverzeichnis

Shutterstock.com/Michael D Brown; **S. 225** Boote Shutterstock.com/AlyoshinE, Abfall Shutterstock.com/siam.pukkato, Regen Shutterstock.com/Helga Khorimarko, Eis Shutterstock.com/Funny Solution Studio; **S. 226** ob.li. Shutterstock.com/Zhiganova Dariaa, ob.re. Shutterstock.com/ONYXprj; **S. 227** mi.re. Shutterstock.com/NextMarsMedia, un.li. Shutterstock.com/Helga Khorimarko; **S. 228** Shutterstock.com/Helga Khorimarko; **S. 229** ob.re. Shutterstock.com/Nadya_Art, mi.re. Shutterstock.com/Tienuskin; **S. 230** Shutterstock.com/Alastair Wallace; **S. 231** Torte Shutterstock.com/Pete Saloutos, Erdbeere Shutterstock.com/Tanya Sid, Erbsen Shutterstock.com/valzan, Tomate Shutterstock.com/Indigo Photo Club; **S. 232** Weißbrot Shutterstock.com/Dan Kosmayer, Schwarzbrot Shutterstock.com/de2marco, Reis Shutterstock.com/Anna Shepulova, jonglieren Shutterstock.com/dompr; **S. 233** Geschenk Shutterstock.com/Rustle, Wurst Shutterstock.com/stockcreations, Salat Shutterstock.com/kochabamba, Packung Brot Shutterstock.com/JocularityArt; **S. 235** ob.re. Shutterstock.com/paulista, un.re. Shutterstock.com/Nataly Studio; **S. 257** Shutterstock.com/Laurie Barr; **S .258** Shutterstock.com/HitToon; **Umschlagseite hinten (U3):** Karte: stock.adobe.com/lesniewski

Typical tasks

Typical tasks	Häufige Arbeitsanweisungen
Act out the conversation / song / story.	Führt das Gespräch / das Lied / die Geschichte vor.
Answer the questions / partner B's questions.	Beantworte die Fragen / Partner Bs Fragen.
Before you read / listen / watch	Bevor du liest / (zu-)hörst / anschaust …
Check the spelling / your answers / ideas (with a partner).	Überprüfe deine Rechtschreibung / Antworten / Ideen (mit einem/r Partner/in).
Choose the correct answer / word.	Wähle die richtige Antwort / das richtige Wort aus.
Compare the pictures / your answers / … with a partner.	Vergleiche die Bilder / deine Antworten / … mit einem/r Partner/in.
Complete the table / list / sentences / …	Vervollständige die Tabelle / Liste / Sätze / …
Copy the table / list / notes.	Schreibe die Tabelle / die Liste / Notizen ab.
Correct the false / wrong sentences / answers.	Berichtige die falschen Sätze / Antworten.
Describe the picture / your room / …	Beschreibe das Bild / dein Zimmer / …
Draw pictures.	Male / Zeichne Bilder.
Find the answers / the correct / right / wrong words.	Finde die Antworten / die richtigen / falschen Wörter.
Finish the sentences.	Vervollständige die Sätze.
Give feedback.	Gib Feedback / eine Einschätzung.
Interview your partner.	Stelle deinem/r Partner/in Fragen.
Look at the board / at page …	Schaue an die Tafel / auf Seite …
Look at the photos / pictures / map / title.	Sieh dir die Fotos / Bilder / Karte / die Überschrift an.
Listen and check / practise / repeat / guess.	Höre zu und überprüfe / übe / wiederhole / rate.
Listen again.	Höre nochmals zu.
Listen to the story / conversation / dialogue.	Höre dir die Geschichte / das Gespräch / den Dialog an.
Make groups (of six / … students).	Bildet Gruppen (zu je sechs / … Schüler/innen).
Make sentences / notes / lists / a mind map.	Fertige Sätze / Notizen / Listen / eine Mindmap an.
Match the sentence parts / what the friends say.	Verbinde die Satzhälften / das, was die Freunde sagen.
Practise with a partner.	Übe mit einem/r Partner/in.
Put it in you Dossier.	Hefte es in deinem Dossier ab.
Put the sentences / dialogue in the correct order.	Bringe die Sätze / den Dialog in die richtige Reihenfolge.
Read about …	Lies über …
Read the conversation / text / story / article.	Lies den Dialog / Text / die Geschichte / den Artikel.
Stand up when you hear …	Wenn du … hörst, stehe auf.
Swap (cards) with a partner.	Tausche (die Karten) mit einem/r Partner/in.
Take turns.	Wechselt euch ab.
Talk about …	Sprich / Sprecht über …
Talk to a partner.	Sprich mit einem/r Partner/in.
Tell your partner / the class.	Erzähle / Sage es deinem/r Partner/in / der Klasse.
True or false? / True, false or not in the text?	Wahr oder falsch? / Wahr, falsch oder nicht im Text?
Say the four / … sentences.	Sage die vier / … Sätze.
Use your notes / the words in a).	Benutze deine Notizen / die Wörter aus Aufgabe a).
Walk around.	Gehe (im Raum) herum.
Watch part / scene 1 / all the film.	Sieh dir Teil / Szene 1 / den ganzen Film an.
Watch again.	Sieh es / sie / ihn nochmals an.
Work alone / with a partner / in groups.	Arbeite allein / mit einem/r Partner/in / in Gruppen.
Write the correct answers / sentences / words.	Schreibe die richtigen Antworten / Sätze / Wörter (auf).
Write (more) about …	Schreibe (mehr) über …

Classroom English

You and your teacher — Du und deine Lehrerin / dein Lehrer

Good morning, Mr / Mrs / Ms … (bis 12 Uhr)	Guten Morgen, Herr / Frau …
Good afternoon, Mr / Mrs / Ms … (ab 12 Uhr)	Guten Tag, Herr / Frau …
Sorry, I'm late.	Entschuldigung, dass ich zu spät komme.
Can I open / close the window, please?	Kann ich bitte das Fenster öffnen / zumachen?
Can I go to the toilet, please?	Kann ich bitte zur Toilette gehen?

Homework and exercises — Hausaufgaben und Übungen

Sorry, I have no exercise book.	Es tut mir leid, ich habe mein Schulheft nicht dabei.
I don't understand this exercise.	Ich verstehe diese Übung nicht.
I can't do number 3.	Ich kann Nummer 3 nicht lösen.
Sorry, I haven't finished.	Entschuldigung, ich bin noch nicht fertig.
I have … Is that right?	Ich habe … Ist das richtig?
Sorry, I don't know.	Es tut mir leid, das weiß ich nicht.
What's for homework?	Was haben wir (als Hausaufgabe) auf?

You need help — Du brauchst Hilfe

Can you help me, please?	Können Sie / Kannst du mir bitte helfen?
What page is it, please?	Auf welcher Seite sind wir / steht das?
What's … in English / German?	Was heißt … auf Englisch / Deutsch?
Can you write it on the board, please?	Können Sie das bitte an die Tafel schreiben?
Can I say it in German?	Kann ich das auf Deutsch sagen?
Can you speak louder, please?	Können Sie / Kannst du bitte lauter sprechen?
Can you say / play that again, please?	Können Sie das bitte noch einmal sagen / abspielen?

Work with a partner — Partnerarbeit

Can I work with Julian?	Kann ich mit Julian arbeiten?
Can I use your (pen), please?	Kann ich deinen (Stift) benutzen?
Yes, here you are.	Hier, bitte.
It's my / your turn.	Ich bin / Du bist dran.
Let's make / draw a …	Lass uns ein … machen / zeichnen.
Let's act out the story / dialogue.	Lass uns die Geschichte / den Dialog spielen.

What your teacher says — Was deine Lehrerin / dein Lehrer sagt

Let's go.	Lasst uns anfangen. / Los geht's.
Listen, please. / Quiet, please.	Hört bitte zu. / Ruhe bitte.
Open your books at page 24, please.	Schlagt bitte Seite 24 auf.
Do exercise 5 for homework, please.	Macht bitte Übung 5 als Hausaufgabe.
Write the correct words.	Schreibt die richtigen Wörter (hin).
Correct the false sentences.	Korrigiert die falschen Sätze.
Where's your book, David?	Wo ist dein Buch, David?
Try again!	Versuche es noch einmal!
That's all for today. You can go.	Das ist alles für heute. Ihr könnt gehen.